Discovering the Attitudes and Mindsets of God

The Bible reveals God's Attitudes
About Trends in America Today

RON ELY

Copyright © 2024 by Ron Ely.

All rights reserved. No part of this publication may be reproduced, distributed, or transmitted in any form or by any means, including photocopying, recording, or other electronic or mechanical methods, without the prior written permission of the author, except in the case of brief quotations embodied in critical reviews and certain other noncommercial uses permitted by copyright law.

Edited by Patricia R. Ely

All Scripture references from the
NEW KING JAMES VERSION (NKJV) Bible
Copyright 1982 by Thomas Nelson, Inc.
Unless otherwise noted

All photographs by the author and/or editor
Unless otherwise noted

Printed in the United States of America.

Library of Congress Control Number: 2023931527

ISBN	Paperback	978-1-965881-63-7
	eBook	978-1-965881-64-4

Boundless Script Inc.
99 Wall Street #210
New York, NY, 10005

www.boundlessscript.com

CONTENTS

Preface v
Introduction xi

Chapter 1: Getting Acquainted With My Lord And Savior 1
Chapter 2: Majoring In The Minors 12
Chapter 3: The Bible Versus The Doctrine Of Man 16
Chapter 4: The Charismatic Renewal 27
Chapter 5: Remnants Of The Charismatic Renewal Still Exist 42
Chapter 6: Why Did The Great Revivals Of The Past Fade Away? ... 49
Chapter 7: What About The Condition Of The Church In
America Today? 55
Chapter 8: How We Can Bring In And Sustain The Next Great
Revival 62
Chapter 9: God's Extreme Love For Us Evident Through
His Creation 77
Chapter 10: The Love And Wrath Of God 86
Chapter 11: "…Be Holy, For I Am Holy" -1 Peter 1:16 101
Chapter 12: The Kingdom Of God 110
Chapter 13: God's Provision For The Healing Of Our Bodies 132
Chapter 14: Praying For A Miracle 140
Chapter 15: If God Loves Me So Much, Why Did He Let
That Happen To Me? 155
Chapter 16: Dealing With Satanic Forces 162

Chapter 17: How Do We Maintain A Growing Relationship
    With God?... 167
Chapter 18: What Does The Bible Teach About Predestination?....... 170
Chapter 19: Is It Possible For A Christian To Forfeit His Salvation?.. 178
Chapter 20: God's Attitude Towards Marriage And Divorce 181
Chapter 21: God's Attitude About Homosexuality 185
Chapter 22: God's Attitude Towards Parenting And Children........... 189
Chapter 23: God's Attitude Towards Our Handling Money 196
Chapter 24: And The Glory Which You Have Given Me,
    I Have Given Them, That They May Be One,
    Just As We Are One…John 17:22 200
Chapter 25: Why I Believe The Bible Is True.................................... 207
Chapter 26: In Conclusion 210

Appendix... 221

PREFACE

You may discover in this book a lot of Bible verses you never heard from a pulpit and interpretations of some verses you never heard. If you are like many Christians who don't spend much time studying their Bible seriously for themselves but depend on others to teach and interpret the Bible for them, you will find some big surprises in this book. Having spent many years in many different types of churches, I can tell you that it is very likely that you have been fed a lot of man's doctrine, rather than Bible truth, and have never heard many important verses of the Bible. Television pastors are much the same way. I only know a couple that I would spend the time listening to. The doctrine of man has been the biggest enemy of the church from the very beginning. Jesus came to earth to establish His church and refute man's doctrine, but the satanically inspired doctrine of man has continued to slip in and has gotten worse, much worse, recently. After much study of this, I have developed a conclusion. The New Testament Church was led by the Holy Spirit, whereas there is little evidence of the Holy Spirit's involvement in most churches today.

My life changed dramatically following an encounter with God in 1955 that prompted me to start each day at 4:30 AM with two hours of Bible study. As I studied the Word for myself and endeavored to make it real in my life, I was dumbfounded by how much of the Bible had not been taught in the church. I have since realized that if I had stayed away from the church the first 10 or 15 years after I started studying the Bible for myself, I would have grown in my understanding of the Bible much faster than I did. No doubt trying to grow in my understanding of the

Bible and my relationship with God was greatly hindered by my church attendance and participation during that time. It appears to me that most pastors and teachers are more concerned about *not* saying something that someone may not like than they are about teaching the whole Bible truth. The drive to protect and build their following becomes more important to them than teaching all the Bible. Thus, the listener receives a distorted and incomplete picture of God.

I was born in eastern Tennessee on December 1, 1930, during the great depression. I was the first of three boys born to my parents. I give you that information to let you know that I have seen a lot of history in my almost 92-year journey on this earth. The sad thing is that I have witnessed in my journey a gradual deterioration of the Christian church, and the United States of America, two institutions that are very close to my heart. World War II started a few days after my eleventh birthday, and although the war ended before I would have been old enough to fight in it, the memories of it are very vivid in my mind.

The biggest thing I remember about the war at home was how strong the nation became united to win the war at all costs. We gladly did without many commodities, such as cars, gasoline, meat, milk, cheese, leather, steel, aluminum, etc., because we knew they were needed by our brave military members, including family members, who were over there fighting for the survival of our country. Many young men volunteered to join the fight, some lying about their age and going in at 16 and even 15 years old. Some of them got sent home within weeks, but many got away with it. Mom and Dad were air-raid wardens. My next youngest brother and I were Boy Scouts, collecting scrap paper, aluminum, and tin cans. We did a limited amount of close-order drill and survival training; in case the war went on so long we would be brought into it. Dad, my grandfather, and two uncles worked for Tri-State Roofing, roofing the buildings of the new army base thirty miles north of us. After that was finished, Dad helped build merchant ships at the Wilmington, North Carolina shipyard. All of Mom and Dad's younger brothers went to war and came home safely after it ended. Towards the end of the war, when the Wilmington N.C. Shipyard shut down, Dad utilized his early navy experience, went to marine engineering school in New Orleans, and joined the Military Transportation Corps. He served on a hospital ship that brought our wounded military members home from France after the war ended in Europe. My brother, Larry, and I found out late in the war that we had lost a great boyhood friend, "Pully", who had been Dad's helper in his sheet-metal, heating, and roofing business before the war. Dad's shop was between our house and school, so we would stop by and visit with "Pully" on our way home from school, and he would chat with us, make our toys, etc. His tank never made it ashore in the Normandy invasion.

When I was growing up in Tennessee and later in North Carolina, about everyone we knew went to church nearly every Sunday, and all the businesses shut down on Sunday. I have seriously studied the Bible and church history since 1955, and now realize those churches fell well short of the potential that they could have had. But weak as their teaching was, Americans still recognized that Christian training and participation were very important and something to be sought after. As I consider the attitudes of people towards the church and towards the United States of America today, as compared to my boyhood experience, it is very, very, heart-breaking.

In my opinion, based on my experience and participation, I see our government and the church as the big problems today, because our government and churches are staffed by-products of our education system, and are staffed with many people who are often more concerned about growing and maintaining their position than doing what is best for our citizens and teaching Bible truths. Please understand that I am generally talking about the majority because we do have a few very important God-fearing, Bible-literate leaders in the government and the church. I see so many in our local and national government who are influenced more by China, Russia, and primarily selfish reasons (satanically influenced) than they are by our national and Christian heritage and the needs of our citizens. The reason this has come about in my opinion is simply that our education system and the Christian church have miserably failed in their responsibility to our once great nation, its founders, and citizens. I hasten to point out that all of us must share responsibility for the sorry state we find our once great nation and once-powerful church in, because we have sat back on our blessed assurance and let satanically influenced individuals aggressively take over some of our churches, education system, government, and most of our media. Selah (go figure). How else can we explain it?

The adage, "the best way to ensure the victory of evil, is for good men (and women) to do nothing", has certainly played out here. We must wake up and realize our once great nation is headed "straight to hell in a hand-basket" if we don't wake up and accept our responsibility as Christians and U.S. citizens, find out what we can do to help reverse the trend, and do it. One thing all Christians can certainly do is pray— pray fervently for our people to turn to God as never before, for our government personnel, and help pray in the next great outpouring of the Holy Spirit. Quickly, very quickly.

This book is an attempt on my part to help reverse the path we see the church and our once great nation on currently. It is also an attempt to share some of what I have experienced and learned in my 91-year journey on this planet and my 65-year study of the Bible, God's Word, as well as church history. I am very confident of this one thing: God loves this nation, like the way He loves Israel, and He wants us as a nation to be victorious, and in love with Him as He is with us. That behooves every one of us who consider ourselves Christians to draw near to Him and seek His counsel on how we should react to the situation we find ourselves in. Check this out:

2 Chronicles 7:14—

If My people who are called by My name will humble themselves, and pray and seek My face, and turn from their wicked ways, then I will hear from heaven, and will forgive their sin and heal their land.

I can only urge you to do everything in your power to draw near to God, pray, study His Word, the Bible, and pray for guidance on what you should do to help stop this terrible downward trend.

Ronald R. "Ron" Ely

INTRODUCTION

"Why me, Lord?" Have you ever asked that question? I have, more than one time. I certainly asked that question one day in early November 2010. On September 11, 2010, my first wife graduated to her reward two months before our 60th wedding anniversary and a little over two months before my 80th birthday. I soon decided that a second marriage was not practical at my age, and I adjusted to a bachelor's life. That lasted two months. In early November I was packing to go teach at a pastors' conference in the Dominican Republic, and I received a very emphatic two-fold Word from the Lord. First, He told me He wanted me to get married, and get married now because I could not do all that He wanted me to do by myself—I needed a helpmate in my ministry. Secondly, He told me to write another book, titled *Attitudes and Mindsets of God*, "because my people do not really know or understand me". Notice there was no time mentioned on the second command.

I tried clumsily to carry out the first part of that word for four months, with absolutely no success. Then God introduced me to a young lady (she was only seventy-three) who lived 107 miles away in the big city of Raleigh, North Carolina. Being a country boy, I was not looking there for a wife. I drove up to Raleigh one Sunday, went to church with her and we spent the day getting to know each other. Before we parted, we felt the need to pray about our new relationship, and to continue talking to God about it until we could make a peaceful decision. The following Wednesday, we shocked our families and friends by announcing that we were getting married. The rest is history. We have lived the past eleven-plus years serving God together and made 12 to 15 mission trips to Haiti and the Dominican Republic together while living life to the fullest. I blame Patricia for our getting married. A couple of years after her first husband died, she prayed, "Lord, please don't let me get bored." So, He gave her me! I assure you I have seen to it that she has not been bored and I could not write this book without her help.

Before the above events, I had written and self-published the book, *"Attitudes and Mind-Sets...of Christians who walk in Peace, Joy, and Victory"*. That book was based on about eight years of my teaching at EBAC Pastors' Conferences in Haiti and the Dominican Republic. It was an effort to help Christians grow in their faith and relationship with God. My good friend and Christian brother, Ronald Sanders, helped me write that book, and another friend, Scott McClintock, published it for me at his cost. For whatever reason, I have had trouble getting started on this current book, while at the same time I have started writing several others, including my autobiography. I guess the main reason for my hesitation was that I felt unqualified. Realistically, the Bible is all about The Mindsets of God and I certainly can't top that important book that God wrote Himself. But one morning recently while I was washing dishes my wife walked by and found me with tears sliding down my cheeks. We had previously discontinued the mission trips due to the pandemic and my medical problems, and for a couple of years, I had felt completely adrift and rudderless—a very miserable situation for me. It was starting to wear on me. That morning, as I washed the breakfast dishes, God spoke to me again through His Holy Spirit, very emphatically. He told me, "It's time—The trumpet has sounded. It is time to write the book 'Attitudes and Mind-Sets of God'". So here I am in 2022, during a very chaotic time in our country when we are in the throes of an attempted socialist takeover of our country by a large group of misguided government leaders. Plus, we are hearing more and more prophecies that indicate that we are on the verge of the greatest outpouring of the Holy Spirit that the country has ever seen.

Again, the question, "Why me, Lord?" I have no college degree, although I did spend three or four years, doing college work, working on a degree part-time, taking other courses, and teaching in community colleges. I have never been to seminary, (for which I am thankful), and am not a scholar, theologian, or even preacher, although I am a licensed minister. I have known about God all my life and have had a personal relationship with Him for seventy-eight years. I guess you could say that we are old friends. I have studied the Bible for sixty-five years, so if you couple that with our long relationship, I guess I qualify as a disciple of Jesus Christ and a minister of the gospel. Over the years I have had many prophecies spoken over me that indicated that my primary ministry would come late in life. I guess that ninety-one years of age qualify as being late in life. Although by the world's standards I am not qualified to write this book, I feel confident God commissioned me to write it, so that is all the reason I need to move forward with it. I pray it will bless you and lead you into a closer relationship with your loving creator Father God, Savior Jesus the Messiah, and your Comforter, the Holy Spirit. A limited amount of material in this book was included in my first book *Attitudes and Mind-Sets of Christians who walk in Peace, Joy, and Victory.* which was published in 2010.

As I studied my Bible, I realized that God is referred to with many titles. Each of these titles indicates an attitude and mind set of God. Here are just some of those titles, referring to God the Father to give you an idea of what I am talking about. I hope to share some of the things I have learned over these many years about who this great God of ours is.

"Papa" (from Greek Abba) in Romans 8:15
"Lord" (from Hebrew Adonai) in Genesis 15:2
"Almighty God" (from Hebrew El Shaddai) in Genesis 49:24
"Ancient of Days" in Daniel 7:9
"Creator" in Isaiah 40:28
"Deliverer" in 2 Samuel 22:2
"The Triune" Elohim in Genesis 1:1
"The God Who Sees" (from Hebrew El Roi) in Genesis 16:13
"Everlasting God" (from Hebrew El-Olam) in Genesis 21:33
"Father" in Isaiah 64:8

"Holy One" in Isaiah 43:15
"I Am" in Exodus 3:14
"Jehovah Lord" (from Hebrew Yehweh) in Deuteronomy 6:4
"The Lord Who Heals" (from Hebrew Yehweh-Rapha) in Exodus 15:26
"The Lord Will Provide" (from Hebrew Yehweh-Jireh) in Genesis 22:14
The Lord Who Sanctifies" (from Hebrew Yahweh-M'kaddesh) Leviticus 20:8
"The Lord God" (from Hebrew Yahweh-Elohim) Genesis 2:4
"The Lord our Peace" (from Hebrew Yehweh-Shalom) in Judges 6:24
"The Lord our Righteousness" (from Hebrew Yehweh-Tsidkenu) in Jeremiah 33:16
"Judge" in Psalm 75:7
"King" in Psalm 10:16
"Lawgiver" in Isaiah 33:20
"Light" in Psalm 27:1
"Most High" (from Hebrew El Elyon) in 2 Samuel 22:14
"Rock" in 1 Samuel 2:2
"Redeemer" in Isaiah 54:8
"Shepherd" in Psalm 23.1
(www.Compellingtruth.org)

About 20 years ago I discovered one of the greatest advantages of growing older: The older you get, the less you care about what other people think about what you say or do. So, brace yourself!

Ronald R. "Ron" Ely

CHAPTER 1

Getting Acquainted With My Lord And Savior

I don't know when I first met Him. I was born on the Cumberland Plateau of the Appalachian Mountains of East Tennessee in 1930—during the "great depression". I don't remember ever not going to church, so I don't remember when I first heard about God or met Him. I know I always recognized the natural environment around me as God's creation, and always loved and appreciated it. The first time I read the first few chapters of the book of Genesis, I saw that it lined up with what I had observed about nature, so I concluded that the Bible must truly be the Word of God. What a blessing. Wouldn't it be great if everyone received those revelations while in childhood? To just "know" that God is the all-powerful creator of the universe, and that the Bible is His instructions for us to live by. Don't ask me why I was so blessed I can't answer that. Growing up in Appalachia during the depression was tough.

Discipline was strong in parents during the depression in Appalachia. Life was hard, and parents felt responsible for making sure their children could "hang tough" when they grew up and make a better life for themselves than they had been able to provide. It reminds me of that Johnnie Cash song about a *Boy Named Sue*.

Dad used a two-inch-wide leather belt to discipline us three boys and could be quite brutal with it. Mom preferred a switch but has been known to use whatever she could get her hands on. All of Mom and Dad's relatives felt obliged to use a switch on us if they felt we needed it. Teachers used a ruler on the bent backhand or a paddle on the bottom when they felt they were needed. When we moved to North Carolina, I got freed from teachers and relatives, so I counted that a big blessing.

My family moved to Wilmington, North Carolina, on the east coast in the summer of 1941 and I became eleven years old that following December. On December seven Japan bombed Pearl Harbor, and we were thrust into World War II. What a traumatic year for a young fellow. The next year also brought about some big changes for me, but they were all good. As I walked along the mile or so home from church one Sunday, I kept thinking about the Sunday School lesson our teacher, Liza Fisher, had taught that morning. By the time I walked through the kitchen door to where Mom was preparing lunch, I had made up my mind. I told her that I had decided to accept Jesus Christ as the Lord of my life and the Savior of my soul, and I wanted to become a member of the church. Mom was quite happy about my decision (I imagine a lot of other people were also), and we continued to discuss it until lunch was on the table. A couple of months after that, I fulfilled my life-long goal of becoming a Boy Scout, so I could enjoy God's creation even more. Not long after that, I got a newspaper route and began making my own money on a regular schedule—financial independence felt so good that I determined not ever to be without it.

In Sunday School we were drilled on the catechism, which I appreciated, and it helped me to learn more about my friend, Jesus, and how to serve Him. I was very sincere about trying to follow God's directions as found in the Bible, but at the same time I was careful not to be labeled as a "goody-goody" or "teacher's pet". After all, I was a boy, and I had a reputation to maintain. I was the oldest of three boys, and Dad drank badly, so I felt responsible for helping Mom keep the home on an even keel. Dad was a good provider and maintained a great work ethic, and he passed those qualities along to us boys. Mom was the strong anchor of the family.

My interest in Boy Scouting was so strong, that I advanced along in leadership positions and attained the Eagle Scout rank. By the time I had reached sixteen years of age, my responsibilities in the home, the Boy Scout troop, school, and my job had become so heavy that I just needed help in handling it all. I found that help in my good friend, Jesus. My Scoutmaster, Charlie Bethea, had previously been a big support, but he was such a good Scoutmaster that he was recruited to be a professional Scout Executive. I then became the acting Scoutmaster most of the time, because our sponsor had trouble recruiting men who were willing and able to do the job, even though they would sign the application, agreeing to do so.

There were open woods ten miles deep and five to ten miles wide within a couple of hundred yards of our house, and my two brothers and I were granted permission by our parents to ramble in them all we wanted to in our free daylight time. And ramble we did. When the pressures of school, home, job, and Boy Scout leadership duties overpowered me, I would simply pack my knapsack on a Friday night, tell Mom I would be home Sunday afternoon, and head off to the woods by myself, often-times after dark. The weather had little to do with my decision to go solo camping. Those trips were always highlight experiences for me. I would spend those times relaxing, enjoying the nature around me, fellowshipping with, God, and "discussing all my troubles" with Him. I always returned from those trips Sunday afternoons refreshed and at peace. As I look back on those outings now and recognize how important they were to me, I marvel at how blessed I was at that period of my life, to have that opportunity and have understanding parents. I continued to enjoy that outlet in my adult life, sometimes going for a week at a time, but always returning home refreshed and at peace. There is just no way of describing how beneficial spending several days at a time completely alone in the presence of God can be. I feel so sorry for people, young and old, who have never had that opportunity.

Fortunately for me, the war ended in 1945, before I graduated from High School in 1949. At around sixteen years of age, I realized I needed to seek God's direction on what profession He would like for me to follow. I told Him I would do whatever He wanted me to do, except be a preacher or missionary. I figured I was "not good enough" for that, but in retrospect, I realize that I was not willing to "be good enough". God respected my choice and asked me to serve Him as a professional Scout Executive with the Boy Scouts of America. We had a deal.

While serving as a District Scout Executive in Alexandria, Louisiana, at age 25, on my first tour of duty, God interrupted me while I was preparing the Sunday School lesson for the teenage class I was teaching the next day. The Holy Spirit spoke up to help me with the lesson. We were studying the "Sermon on the Mount" in Matthew, chapters five through seven. The Scripture we were studying that Sunday was **Matthew 6:19-34.**

[19]**"Do not lay up for yourselves treasures on earth, where moth and rust destroy and where thieves break in and steal;** [20] **but lay up for yourselves treasures in heaven, where neither moth nor rust destroys and where thieves do not break in and steal.** [21] **For where your treasure is, there your heart will be also.**

[22] **The lamp of the body is the eye. If therefore your eye is good, your whole body will be full of light.** [23] **But if your eye is bad, your whole body will be full of darkness. If therefore the light that is in you is darkness, how great is that darkness!**

[24] **No one can serve two masters; for either he will hate the one and love the other, or else he will be loyal to the one and despise the other. You cannot serve God and mammon.**

[25] **Therefore I say to you, do not worry about your life, what you will eat or what you will drink; nor about your body, what you will put on. Is not life more than food and the body more than clothing?** [26] **Look at the birds of the air, for they neither sow nor reap nor gather into**

barns; yet your heavenly Father feeds them. Are you not of more value than they? [27] Which of you by worrying can add one cubit to his stature?

[28] So why do you worry about clothing? Consider the lilies of the field, how they grow: they neither toil nor spin; [29] and yet I say to you that even Solomon in all his glory was not arrayed like one of these. [30] Now if God so clothes the grass of the field, which today is, and tomorrow is thrown into the oven, will He not much more clothe you, O you of little faith?

[31] Therefore do not worry, saying, 'What shall we eat?' or 'What shall we drink?' or 'What shall we wear?' [32] For after all these things the Gentiles seek. For your heavenly Father knows that you need all these things. [33] But seek first the kingdom of God and His righteousness, and all these things shall be added to you. [34] Therefore do not worry about tomorrow, for tomorrow will worry about its own things. Sufficient for the day is its own trouble."

I do not remember everything that was said in our conversation, but I know it changed my life forever in a very dramatic way. As a result of the encounter, I made two life-changing decisions that night:

1…I would try to live my life in such a way that my first consideration/motivation was to please God in everything I did, said, and thought.

2…I would start getting up at 4:30 AM every morning, to study my Bible two hours before preparing for work. I was so thrilled by the Holy Spirit joining me in my Sunday school lesson preparation and all that Holy Spirit showed me through that one Scripture, that I was anxious to uncover more truths in God's word.

You might expect me to say that life immediately got much better after that, and in many ways it did, but it also led to the most frustrating time of my life. "Coincidently", I had just purchased my first new car.

The old 1947 Kaiser Frazer that had trips back and forth to Louisiana as well as the three counties I served in took its toll on the 8-year-old battlewagon. It died. I was so proud and excited about my new 1955 Chevy, that as soon as I got it home, I took the Owner's Manual out of the glove compartment and studied it thoroughly. I did not want to accidentally do anything to mess up this new asset. As I continued to study the Bible, I studied it with the same interest as I had applied to that '55 Chevy Owner's Manual, because I recognized it as the "Owner's Manual" for my life. However, as I studied the Bible this way, I found myself progressively becoming more isolated and confused, because I could not find anyone (including my wife, who was not saved at this point) who considered the Bible in that light. As I read the Bible and tried to live out what it taught, I got more and more frustrated. I consulted with my pastor about it, and he thought I was being foolish. They say that one of the first signs of insanity is when you think you are right and everyone else is wrong. That was exactly where I was.

After three and a half years in Louisiana, I transferred to Athens Georgia, and we received the devastating diagnosis that my wife had rheumatoid arthritis and would likely be crippled within seven years. Our boys were probably three and seven years old. When my wife gave me that news, I felt God was telling me He was not going to let that happen to us. I told my wife that and said I am going to stand on that word. The disease progressed through her body, so that three years later her hands were twisted and gnarled, her knees were badly swollen, and she was in unbearable pain. I called her doctor and asked for an appointment for her with him and his partner to try to alleviate her pain, which he agreed to. After their examination, the two doctors sat us down in a room and gave us the results of their examination. Much to everyone's surprise, they told us that after a thorough examination, they could find no trace of rheumatoid arthritis in my wife's body. They told us there was no question about the fact that she did have it previously after reviewing her file, but she did not have it now. They said they were at a complete loss to explain this very unusual circumstance. My wife spoke up and said, "I can explain it—it was my husband's faith in God's Word". Over some time, all the pain and other symptoms dissipated, and her hands and knees returned to normal.

After five years in Athens, I transferred to Orangeburg, South Carolina. By this time, I had given up on the church of my denomination that I had been a part of all my life. I was searching for fulfillment in any church that I thought might be following the Scripture I was studying. As if that frustration was not enough, the pressure from the BSA professional administration to file false troop applications to help raise more money (this had been an ongoing problem from the beginning of my career,) rather than training leaders on how to develop their program to attract more boys, was getting stronger and stronger. During this period, I was developing inexpensive back-packing equipment so that the disadvantaged troops could afford to have a camping program. I did all that research and development on my own time and at my own expense. I was selected to be part of a survey on how we spent our hours per week on the job, and I discovered that I averaged over 65 hours per week without reporting the time I spent developing the camping equipment. Some of the equipment I developed was featured in BSA books and magazines. I served the black "divisions" (this was the way the "black" Boy Scouts were organized in the segregated south during this period) on all three of my service areas. As I drove from one small rural town to another, I would pray about the plight of the disadvantaged boys. I would get ideas on how to make tents, packs, canteens, etc., and on the weekends, I would purchase the materials and develop the equipment. One day as I was driving towards Bamberg, South Carolina, and praying, the Holy Spirit said to me, "Son, things have gotten so rotten in this profession, that you can serve me better outside of it than in it". That hit me like a ton of bricks! I had to pull off the road and get control of my emotions. A few weeks later my boss demanded I turn in a troop charter by the weekend for a troop that did not exist. I told him he was not big enough to make me lie like that and turned in my resignation.

My life seemed to get rougher after that, working at jobs I did not enjoy, and still struggling with the frustration of not finding anyone who believed the Bible as I did. However, one great thing did happen. A close friend led my wife to accept Jesus Christ as Lord of her life and Savior of her soul, so I gained a real partner in my search for Bible truth. One day I was driving down a rural road to see a customer while struggling with God about my frustration of not finding anyone who believed as I felt He was leading me to believe. My struggle became so intense that I found myself with the Bible that had been laying on the passenger seat, in my hand and considering throwing it out the open car window (no air-conditioned cars back then). Thankfully, instead of following through on that thought, I pulled off onto a tractor path and stopped. I exited the car, found myself in the most beautiful outside cathedral I had ever seen, fell to my knees, and "had it out" with God. To this day, I have no idea what He said to me. I just know that after a few minutes, I got up off my knees with complete peace, and have never doubted God's love nor my total belief in the whole Bible since then.

While working at whatever job I could find to put bread on the table, I was seeking God's guidance as to how I could use my skills and experience to serve Him. I accepted a position as a youth minister on a Christian youth dude ranch in California. We moved out there and the whole family got involved in youth ministry and ranch operation. We introduced many young people to Jesus Christ and had a good ministry. The owners eventually turned against us for some unknown reason, and after several months the whole thing just blew up in our face. So, we limped back to our hometown of Wilmington, North Carolina, and started over.

One evening when I came home from work, my wife told me about a prayer meeting that was happening every Tuesday night in a private home. She named some of the people involved and I knew several of them. But when she told me about some of the things that were happening there, I really got interested. The next Tuesday night I was at that meeting with my Bible in my hand. Finally! I had found a group of people who believed as I did! I sat in awe as the meeting flowed, very obviously under the leadership of Holy Spirit. Some of the participants testified of God's power evident in their lives that week. At the end of the meeting, they prayed for some of the individual participants, and I saw miracles of healing take place right in front of my eyes. This would have been 1967 or 1968 and was my first introduction to the Charismatic Renewal.

After attending these meetings for a few weeks, I realized that everyone at those meetings was baptized in the Holy Spirit except me. I am ashamed to admit it, but most of us in the major denominations (the frozen chosen) looked down on Pentecostals and did not believe the Baptism in the Holy Spirit was still available to us today. I now marvel at how ignorant and how arrogant we were, and how widespread those beliefs were among members of the major denominations in those days. But, after attending a few of those charismatic meetings, I realized I needed to make a major attitude adjustment. I also realized that I had been a member of the so-called "frozen chosen". So, one night after supper, I walked out the back door of our home, through the woods, and up to the top of a barren hill. I looked up into a starlit sky, discussed my change of attitude with my friend, God, repented of my past attitude, and asked God in Jesus' name to baptize me in His Holy Spirit. I did not want to speak in tongues yet because I was not sure about it. I felt nothing emotionally as I walked back home, but I had prayed with such confidence and faith that I did not doubt that I had been filled with the Holy Spirit. I opened my Bible when I returned home, and quickly realized my prayer had been answered because I now had a new power to better understand the Scripture and my Bible was far more revealing and interesting than it had been previously. I had received the Holy Spirit with a power I had not even considered.

A few nights after that experience, my wife and I had gone to bed, and she asked me to pray for her because she was in pain. I asked her where she was hurting, and she answered, "all over." I placed my hand on top of her head, and asked God in the name of Jesus, "to heal her from the top of her head to the tips of her toes." My wife had suffered from leg and hip pain all her life, and only recently found the cause. An Orthopedic doctor from the University of South Carolina examined her and found that she was born with very severe birth defects that had left her with a curvature of the spine and her foot, leg, hand, and arm on one side of her body were all shorter than the ones on the opposite side. He measured one leg a half-inch shorter than the other. We had known that one foot was a full size shorter than the other because she had never found a pair of shoes that were comfortable on both feet—they would squeeze one foot and be loose on the other. The doctor had given her a cork "lift" to wear under the heel of her short leg, and that had relieved some of the pain. When my wife got out of bed the next morning after I had prayed for her, she walked across the room barefooted and was immediately aware that her body had undergone a huge change because she normally could not walk barefoot without pain. She hollered and called me excitedly. I grabbed the tape measure and measured her feet, legs, hands, and arms—they all matched. I checked her spine and found it to be straight. As you might expect, we spent most of that Saturday morning rejoicing, praising God, and thanking Him for the greatest healing miracle we had ever witnessed or even considered possible. As you ladies would understand, my wife celebrated that afternoon by going to town and buying new shoes!

A few weeks after that great event, I had become educated on speaking in tongues, so I went up on that familiar hilltop one night and told God I had changed my mind about "tongues" after getting educated about it. I asked Him to enable me to speak in tongues. I walked back home speaking in tongues. I realize that at this point, many of you are freaking out about the order of events and how I experienced them and think that I am confused about when I was baptized in the Holy Spirit. Well, just relax and don't worry about it. "Don't confuse me with the facts, because my mind is made up already". I know what I experienced, and God and I are happy about it.

About this time, I realized how deprived and how misinformed the billions of other "frozen chosen" had been for so many years. We had been blindly following long-dead Bible illiterate church denomination leaders who did not know or understand certain Scripture enough to make it real in their lives. They were easy targets for demonic spirits to convince them to take a portion of Scripture out of context and twist it to conform to their thinking. The way that those Scriptures were misinterpreted often defied all reasonable rules of Scripture interpretation. Their followers swallowed it "hook, line, and sinker". I have since been heartbroken for the billions of misguided "frozen chosen" Christians through the ages and currently who have been denied the power and the fellowship of the Holy Spirit in their lives, simply because they believed the doctrine of man rather than sound Bible doctrine. Those leaders who originally made those erroneous interpretations of the sacred Scriptures remind me of the rebellious dog in the meadow who could not eat the grass but would not let the sheep eat it. This work is one of many I have started to try to wake up the billions of Christians who have been misinformed about the power and fellowship of the Holy Spirit that is freely available to them for the asking. They have been unintentionally lied to by ill-informed church leadership. This is an attempt to expose something that is often missed in many Christians' lives.

I did not think about it at the time, but I was a prime candidate for the Charismatic Renewal when I found my way to that meeting that night that changed my life. I am convinced that God led me to that meeting. I had been faithfully studying the Bible two hours every morning for twelve or thirteen years, trying to pattern my life according to the instructions in the New Testament, and getting more and more frustrated because I could find no one else who believed as I did. I was a very mature 35-37 years old seeker of truth. It was obvious that those folks at that meeting that night, believed as I did. There is no way of explaining the exciting relief I felt at and following that meeting.

CHAPTER 2

Majoring In The Minors

During my career as a District Scout Executive with the Boy Scouts of America, the term, "majoring in the minors" was very popular among the professional staff. Our job description included many responsibilities, and some were critically important, "major", and others were "minor" by comparison. With the workload we were responsible for it was very difficult to do everything as well as we wanted to. With many of those responsibilities being more enjoyable than others, as well as some more important than others, the temptation was always there for us to spend more time on the more enjoyable responsibilities at the cost of the more important, or less enjoyable ones. Hence the term "majoring in the minors".

While trying to live our lives to the fullest, our lives have become more and more complex, and technology has given us more and more tempting activities. The opportunities and temptation to "major in the minors" have been increasing steadily lately. Perhaps the time has come for us to review how we are spending our time, as it relates to what is important to us in the long run.

Jesus gave us a good clue to this in **Matthew 10:28—And do not fear those who kill the body but cannot kill the soul. But rather fear Him who is able to destroy both soul and body in hell.**

In case you haven't figured out who the "Him" is in that Scripture, only God, the creator of the universe, has that power—not Satan or anyone else. Once some years ago, my late wife was talking to a fellow camper about the importance of believing what the Bible says about heaven and hell, and his answer was, "I don't believe in hell". She replied: "Eternity is an awfully long time. What if you are wrong?" Selah (go figure)

What most folks fail to realize is, that living according to God's standard makes life so much more pleasant now, before we die. I have done it so long now I can't imagine trying to live on this earth in this day and time without His fellowship and direction. The following chapters of this book will show you the many great advantages available to "those who believe" here and now, as well as the future eternity. <u>Jesus came to this earth to walk among mankind 2000 years ago to show us how to live in peace, joy, and victory on this earth in The Kingdom of God, and graduate into the ultimate fullness of The Kingdom of God when we leave.</u> It seems that many people never come to realize that Jesus provided so much for our life here and now, as well as the opportunity to spend eternity with Him in paradise.

The choice of whether you spend your life now in fellowship with God through His Holy Spirit or not, as well as eternity in heaven or hell later, is yours to make. It simply concerns your decision to believe the promises as expressed in the Bible and then to live your life in obedience to God based on those promises. It is true that you can make that decision any time before you die but is it worth the risk of waiting till later? Consider the fact that you could miss the opportunity of a much more enriched life now and miss the opportunity to decide before your life ends here.

I think about the comparison between my father's life and my life. My father made little effort to follow the Bible's direction and lived what appeared to me to be a very miserable life. That was because he didn't have companionship with God through the Holy Spirit when he needed it. His drinking and bad temper caused him to lose friends often. He lived with the fact that many people, even those in his own family, disliked him. All in all, my father possessed a lot more skills and abilities than most men, including me, so from that standpoint, he should have had a better life than me. But. I have experienced more peace, joy, and victory in my life than Dad did.

From what I have observed in associating with thousands of people in my 91-year journey, people who love God live a much happier and more contented life than those that don't. That doesn't mean that they have not dealt with hardships, frustrations, and pain. It does mean that they were able to deal with them without being destroyed by them because they had the companionship of God's Holy Spirit to guide them through them. I know that has certainly been the case for me.

So, it all comes down to this: What motivates you; why do you do what you do? That sounds simple enough. What is also simple, is the fact that you only have two choices: God's way or Satan's way. A lot of people never figure that out. They think there can be more than those two, but when you study it, you find that two are all there is. Every motivation is related to one or the other.

What happens often, is people try to dabble in both and not make a conscious decision to serve one or the other. That is not what God asks of us. His command is clear: **Matthew 22:36-40—**

[36] "Teacher, which *is* the great commandment in the law?" [37] Jesus said to him, "'You shall love the LORD your God with all your heart, with all your soul, and with all your mind.' [38] This is *the* first and great commandment. [39] And *the* second *is* like it: 'You shall love your neighbor as yourself.' [40] On these two commandments hang all the Law and the Prophets."

I assume that "all" means "all". I am afraid that far too many people miss that and accept God's motivation only sometimes. I simply do not see how Jesus could have stated it any simpler and clearer than what He did in that Scripture.

It is not complicated. It is actually very simple. Your Creator, the Creator of the universe, gives us a simple formula to have a successful journey on this planet, as well as eternity in Heaven with Him rather than in Hell. That is the formula in **Matthew 22:37-40.** You have the privilege of choosing your journey on this earth and your destination when it is over. God even went further by writing an Operator's Manual to guide you through your journey here on earth. It is called The Holy Bible. But, just like that operator's manual for your car, you must read it to get any benefit from it. Choose wisely because it is the most important decision you could ever make. Remember, "all" means "all".

CHAPTER 3

The Bible Versus The Doctrine Of Man

The doctrine of man was a big problem in the Jewish religion when Jesus started His ministry on earth, and it certainly is a big problem in the church today. The biggest problem was caused by the Jewish religious leaders who were not content with the original law as laid down by God to Moses on Mount Sinai but were continuously tweaking, expanding, adding to it, and outright changing it. A second problem was one that we often see in government and the church today, and that is some individuals got so impressed by their own prestige and lifestyle afforded by their office that protecting that prestige and power became a major motivation. By and large, man's doctrine is false doctrine. We see the disciples fighting false doctrine from the book of Acts through the book of Revelation. The fact that we probably have several thousand different denominations of the Christian church in America today is just the tip of the iceberg. Practically all of them are based on man's doctrine (many times one man's doctrine) and those doctrines are nearly all unbiblical false doctrines. Again, the religious leaders are the culprits in creating this man's doctrine. We have the problem because most folks do not recognize false doctrine when they see it, simply because they are not familiar enough with the Scripture. Sometimes people recognize false doctrine but are reluctant to "make waves" by questioning it. Frankly, that simply perpetuates the problem.

As you read the book of Acts and the books that follow, you can see that the Christian church was what we refer to today as charismatic. By charismatic we mean that it was very much led by the Holy Spirit working through the leaders and members, with signs and wonders of the power of the Holy Spirit working through them.

A very interesting book by Bishop Eusebius, *Eusebius' Ecclesiastical History*, written around the year 350, reveals how the fledgling church was persecuted unmercifully yet spread like wildfire. To protect itself against persecution from the Jewish religious leaders and the Roman Empire, the church took steps to organize itself against the persecution. These steps often proved to be man-made rather than Holy Spirit-inspired. This was evidenced by the fact that morals and evidence of the power of the Holy Spirit gradually eroded. Man's doctrine was a big problem, but the church leaders managed to reject it in most cases, and the church remained somewhat charismatic. Eusebius' book tells how Emperor Constantine accepted the Christian faith and made Christianity the official religion of the Roman Empire. That action brought an end to the severe persecution of the Christians and caused a quick expansion of the church. That all sounds pretty good, and it would have been had Constantine left it alone in the hands of the Holy Spirit's anointed leadership. But in his enthusiasm to "help" the church of his new faith, he caused the demise of the charismatic nature of the church, and it didn't take very long. Constantine injected himself into leadership roles of the church and that caused politicians to join the church (even though they kept their heathen nature) to gain favor with the emperor. Constantine changed the leadership of the churches to a business model, paid salaries, and built church buildings with a stage and pulpit on the order of a royal throne. He thus established the ministerial staff as separate from the laity. Political and business principles are simply incompatible with Charismatic Christianity. You might say Emperor Constantine pushed the Holy Spirit aside and injected himself and other political and business leaders into His place. There simply is no way he could make those three systems work together as one. We turn to the book, *"2000 Years of Charismatic Christianity"* by Eddie L. Hyatt to see the final effort to remove the Holy Spirit from the church. The Holy Spirit was officially kicked out of the church at the Council of Constantinople in 381, when the Montanists, the biggest group of churches who still experienced evidence of the gifts and power of the Holy Spirit, were declared pagan! From that point on, if a church wished to have Holy Spirit-directed services, it had to do it outside of "the church". That is when monasteries and convents came into being. Basically, the New Testament Church went underground, and thus never died. The aforementioned book by Eddie L Hyatt gives you the history of the "underground" charismatic church. It wasn't until the Azusa Street Revival in the early 20th century, that Pentecostal and Holiness denominations were formed, and become officially part of "the church". So, when you consider all this, you can see how and why we basically have two distinctly different churches today, with many churches operating somewhere in between the two. We have the New Testament Church, the Council of Constantinople Church, and many which attempt to have the gifts of the Holy Spirit evident in their services, but basically do not give up Emperor Constantine's organizational pattern. The hierarchy of leadership in the individual churches as well as denominations, plus the financial entanglements, simply closed the door on God and His Holy Spirit having free rein.

"The church" has never gotten itself right since. Oh, it has grown in numbers all right, but it has never regained its power and effectiveness under the leadership of the Holy Spirit since Emperor Constantine pretty much freed the church from persecution and caused a rapid expansion of it. But, by increasing the tendency towards organization and rituals, he virtually made the Holy Spirit unwelcome in church operations and services. Just like in the Old Testament, God always was able to maintain a remnant of true believers, despite whatever turmoil His people were going through. He has done so with His charismatic church which He established 2000 years ago with His original Apostles. We see remnants of it all around us today, we saw it break out in the great awakening of the 18th century, the second great awakening of the 19th century, and on Azusa Street in Los Angeles in the early 20th century. We saw it break out around the world in the 1960s with the Charismatic Renewal, and we are about to see the biggest breakout of it ever very soon, according to many prophecies.

Early in His ministry, Jesus explained His somewhat new doctrine in the "Sermon on the Mount" in **Matthew chapters 5, 6, and 7**. It was His interpretation of the old Jewish law. He later simplified or condensed it which we find in **Matthew 22:35-40**, which we quoted in the previous chapter.

If you have not seriously studied **Matthew 5-7** lately, now would be a good time to start. Being that His doctrine for His church is laid out so clearly there, it makes for very important reading.

The doctrine of man has grown so rapidly and become so prevalent in recent years because so few of the church members see the need to study the Bible for themselves. Consequently, they simply accept whatever the preacher or teacher says, assuming they are qualified and truthful. The problem with that situation is that the need to build up a following often outweighs the responsibility of teaching Bible truth. I have even heard of preachers admitting this. They "don't want to scare them away". Unlike the apostle Paul, they depend on their expertise in oratory excellence rather than Bible truth to attract and hold a following. Look at **1 Corinthians 2:1-7**—

¹And I, brethren, when I came to you, did not come with excellence of speech or of wisdom declaring to you the testimony of God. ² For I determined not to know anything among you except Jesus Christ and Him crucified. ³ I was with you in weakness, in fear, and in much trembling. ⁴ And my speech and my preaching *were* not with persuasive words of human wisdom, but in demonstration of the Spirit and of power, ⁵ that your faith should not be in the wisdom of men but in the power of God. ⁶ However, we speak wisdom among

those who are mature, yet not the wisdom of this age, nor of the rulers of this age, who are coming to nothing. ⁷ But we speak the wisdom of God in a mystery, the hidden *wisdom* which God ordained before the ages for our glory,

The sad, but the obvious truth is, that today far too many pastors and teachers place more importance on building and maintaining their following or their church building and are not faithful enough to their calling to depend on the Holy Spirit for power. Instead, they put that faith in their own oratory skill. I realize you may think I am being cruel and mean, but I am simply telling you what I have observed in my long search for a true New Testament church. Far too many pastors are very careful not to say anything, even if it is Scripture, that might offend someone in any way and "scare them off". Sometimes they seem to have the same attitude about their sermons as Hollywood has about producing a movie about God: "Don't mess up a good story (or sermon) with the truth". That is why I have left far more churches than most Christians have ever attended, and why I seldom turn on our TV. I do selectively check out the news and weather on my smartphone. "Way back when" there was little available to do in "spare time", people would read their Bible regularly, even if they had to do it by the light of a kerosene lamp or the moon. By comparison, the television is often blaring all over the house day and night, smartphones are tempting with an abundance of social media. The sad truth of the matter today is, that consciously or not, most Christians spend more time staring at social media on their smartphone than they do reading their Bible. That leaves the preacher and teacher to teach anything they want to because their listeners do not know enough Bible to know the difference between sound Bible doctrine and the doctrine of man. So, we should not be blaming the preacher and teacher, because they are simply giving us what we ask for. Personally, I have no respect for a spineless preacher or teacher who will not place more responsibility on teaching total Bible truth than on appealing to the audience, and I do not envy they're having that on their resume when they stand before the great white throne judgment. For the Christian in the pew, we simply get what we ask for if we take it.

Jesus said several seemingly harsh things, that you probably won't hear about if you do not study them for yourselves. God has some strong Attitudes and Mindsets, which at first glance seem very harsh. You will find several of those in this book, and here is one: —

Matthew 10:34-39— [34]**"Do not think that I came to bring peace on earth. I did not come to bring peace but a sword.** [35] **For I have come to 'set a man against his father, a daughter against her mother, and a daughter-in-law against her mother-in-law';** [36] **and a man's enemies will be those of his own household.'** [37] **He who loves father or mother more than Me is not worthy of Me. And he who loves son or daughter more than Me is not worthy of Me.** [38] **And he who does not take his cross and follow after Me is not worthy of Me.** [39] **He who finds his life will lose it, and he who loses his life for My sake will find it."**

Is that strong and radical, or what? He made it perfectly clear that the doctrine He was bringing to His people was so strong that it would cause division in families because He was going to expect His followers to die to selfish desires every day and make pleasing Him, rather than themselves and their families, the object of their life daily. You could even say that He was saying He wanted your complete, total, loyalty, or nothing. <u>Man, that is radical!</u>

Remember that Jesus made His intentions for His earthly ministry primarily to the Jews first, and His "doctrinal statement" which you might call **Matthew chapters 5-7**, was clearly contrary to what the Jewish religious leaders had been teaching. However, what He was teaching in the Sermon on the Mount, was simply His interpretation of the Ten Commandments and the rest of the Old Testament law, as opposed to the way the Jewish leaders had twisted it. He was expecting loyalty to Him as opposed to loyalty to the Jewish leaders, even if that would cause division within a given household. I believe God always demanded "all or nothing," but the Jewish religious leaders twisted His words so much that the message DID NOT COME THROUGH. That is how strong a demand He made on followers then, and I can only assume that same demand still holds today. The Jewish religious leaders of Jesus' time had so perverted the Jewish law, as spelled out in the first several books of the Bible, that He knew that some within the same household would choose to follow Him, while others in that same household would continue to follow the false doctrine of the religious leaders. Jesus made the rash statement that we should love Him more than even family members. "Die to self" is a theme Jesus repeated quite often, and that is the message of **Matthew 10, verses 38 and 39** in the above Scripture. At that time, a man with a cross on his back had a death sentence on his head. "He who loses his life for My sake shall find it!"

Please note that this does not contradict the angel's announcement in **Luke 2:14—**

"Glory to God in the highest, and on earth peace, goodwill toward men!"

Jesus was bringing a means of goodwill between God and man because man had not been on good terms with God. This was certainly borne out in His ministry—consider the Kingdom of God that He would introduce later. Look at the ultimate relationship He wanted to establish with His followers in **John 17:20-23—**

"I do not pray for these alone, but also for those who will believe in Me through their word; [21] that they all may be one, as You, Father, *are* in Me, and I in You; that they also may be one in Us, that the world may believe that You sent Me. [22] And the glory which You gave Me I have given them, that they may be one just as We are one: [23] I in them, and You in Me; that they may be made perfect in one, and that the world may know that You have sent Me, and have loved them as You have loved Me."

Matthew 10:34-39 (previously quoted) is just one of many Scriptures we will point out in this book, that describes some very strong and serious Attitudes and Mindsets that Jesus made clear, that many preachers and teachers avoid teaching. The fact that they are rarely taught does not make them any less real or important.

God's love for us is stronger than we can understand, and He is completely justified in expecting us to love Him as much as He expects us to. He makes that Attitude and Mindset very clear to the lukewarm Laodicean church in **Revelation 3:14-16—**

[14]"And to the angel of the church of the Laodiceans write, 'These things says the Amen, the Faithful and True Witness, the Beginning of the creation of God: [15] I know your works, that you are neither cold nor hot. I could wish you were cold or hot. [16] So then, because you are lukewarm, and neither cold nor hot, I will vomit you out of My mouth."

Now, that is strong language. Like it or not, that is one of God's Attitudes and Mindsets that the Bible is very clear about, but you seldom hear about. I hasten to point out, that Jesus went on to tell them how to redeem themselves, and that Scripture will be quoted later.

"The church", has fed us so much false doctrine that very few church attendees have a true and accurate knowledge of God's Attitudes and Mindsets. When you really get to thinking about the consequences of it, that is very scary. Nowhere in the Bible do I see ignorance listed as an excuse for not following Jesus' teaching. YOU are responsible for understanding YOUR salvation.

Perhaps the biggest and most blatant false doctrine that has been perpetuated for no telling how long, and to no telling how many (billions!) oblivious Christians, is the outright lie that the gifts and miracles associated with the Baptism in the Holy Spirit ended with the original Apostles. I say outright lie because there is no Scripture to support it and a big part of the New Testament proves it just is not true. If that lie were a fact, much of the New Testament would be unnecessary. I have not researched how it got started, and for the life of me I cannot figure out why anyone would believe it, let alone go so many years without being absolutely refuted. I believed that lie for the first 37 years of my life when I was in a major denomination church. But, after studying the Bible for two hours a day for 12 years, and attending meetings with Christians who knew better, I quickly repented, got my thinking straight, and started growing in the life Jesus made available to me. There have been <u>billions of miracles</u> in the last 2000 years that prove the miraculous power of the Baptism in the Holy Spirit is alive and well among His followers today, and I personally have received and witnessed hundreds of miracles of healing and provision. I have trouble understanding how that blatant lie has been perpetuated for so long.

The only explanation I have ever heard for the basis of that false doctrine is so shallow I don't understand how anyone could ever believe it in the first place. It obviously has only survived because of biblical illiteracy. It is this Scripture from **1 Corinthians Chapter 13**, known as the love chapter. I will quote the whole chapter.

¹Though I speak with the tongues of men and of angels, but have not love, I have become sounding brass or a clanging cymbal. ² And though I have *the gift of* prophecy, and understand all mysteries and all knowledge, and though I have all faith, so that I could remove mountains, but have not love, I am nothing. ³ And though I bestow all my goods to feed *the poor,* and though I give my body to be burned, but have not love, it profits me nothing.

⁴ Love suffers long *and* is kind; love does not envy; love does not parade itself, is not puffed up; ⁵ does not behave rudely, does not seek its own, is not provoked, thinks no evil; ⁶ does not rejoice in iniquity, but rejoices in the truth; ⁷ bears all things, believes all things, hopes all things, endures all things.

⁸ Love never fails. But whether *there are* prophecies, they will fail; whether *there are* tongues, they will cease; whether *there is* knowledge, it will vanish away. ⁹ For we know in part and we

prophesy in part. ¹⁰ But when that which is perfect has come, then that which is in part will be done away.

¹¹ When I was a child, I spoke as a child, I understood as a child, I thought as a child; but when I became a man, I put away childish things. ¹² For now we see in a mirror, dimly, but then face to face. Now I know in part, but then I shall know just as I also am known.

¹³ And now abide faith, hope, love, these three; but the greatest of these *is* love.

As I understand it, the original perpetrators of the lie say that verses 8-12 indicate that prophecies, tongues, and knowledge will all pass away when the perfect has come, which they say is the Bible. There are many things indicating this is false doctrine:

1.. They commit the major sin of Bible interpretation, by taking those verses out of context. Chapter 13 is clearly placed between chapters 12 and 14, to show the proper way of exercising the things described in chapters 12 and 14. Thus they have perverted one of the most beautiful chapters in the Bible.

2.. They say the Bible is the "perfect" referred to. Really? Do they mean that all knowledge has become nil since the Bible was written? Come on! God has been enhancing man's knowledge for years.

3.. Why would the Apostle Paul waste his time writing chapters 12 and 14, not to mention the rest of his writings, if everything there is shortly to be done away with?

4.. I think the "perfect" in this Scripture refers to the completion that we will enter after we leave this life. In my opinion, that is the only thing that fits the word "perfect."

The root cause of all false doctrine is obviously satanic, and we need to be sharper at recognizing it. We do that by seriously studying the Bible for ourselves, asking the Holy Spirit to help us understand and interpret it, rather than depending on someone else to tell us what it says. The sad truth is, that most church attendees never question the motive or Bible knowledge of the preacher or teacher. They can't question it, because they haven't read the Bible enough to know the difference between Bible truth and false doctrine. They simply assume that the preacher and teacher are saintly men or women with high motives and complete knowledge of the subject matter. As a friend of mine once said, "if the ignorant lead the ignorant, everyone gets more ignoranter!". (He was referring to the need for properly trained trainers of Boy Scout troop leaders.) Jesus said something like this in **Matthew 15:14 "Let them alone. They are blind leaders of the blind. And if the blind leads the blind, both will fall into a ditch."** Jesus was referring to the religious leaders of the day.

Jesus spent 3½ years walking this earth, putting up with enormous ridicule and verbal abuse; then suffered the cruelest torture and death that the evil religious leaders and the Roman emperor could contrive. I believe He did all this because Father God and Jesus figured that was the only way to get the job done: to show us how to have peace, joy, and happiness in this life, then graduate to an eternal paradise with Him. It is hard to wrap your mind around that kind of love. To top that off, they decided to send Holy Spirit to live in each one of us, so that we could exercise the same power and wisdom that Jesus had when He walked this earth. If we don't study the Bible to understand this free gift that has been given to us, we are as pitiful as a poor destitute European widow I read about. The story took place over a hundred years ago in England. She had been a loyal servant to a wealthy landowner. Before his death he had given her a certificate, without realizing she could not read. She became bedridden her pastor visited her, read the framed certificate that was hanging on the wall. He discovered that she had received a very large inheritance. But, because of not being able to read, she was living in poverty while being very wealthy. Just think of the billions of people who have not taken the opportunity to study their Bible to understand how wealthy they could be if they just took advantage of the opportunity to do so.

CHAPTER 4

The Charismatic Renewal

The Charismatic Renewal was the outgrowth of the Azusa Street revival and Welsh revivals that occurred early in the twentieth century. There are many interesting books available on those events. The Azusa Street Revival birthed most of the Pentecostal and Holiness denominations that we have in America today. That revival drew interested people from all over America to Los Angeles, and seekers in foreign lands boarded ships to come to the revival. When the Azusa Street Revival played out after several years, it left a rumbling that eventually erupted into the Charismatic Renewal on the West Coast in the early 1960s. It finally reached us here in the East in the mid-1960s. There is a good book available on the history of charismatic activities in the twentieth century titled, *The Charismatic Century,* written by one of my favorite Bible teachers, Jack W. Hayford, and S. David Moore. This book was published in 2006.

The Charismatic Renewal was not started by any one denomination, but by individuals and groups from several different denominations. I have often said and do believe, that God got frustrated with the church and reached out to seeking individuals in many different church denominations to start a movement among strong followers from those many different churches. However, the door was left open for churches to become part of the movement if they wanted to. Many churches from various denominations did join in eventually. The Charismatic Renewal featured very limited leadership and finances with no building ownership. A study of church history reveals that church government, programs, and finances have affected the church much more negatively than they have positively.

The people involved in the Charismatic Renewal were people like me, who had studied the Word enough for themselves that they became dissatisfied and malnourished by their church and looked elsewhere for nourishment. We see the same situation in play today, so many of us are praying for and expecting another great outpouring of the Holy Spirit to bust out soon. Most participants in the Charismatic Renewal stayed active in their home church but looked to the Charismatic Renewal meetings for fulfillment. The weekly home Bible study meetings were the heart of the movement, but in the cities and towns, there were also monthly community-wide meetings of the Full Gospel Businessmen's Fellowship and Women's Aglow. They usually ended with several people receiving miracles of healing. These meetings usually were built around the testimony and ministry of a well-known person with an outstanding testimony, included a meal, and often drew big crowds.

That first weekly Bible study that I attended was the first meeting, or church service, that I had ever attended that somewhat followed the only outline I have found in the Bible for a church service.

1 Corinthians 14:26-33:

[26] How is it then, brethren? Whenever you come together, each of you has a psalm, has a teaching, has a tongue, has a revelation, has an interpretation. Let all things be done for edification. [27] If anyone speaks in a tongue, *let there be* two or at the most three, *each* in turn, and let one interpret. [28] But if there is no interpreter, let him keep silent in church, and let him speak to himself and to God. [29] Let two or three prophets speak, and let the others judge. [30] But if *anything* is revealed to another who sits by, let the first keep silent. [31] For

you can all prophesy one by one, that all may learn, and all may be encouraged. ³² And the spirits of the prophets are subject to the prophets. ³³ For God is not *the author* of confusion but of peace, as in all the churches of the saints.

The seating at those weekly Bible studies was usually a circle, with no designated seats. After a time of gathering and greeting, everyone would take a seat, and the room would gradually become quiet. Then someone would start softly singing a chorus, after which others would join in. After a few runs of that one, someone else would start another. This would keep up for twenty or more minutes, with the choruses gradually moving from praise to worship. Once we "crossed that line" from praise to worship, we never turned back to singing about God rather than to Him. These were choruses of popular hymns or Scripture set to music. They were usually only one to three lines, so were easily learned—no printing, projecting, or leading needed. Several different things could happen after the singing, without any apparent leadership or order. This could include prophecies, words of knowledge, words of wisdom, exhortation, a message in tongues, interpretation of tongues, testimonies, or whatever—no particular order. When things eventually quieted down, the teacher would lead a Bible teaching, never a sermon. Occasionally, there would be so much individual participation that there just would not be enough time left for teaching, and the teacher was always able to adjust his teaching to end at a reasonable time. If there was no time for Bible teaching, neither the teacher nor anyone else would be concerned about it. After the Bible teaching, someone would then close that part of the meeting with prayer. We would then place a chair in the middle of the room and offer it to anyone who wanted us to pray for them. It was not unusual to see miracles of healing or other manifestations of Holy Spirit resulting from this. Seldom have I ever participated in worship as strong as we had in those meetings. We always left the meeting uplifted and looking forward to the next one. Although those weekly meetings were nearly always referred to as "Bible studies", I now believe it would have been more accurate if we had referred to them as "home church meetings". The reason they were not referred to as "home church meetings" was that the charismatic leadership often emphasized that we were not to do anything to hurt or interfere with the established churches in any way. As I look back on that now, I believe that we should have "quit whipping the dead horses" and looked after our own spiritual growth. If we had just left those dead churches and put all our effort and support into the "home churches", we would be much stronger followers of Jesus today, we would have impacted far more people, and the Charismatic Renewal may well have been stronger and better today than it ever was. That's my opinion, and I'm sticking with it.

I have always been a lover of God's Creation and am most comfortable out in it. After working inside a building with no windows for several years and participating in the traffic rat race getting to work every morning, I reached the breaking point. I took a week's camping vacation to Florida with my wife and youngest son and obtained a job as a Florida State Park Ranger at Manatee State Park, near Chiefland, Florida. We found a charismatic home Bible study about thirty-five miles from the park, and participation there was quite fulfilling. Not finding anything near the park in the Chiefland area, we decided to fill that need ourselves. So, we started a weekly night Bible study in our home in the park, and my wife started one for the ladies in the mornings. After a few months, we started a Full Gospel Businessmen's Fellowship Chapter in the nearby town of Chiefland. It was a very uplifting time of spiritual growth as well as ministry.

We witnessed God's power in nearly all those meetings and had a very effective ministry. We saw people saved and receive miracles of healing. The one miracle that stands out the most was the older lady that some of the regular attendees talked into coming to a meeting one night. She very obviously had a severe case of emphysema, to the extent that after she climbed the three or four steps up to our house, she had to rest several minutes before she could talk. Her natural breathing was so labored, that her problem was constantly obvious to everyone in the room. I taught on healing that night, and when we offered to pray for individuals at the close of the meeting, she was the first one to request prayer. We commanded the disease to leave her body in the name of Jesus. Her breathing immediately became normal. She vacated the "hot seat" and took a chair over in the corner, completely overwhelmed by the miraculous healing she had just received. As we progressed on to praying for other individuals, I became aware of the fact that the lady's breathing had again become labored. I slipped away from ministering to the individual in the "hot-seat", leaving it for others to finish, eased over to the lady breathing heavily, placed my hand on her head, rebuked that demon of emphysema, and commanded it to leave in the name of Jesus. Her breathing immediately became normal. She left the meeting that night rejoicing and continued to attend the meetings regularly until she returned to her home in Indiana that spring.

The next fall I happened to see that lady in a store in Chiefland, and she looked so much healthier and younger than she had the past spring. I asked her if she would give her testimony at the upcoming Full Gospel Businessmen's Fellowship Meeting, and she gladly accepted. At the meeting, she told how God miraculously healed her that night, and a demon tried to rob her of her miraculous healing. She said that occurred one more time when she was alone, but she remembered how we dealt with it that night and she rebuked the demon in the name of Jesus and has been completely free of the disease ever since. She stated that prior to that night she had been sleeping in a chair for several years, but since that night she had slept in her bed every night. She had lost weight and looked many years younger.

The recession of the mid-seventies caused inflation to eat so deep into my paycheck that I was again forced out of a profession I loved. I began my profession as an office machine technician back in Wilmington, then took a job as service manager with an office machine dealer in Roanoke Rapids, North Carolina, in the northeast of the state. We found a Bible study group that worked for us although not as fulfilling as what we had in Florida. I got involved in the local Full Gospel Businessmen's Fellowship Chapter, and my wife got involved in the local Women's Aglow Chapter. We visited several churches and following a service one morning, a fellow asked me to pray for his left ear, as he was completely deaf in that ear. I commanded that ear to be opened in the name of Jesus, and added, "according to your faith be it unto you", and he could immediately hear perfectly out of both ears. All praise to God!

After visiting around for a while, we found a very satisfying church home. It was a Pentecostal denomination church that was open to the evidence of the gifts of the Spirit in action. We became very much involved in the ministry of the church, more so than involvement in the home Bible study meetings. That, along with our involvement in the Full Gospel Businessmen's Fellowship and Women's Aglow, kept us very active and spiritually satisfied. The Charismatic Renewal was gradually fading out at this point, and that church along with the Full Gospel Businessmen's Fellowship and Women's Aglow Chapter were the last remaining bastions of the Charismatic Renewal in Roanoke Rapids that I was aware of.

Let's look back at the early church that the disciples started. It very closely resembled what we experienced in the Charismatic Renewal. Church history indicates that the church operated that way to at least some extent up to the time Emperor Constantine put a stop to the serious persecution of the Christians, enabling the rapid spread of the Gospel. The Holy Spirit was mostly kicked out of the church in 381 when the Council of Constantinople declared the Montanists as pagan. Montanists were followers of Montanus, who had been outstanding in his success of experiencing the evident power of the Holy Spirit, was regarded as a saint by his followers, but as a heretic by others. From that time, the charismatic church operated underground and was completely ignored by most historians for hundreds of years.

We must understand that Peter, John, and Jude who was a half-brother of Jesus, all were members of the Jerusalem church, and the Jerusalem church was mostly comprised of Jews. The Apostle Paul was the one who organized most of the basically gentile churches out in the area away from Jerusalem. Peter started one in Caesarea according to chapter 10 of Acts. Others started some gentile churches, but they all evidently came to be under Paul's jurisdiction. These outlying churches were mostly gentiles although some of them had a few Jews in them. We have to say that there's a difference between the mostly Jewish Jerusalem church and the other mostly gentile churches. If you go back to Acts chapters 2 through 4 you see that the Jerusalem church right from the outset had over 8000 people in it, and it probably grew bigger even than that. There is no evidence in the Bible that the gentile churches ever had anywhere near numbers like that. So, we have to say that there are two different types of churches: the huge Jerusalem Jewish church of the first 10 chapters of the book of Acts, and the smaller gentile churches where Paul's and Jude's letters are addressed to. 1 John, James,1 and 2 Peter are probably addressed to all the churches. The other epistles are addressed to individuals.

Let's first consider the Jerusalem church. The first few chapters of the book of Acts only mentions the outer court of the temple as their main meeting place. I seriously doubt they could do any worship or training there under the nose of the Jewish religious leaders, and I doubt the Jewish religious leaders tolerated their meeting there very long. The outer court was most likely only used for fellowship and communication. Otherwise, they probably either met outside or in homes. The only other place that is mentioned in the Bible that they probably used was the upper room and from what I have been able to find out, probably about 200 to 300 people was all that it could accommodate. They met somewhere as a big group for eating because we get that from chapter three. It was possibly an outdoor setting even for meals and any activities because they do not receive much rain or cold weather there. Homes were very small so the capacity inside the homes was very limited. Remember that they had no electricity or electronics back then and no amplifiers to broadcast to a larger crowd.

Paul's letters, particularly First Corinthians and Ephesians, tell us much about the operation of the gentile church, so we may draw some conclusions from those and other writings of Paul. We will check out some of those Scriptures and insert some passages from them to get a picture of how the gentile churches operated.

1 Corinthians 1:26-31—²⁶For you see your calling, brethren, that not many wise according to the flesh, not many mighty, not many noble, are called. ²⁷ But God has chosen the foolish things of the world to put to shame the wise, and God has chosen the weak things of the world to put to shame the things which are mighty; ²⁸ and the base things of the world and the things which are despised God has chosen, and the things which are not, to bring to nothing the things that are, ²⁹ that no flesh should glory in His presence. ³⁰ But of Him you are in Christ Jesus, who became for us wisdom from God—and righteousness and sanctification and redemption— ³¹ that, as it is written, "He who glories, let him glory in the Lord."

1 Corinthians 11:17-22— ¹⁷ Now in giving these instructions I do not praise you, since you come together not for the better but for the worse. ¹⁸ For first of all, when you come together as a church, I hear that there are divisions among you, and in part I believe it. ¹⁹ For there must also be factions among you, that those who are approved may be recognized among you. ²⁰ Therefore when you come together in one place, it is not to eat the Lord's Supper. ²¹ For in eating, each one takes his own supper ahead of others; and one is hungry and another is drunk. ²² What! Do you not have houses to eat and drink in? Or do you despise the church of God and shame those who have nothing? What shall I say to you? Shall I praise you in this? I do not praise you.

1 Corinthians 12:4-14— ⁴There are diversities of gifts, but the same Spirit. ⁵ There are differences of ministries, but the same Lord. ⁶ And there are diversities of activities, but it is the same God who works all in all. ⁷ But the manifestation of the Spirit is given to each one for the profit *of all:* ⁸ for to one is given the word of wisdom through the Spirit, to another the word of knowledge through the same Spirit, ⁹ to another faith by the same Spirit, to another gifts of healings by the same Spirit, ¹⁰ to another the working of miracles, to another prophecy, to another discerning of spirits, to another *different* kinds of tongues, to another the interpretation of tongues. ¹¹ But one and

the same Spirit works all these things, distributing to each one individually as He wills.

¹² For as the body is one and has many members, but all the members of that one body, being many, are one body, so also *is* Christ. ¹³ For by one Spirit we were all baptized into one body—whether Jews or Greeks, whether slaves or free—and have all been made to drink into one Spirit. ¹⁴ For in fact the body is not one member but many.

1 Corinthians 12:27-31— ²⁷Now you are the body of Christ, and members individually. ²⁸ And God has appointed these in the church: first apostles, second prophets, third teachers, after that miracles, then gifts of healings, helps, administrations, varieties of tongues. ²⁹ Are all apostles? Are all prophets? Are all teachers? Are all workers of miracles? ³⁰ Do all have gifts of healings? Do all speak with tongues? Do all interpret? ³¹ But earnestly desire the best gifts. And yet I show you a more excellent way.

Chapter 13, the love chapter follows the above Scriptures.

The above Scriptures prompt me to believe the gentile churches mostly met in small groups that we refer to today as "home churches", or "home groups." If nearly everyone present had a part in the meetings, that would limit the number of participants. In a bigger setting, the timid members would be reluctant to participate. Note also in that last scripture that the spiritual gifts were bestowed by the Holy Spirit.

This is what I referred to earlier when I talked about the home Bible studies that I attended during the Charismatic Renewal. We depended on the Holy Spirit to lead the meeting and He led it through many different people. Most of the people in the meeting would take part because they obviously studied the Bible and understood how to participate with whatever gift of the Spirit the Holy Spirit chose to utilize through each individual participant.

This brings me to a very interesting comparison of "the church" to the once huge Boy Scouts of America organization that I was active in from 1943 to 1968, with part of that time serving as a professional District Scout Executive. It appears to me that in the early church the small groups were the heart of the church where growth in the faith mostly took place. That was also the way that we operated during the charismatic renewal. The heart of the movements was not the big meetings, but it was the small meetings that drove both movements. I compare this to my Boy Scouting experience. Boy Scouting, the program established by Lord Baden Powell in England in 1908 and that came to America in 1910 was completely different from the way the program usually plays out today. The program was centered around the patrol, not the troop. A troop was organized into patrols of 5-9 boys each. The boys in the patrol elected their patrol leader, and he in turn assigned each boy in the patrol with responsibilities such as Assistant Patrol Leader, Scribe, Quartermaster, Cook, etc. When a troop camping trip was scheduled, (usually once a month) the patrol would meet and plan their participation. They would decide what they would eat, make up the grocery list, put their money together to buy the food, plan the purchasing of the food, decide how it would get to the campsite, how it would be cooked, and the utensils needed, cleanup, etc. The Scoutmaster's job was basically to train his "junior" troop leaders and Patrol Leaders in how to lead and let them lead. The problem came when the national professional leadership abandoned the basic plan and put pressure on the local professionals to spend the bulk of their effort on increasing membership and raising money, rather than training the adult leaders to train the boy leaders. Today that once great organization is in shambles.

Evidently in the New Testament gentile church, the small home church was the basic unit, and local bishops led and trained the leaders of the home churches.

Francis Chan has written some books, including *Letters to the Church*, and has thoroughly researched the home church concept. He was pastor of a megachurch up until a few years ago when he resigned and went back to working just with the home church concept. He has written several books on the subject.

Basically, "the church" that we are familiar with today, generally has no resemblance to the church of the New Testament. *Eusebius' Ecclesiastical History* offers us the most insight into what went on in the church's early years. Eusebius lived from about 280 to 360, was an influential leader and historian of the church, and was well acquainted with Emperor Constantine. He points out that the power and miracles of the Holy Spirit were still in evidence in some churches during his lifetime in chapter 7 of book 5. He also indicates that their occurrences were in decline. He quotes from many lost manuscripts that are no longer available.

I believe that the home church meetings of the Charismatic Renewal were a good example of the New Testament Church, with remnants still functioning in individuals and scattered bodies of believers today. I am referring to individuals and churches in whom God's power and glory through the fruit and gifts of the Holy Spirit, are still evident in the lives of the believers and the church. They still see operation of the gifts and the fruit of Holy Spirit, miracles of healing, and provision, like those recorded in the New Testament. Even some Pentecostal denominational churches today, which claim to be New Testament Churches, are often void of much evidence of the power of the Holy Spirit.

The New Testament modeled churches and their members are experiencing the Kingdom of God now, whereas the members of the other churches, for the most part, are not. If a church belongs to a denomination, they face both a challenge and a benefit. A denomination has certain criteria that each individual church is required to adhere to. This could be doctrine, ways of organizing, selection of leadership, procedures, and protocols. In some cases, this could partially or completely stifle the work of the Holy Spirit in that church. On the other hand, belonging to a denomination provides checks and balances of accountability that could discipline leadership gone astray from the work of the Holy Spirit. All this is to say, that the New Testament church model could flourish wherever united hearts want it to. It more likely happens in a smaller group, but we also don't want to put God in a box, saying that Holy Spirit can't work fully through larger bodies of Christ.

I often hear the expression, "we are saved by grace, not works". I agree with that statement. However, I do not see that as an excuse not to be holy. The Bible clearly teaches that we should love God enough to cause us to be holy because He is holy and loves us so much. Chapter 11 will discuss this subject in more detail. I mention that here because history shows us that a decline in holiness, accompanies a decline of the fruit of the Holy Spirit (Galatians 5:22-23) as well as the gifts of the Holy Spirit.

WORSHIP MUSIC OF THE CHARISMATIC RENEWAL

I have never experienced such an encouraging music worship time that matched that which we experienced at those weekly home Church meetings during the Charismatic Renewal. I had some files with the words on them, but in the process of downsizing from a house to an RV, I regretfully lost them. I consider them so important to meaningful worship in song that I am going to print some of them here, particularly the ones based on Scripture. These were formulated in the early 1960s before we were nearly drowned in so many different translations of the Bible. So, these all come from the King James Version of the Bible. They were basically divided into three groups: exhortation, praise, and worship. We generally sang them in that order. We would usually start with exhortation, then ease into praise, and finish in worship. If someone accidentally started a praise chorus (singing about God) or exhortation chorus, after we had started singing worship (singing TO God) choruses, it usually interrupted the flow of worship. The words sometimes varied slightly from Scripture, to fit the chorus.

EXHORTATION

Matthew 6:33 & 7:7 Karen Lafferty
Seek ye first the kingdom of God,
And His righteous-ness
Then all these things shall be added
    unto you
Al-le-lu allelu-ia

Ask and it shall be given unto you
Seek and you will find,
Knock and the door will be opened
    unto you
Al-le-u alleu-ia

Ephesians 5:18-20
Be filled with the Spirit
Speaking to yourselves
In Psalms and hymns
And spiritual songs,
Singing and making melody
In your heart to the Lord

Isaiah 40:31
They that wait upon the Lord
Shall renew their strength
They shall mount up
With Wings as Eagles
They shall run and not be weary
They shall walk and not faint,
Teach me Lord, teach me Lord
To wait.

Psalm 34:1-4
I will bless the LORD at all times;
His praise shall continually be in my mouth.
My soul shall make its boast in the LORD;
The humble shall hear *of it* and be glad.
Oh, magnify the LORD with me,
And let us exalt His name together.
I sought the LORD, and He heard me,
And delivered me from all my fears.

Acts 3:6-8
Silver and gold have I none
But such as I have, give I thee,
In the name of Jesus Christ
Of Nazareth, rise up and walk.
And he went walking and leaping
And praising God
Walking and leaping and praising God
In the name of Jesus Christ
Of Nazareth, rise up and walk.

PRAISE

Psalm 30:1-2
I will extol thee oh Lord
For Thou hast lifted me up
And hast not caused my foes
To rejoice over me
O Lord my God
I cried unto thee
And Thou hast heard me
And thou hast heard me
(repeat first 4 lines)

Psalm 3:3-4
My glory and the lifter of my head,
My glory and the lifter of my head,
For thou oh Lord art a shield to me,
My glory and the lifter of my head.
I cried unto the Lord with my voice,
I cried unto the Lord with my voice.
I cried unto the Lord with my voice,
And He heard me from His holy Hill.
(repeat first three lines)

Psalm 103:1-3
Bless the Lord, oh my soul,
And all that is within me, bless His Holy Name.
For He hath done great things,

Alleluia
Alleluia, Alleluia, Alleluia, Alleluia.
(may repeat)

Lord I love You, Lord I love you
Lord I love You, Lord I love you,
Lord I praise You, Lord I praise You,
Lord I praise You, Lord I praise You.
(you can do several different things with this simple chorus.)

Father, We Adore You Terrye Coelho
Father, we adore You,
Lay our lives before You,
How we love You
(Repeat with Jesus and Spirit)

WORSHIP

I love you Lord
And I lift my voice
To worship you
Oh my soul, rejoice
Take joy my King
In what You hear
May it be a sweet, sweet song in Your ear.

Heavenly Father, We Appreciate You
Heavenly Father we(I) appreciate you,
Heavenly Father we(I) appreciate You,
We(I) love You, adore You,
We(I) bow down before You,
Heavenly Father, we(I) appreciate You.
(Repeat with Lord Jesus and Holy Spirit)

Thy Loving Kindness
Thy loving kindness is better than life.
Thy loving kindness is better than life.
My lips shall praise Thee, thus will I bless Thee,
I will lift up my hands in Thy name.
I will lift up my hands in Thy name.
I will lift up my hands in Thy name.
My lips shall praise Thee, I will lift up my hands in Thy name.

Most of these choruses and many more, with the music, can be found in DOVE SONGS,

Published by Presbyterian Charismatic Communion.

CHAPTER 5

Remnants Of The Charismatic Renewal Still Exist

Getting back to my personal experiences during and after the Charismatic Renewal, we spent five years in Roanoke Rapids, moving from there in 1982. After renting an apartment back in our hometown of Wilmington, North Carolina for a while, we bought five and one-half acres of beautiful woodlands near Burgaw, thirty miles up interstate forty from Wilmington. We found a charismatic church in Burgaw, attended some Full Gospel Businessmen's Fellowship meetings in Wilmington, and my wife started a Women's Aglow Chapter in Burgaw.

Even though the Charismatic Renewal had somewhat faded out by this time, we still witnessed the power of the Holy Spirit somewhat as we had back in the seventies. My wife was again afflicted with rheumatoid arthritis and again was miraculously healed by God. One night at church, Pastor Elmer taught on healing, and at the close of his message invited anyone who wanted to be healed to come forward for prayer. One of our members went forward and asked to be healed of severe back pain. I felt led to go forward and pray for him. I placed my hand on his back, rebuked the pain, and commanded his back to be healed in the name of Jesus. He said his back felt better, so we both returned to our seats. I visited with Forrest in his home a few weeks later and was surprised to find out what a miracle he had received that night. He had hurt his back while working on his chicken farm and had become completely disabled. He had to give up raising chickens and could no longer do manual work. He spent most of the day and night in a recliner. He said that night when I prayed for him that I put my hand exactly on the spot that was injured, and he felt a sensation when I prayed. He said he was instantly, completely healed and soon returned to full mobility. We were all amazed and praised God for the great miracle.

I followed the evangelist Benny Hinn for a couple of years on television and became a supporter. In the spring of 1998, I took off a week to camp by myself in the Everglades and attend a four-day Benny Hinn supporters rally in Miami, Florida. I spent the first part of each day kayaking on one of the canoe/kayak trails. or photographing alligators and water birds on the Anhinga Trail. About mid-afternoon I would return to my tent and take a bath with that new popular item, "baby wipes". There were no showers at the Long Pine campground. I would then drive into downtown Miami for the conference. I was spiritually fed at the conference with good Bible teaching but became intrigued by Benny's description of the Holy Land Tour he would be leading in the fall. The fact that 1998 was Israel's first Jubilee Year since David was King, really intrigued me. Benny had made friends with King Abdulla of Jordan and his son and had received permission from the king to take a Christian tour into Jordan for the first time in many years. That also intrigued me. At the end of the week, I packed up and headed back to Burgaw.

I had wanted to visit the Holy Land for years but had never felt I had the time or could afford it. As I headed North, I couldn't get that Holy Land Tour off my mind. I started praying about it as I drove. I must confess that my praying eroded into begging. As I passed Fort Pierce Florida, I received the answer to my begging prayer: "OK, you are going". It was all I could do to keep that little pickup truck between the lines as I barreled up I-95. I had no idea where I was going to get the money for the tour, so I did the only thing I could think of. I went before the approximate two-hundred-member congregation of the church I was attending at that time and asked for help. Within a few weeks, there was more than enough money in the account for the trip. My wife was not physically able to go.

The ten-day Holy Land Tour turned out to be everything I had hoped for and more. The Empty Tomb, the Upper Room, the Dead Sea Scrolls site and museum, the Museum of the Bible, the Holocaust Museum, Petra (The Rose City) in Jordan, the Sea of Galilee, the Dead Sea, the Golan Heights, my baptism in the Jordan River, and my planting a tree in honor of my deceased kid brother, all impacted me greatly. The friends I made on the tour and the Bible teaching were great. Following that experience and after making several mission trips, I have said many times, "Every Christian should try to make a trip to the Holy Land and a mission trip to a third-world country." They are very educational and soul-enriching experiences.

The day after I returned home from the tour, as I was unpacking my luggage, I was thinking about the events of the trip and thanking God for the experience. I asked God about two experiences I had on the trip that I did not understand. The first was as I slowly walked around the displays in the museum of the Bible, which were arranged in a circle, I would start sobbing every time I passed a certain Bible on display. I couldn't read the description in the Bible because my eyes would grow blurry as I approached. I thought the phenomenon was so strange at the time, that I walked back and forth several times and had the same reaction every time, which I did not understand. That day as I was unpacking God told me that was the oldest copy of the Old Testament in existence, and the one the several translations I had studied were based on. He told me that my love and appreciation of the Scripture is what made it so impactful. Of course, that created another reaction.

The other experience I had on the trip that puzzled me had to do with the baptism in the Jordan River. I had already been baptized twice: Presbyterian, which, after studying the Bible, I personally did not consider a baptism at all; and Baptist. So it wasn't that I felt a spiritual or religious need to be baptized. But the idea of the opportunity to be baptized in the same river where my Lord and Savior was baptized, just seemed like an opportunity I didn't want to pass up. Everyone on the tour that signed up for it was issued white robes and lined up. Benny Hinn was doing the baptizing by pushing you back into the water, but he had an assistant on each side of you take your hand and pull you back up. When my turn came, as I approached Benny Hinn and he reached for my forehead, my knees buckled and I sat down in the water, completely submerging my head. Of course, when I came back up everyone had a bewildered look on their face—me most of all. I had no idea why my knees buckled. I did not consciously do anything to cause them to buckle. I walked away wondering what had just happened. So, when I asked God that morning what happened on that occasion, He told me simply, "I wanted to baptize you Myself". Wow! It took me a while to get over that!

Please try to understand why I am relating these very personal events to you in this book and try not to read anything into it that isn't there. I hesitated to relate them because they are very personal and I do not want to be construed as bragging, which I am not. I relate them to show you the depth of the relationship, your Lord and Savior wants to have with you and how He wants to love you. I am sharing with you only a fraction of some of the ways God has blessed me through the years. The Apostle, John, lays out a key Attitude and Mindset of God in **1 John 4:7-8— ⁷Beloved, let us love one another, for love is of God; and everyone who loves is born of God and knows God. ⁸ He who does not love does not know God, for God is love.** (emphasis mine).

We must know and understand that much about God at the least if we are going to have an understanding and relationship with Him. The depth of His love for us is unfathomable, but the next Scripture shows a little more of the depth of that love.

Revelation 3:20-22— ²⁰Behold, I stand at the door and knock. If anyone hears My voice and opens the door, I will come in to him and dine with him, and he with Me. ²¹ To him who overcomes I will grant to sit with Me on My throne, as I also overcame and sat down with

My Father on His throne. **[22] "He who has an ear, let him hear what the Spirit says to the churches."**

This Scripture reflects an Attitude and Mindset of God that He has towards all people. He asks you to invite Him into your life in every situation. He doesn't generally simply step in and take over, but He asks you to invite Him in. My experience has been that I am free to "go it alone" anytime I want to, but I always can invite Him to participate with me. The above Scripture makes clear what His choice is, but He is such an extreme gentleman that He will not participate if He is not invited.

Notice that these events I just referenced took place in 1998, sixteen years after the Charismatic Renewal had nearly ended. But there were individuals and ministries that evidently didn't know it was over.

In 2000 I discovered a new satellite TV service called "Sky Angel", which had an all-Christian satellite format. That appealed to me, so I bought it and managed to pray my way through installing it myself. It was great, and I wish it were still around. As I started watching it, I found a Bible teacher I had never heard of, Andrew Wommack. His teaching style and knowledge of the Bible appealed to me, so I spent the next several years being mentored by him. I heartily recommend any seeker of a deeper understanding of the Bible, particularly the power of the Holy Spirit within you, to check out his website at awmi.org. If you have access to Christian television stations, you may be able to find his daily Bible teaching. In 2017 my bride and I were exploring the Western U.S. in our motorhome and were able to schedule a few days at AWMI's Charis Bible College in Winter Park Colorado, for their annual "Healing School". It was a fantastic experience.

I experienced many manifestations of the power of the Holy Spirit to heal since 1982 as the charismatic renewal seemed to slow down. About 20 years ago, I started having pain in my left hip. I didn't think too much about it at the time because I have managed to lift something wrong more than once, which resulted in a pinched nerve that caused temporary pain.

I figured that was all it was, and that it would dissipate. It didn't. After a couple of days, I asked God to heal me of the pinched nerve. It gradually got worse over the next several days, so it became very painful to walk at all. After several days I cried out "Lord, why have you not healed my pinched nerve?" His answer came back very promptly and clearly, "You do not have a pinched nerve. You have walked, ran, and ridden a bicycle many miles in your lifetime. You have simply worn your hip joint out". Wow! So, I asked Him to restore my worn-out hip joint in the name of Jesus. The next morning my hip joint was completely free of pain and has remained that way. A few weeks later I started having the same pain in my right hip, so I simply asked Him to restore my right hip joint, and He did. At the age of ninety-one, I still have not experienced any more pain in either hip joint.

On another occasion, I was helping a friend tear down and dismantle a twelve by sixteen-foot storage building. As we were flattening the bare frame, I managed to get my right hand crushed as it fell. The corner edge of the crossbeam that supported the rafters and roof of one side came down across the knuckles of my right hand, and the underside of those knuckles was against the corner edge of the beam that had topped the studs—a "perfect storm". When my friend helped me lift the roof section off my hand, my hand went up with it because a twenty-penny galvanized nail had gone through my wrist. Yes, it was quite painful, and very quickly swelled up and turned colors. Rather than go to the hospital which was only a couple of blocks away (I had previously had a very bad experience with its emergency room), I elected to trust God to heal it. I encouraged the puncture wound to bleed freely but did nothing else for it. My hand and wrist were badly swollen and discolored and very painful. When I returned home and was eating supper, the pain grew so intense that I became nauseated. I excused myself from the table and sat down in my recliner and prayed. As I prayed "Father I know that you are aware of how badly my hand hurts", before I could finish God replied, "Yes, son, I know exactly how much your hand hurts. But what I want you to understand is, that when I hung on that cross atoning for your sin, pain, and suffering, I hurt in every single joint of my body, including between every vertebra, just the same as your hand hurts right now". Wow! The memory of that conversation is one of my most valued assets. That accident happened on a Friday afternoon. By the following Wednesday, there was no evidence the accident had ever happened—no visual evidence and no pain. I have experienced no discomfort from the accident since that day, and my hand and fingers are fully functioning.

A year or so ago, I developed chronic pain in my lower back, on the right side. For whatever reason, for which I will not attempt to explain, my faith to believe in God to heal me at that time was bottomed out. The pain got so severe that I could not get comfortable in the motor home that we were living in at the time, so I went outside to seek comfort in a "gravity chair". It was a very hot day, and I still could not get comfortable. I started feeling nauseated, so got up and started back inside, but passed out and fell through the doorway. My wife called 911, and I was transported to the hospital. X-rays revealed that my right sacroiliac joint was inflamed, and the bones had deteriorated from deteriorating bone disease. I had been aware that I had the disease for years. Although I had not suffered a lot of pain from it, except for headaches originating from neck problems, my height had dropped from 5'11" to 5'6" as I aged. The emergency room staff offered no solution for the problem, except to give me a shot to temporarily relieve the pain. Two days later the pain was completely gone. So. What happened? I credit my wife for praying for my healing and mustering all our friends to pray with her, which resulted in God healing me. I was not up to the task at the time myself. A few months after that incident, I started having the same pain on the other side of my back. By then I had built my faith up to the task, so I prayed, and God healed. I have experienced no more recurrence of that same pain.

CHAPTER 6

Why Did The Great Revivals Of The Past Fade Away?

I don't really know all the answers to that question. But being I was a mature adult and very actively involved in the last one (the Charismatic Renewal), I can offer some observations and speculations. Perhaps the main reason was that the same attitudes that were present in the hearts of believers that brought about the revival in the first place did not persist as the revival lasted and dwindled.

One thing I observed during the Charismatic Renewal, was that ministers who became the most successful in praying for people to be healed quickly became the most popular. I participated in carpools to visit certain venues because certain ministers would be ministering. That doesn't sound too bad when you first think about it, but could it be that we got more interested in the ministers who were the most successful in accessing God's power, than in the One who was the source of that power? Were we more thrilled by seeing the miracle, than being thrilled by having a heavenly Father who loved us so much that He would bless us that way? Selah (go figure)

I remember that satanic forces infiltrated our marriage and the church in which I was involved in Roanoke Rapids, in 1982. They very obviously tried to destroy both the church and our marriage and nearly succeeded. I know from experience, as well as from the study of the Bible and church history, that Satan always dispatches his demons to hot spots of Christian progress, wherever they occur. That experience, and many experiences similar since that time, convince me that satanic forces always have and always will fight against any perceived progress of the church. If we fail to recognize it and actively fight back, guess who wins? Just take a close look at church history and see how often the forces of Satan have always tried to destroy the church when it appeared to be progressing, But, just as the Old Testament and church history illustrate, God has always maintained a remnant of true believers to keep the movement alive. The New Testament from beginning to end shows evidence of demonic forces trying to destroy the church, but you must look for it to find it. Jesus encountered them mostly through the Jewish religious leaders, as did the first Apostles, as recorded in the book of Acts. Nearly all the epistles record instances of satanic forces fighting the new church. During the eighties, demonic forces seem to get the upper hand on many occasions. Satan always has been and always will be fighting the church, until the final battle, which Satan loses.

Another thing I remember as happening in the waning years of the Charismatic Renewal, was that some of the evolving leaders formed a sort of alliance and started advocating the importance of every member being under a recognized "covering". That included every "Home Church" and every individual in the church, including unmarried women being under the covering of some man. That came to be known as "the Shepherding Movement". It caused a lot of confusion and division and played into the gradual deterioration of the Charismatic Renewal. I hasten to point out the history of the several revivals, which have consecutively lasted longer than the previous one. I see that as a very good indication that we are gradually becoming more successful in maintaining them.

Another possibility, (that occurred to me as I was writing this chapter and I referred to in a previous chapter) for the decline of the Charismatic Renewal, was the fact that most of the participants in the Charismatic

Renewal never left or quit supporting their original home church. The various leaders of the movement encouraged this, emphasizing that we didn't want to do anything to weaken the established churches. At first glance that seems like a good thing, but when I think it through, I can see problems with it. It is a proven fact that you cannot stay closely in fellowship with the Holy Spirit if you spend too much time with folks who don't even believe it is possible for us to do so. They will drag you down, while you are trying to pick them up. I believe that our loyalty to our old church and denomination is usually so strong that we have trouble walking away from it. After all, look at the time and money we have invested there, and all the friends there that we love and like to spend time with.

By the time the Charismatic Renewal had wound down, I had already become completely disgusted with the denominational church. I saw it as completely out of touch with the Bible, and for the most part, a waste of my time. I felt no loyalty to any denomination. I looked for small churches where I could participate that were at least trying "to get their act together." If none were available, I did not waste my time going to church at all. I would either spend Sunday morning in Bible study or listen to a good teacher on the television. I learned to be a better steward of my time than folks who waste time going to a dead church just because that "was the thing to do". That probably is the main reason I have continued to walk in fellowship with God's Holy Spirit and experience his power in my life. I refuse to waste my time in dead churches. I have come to realize I am somewhat of an exception to the general rule, in more cases than one.

Most participants in the Charismatic Renewal did not do as I did but continued to "whip the dead horse" denominational church they had a history with, with hopes of bringing it to life. They wound up as spiritually dead as the church they were trying to revive, instead of nourishing the live "church" they had been involved in during the Charismatic Renewal. By staying loyal to their previous church home, their divided loyalty sucked the Holy Spirit right out of them, and they reverted to their previous level of faith and victory. I believe if they had stopped supporting the previous church and given all their support and attention to the Charismatic Church, the chances of survival of the charismatic movement would have been much better. By leaving my dead church and never looking back, I have managed to continue to grow in my relationship with God through my companion, the Holy Spirit. That might have caused some negative effects for my previous church, but if that church was not fulfilling its mission, so what? Thankfully, many of those participants in the Charismatic Renewal did as I did or started a New Testament church or ministry. One of the hallmarks of a New Testament church was the demonstration of the "Fruit of the Holy Spirit" which I have mentioned before. 1 Corinthians 13 touches on the fruit, but Paul gave a clearer definition of it in **Galatians 5:22-25—**

[22]But the fruit of the Spirit is love, joy, peace, longsuffering, kindness, goodness, faithfulness, [23] gentleness, self-control. Against such there is no law. [24] And those *who are* Christ's have crucified the flesh with its passions and desires. [25] If we live in the Spirit, let us also walk in the Spirit.

That is why we still have individuals, ministries, and churches alive today who regularly exhibit the Gifts and the Fruit of the Holy Spirit. It is hard for me to completely understand why so many people have so much difficulty in quitting worshipping sacred cows when they are not getting any milk from them. The biggest reason I can think of is they do not study the Bible seriously for themselves, and consequently are so Bible illiterate they do not realize how badly their church is failing them spiritually.

There are many references in the New Testament to the predominance of the home church:

Acts 2:46-47— [46]So continuing daily with one accord in the temple, and breaking bread from house to house, they ate their food with gladness and simplicity of heart, [47] praising God and having favor

with all the people. And the Lord added to the church daily those who were being saved.

Acts 5:41-42— [41]So they departed from the presence of the council, rejoicing that they were counted worthy to suffer shame for His name. [42] And daily in the temple, and in every house, they did not cease teaching and preaching Jesus *as* the Christ.

Acts 20:20— how I kept back nothing that was helpful, but proclaimed it to you, and taught you publicly and from house to house,

Romans 16:3-5—Greet Priscilla and Aquila, my fellow workers in Christ Jesus, [4] who risked their own necks for my life, to whom not only I give thanks, but also all the churches of the Gentiles. [5] Likewise *greet* the church that is in their house. Greet my beloved Epaenetus, who is the firstfruits of Achaia to Christ.

1 Corinthians 16:19— The churches of Asia greet you. Aquila and Priscilla greet you heartily in the Lord, with the church that is in their house.

Colossians 4:15—Greet the brethren who are in Laodicea, and Nymphas and the church that is in his house.

Philemon 1:2—to the beloved Apphia, Archippus our fellow soldier, and to the church in your house:

I believe that gives us enough evidence to indicate that the gentile church basically met in homes, being there is no Scripture naming any other building for the gentile church, and little mention of it in history, up until the time of Constantine. Frankly, I have no intention of wasting my time in churches not led by the Holy Spirit with evidence of His power. I am too old to sit meekly by when another man yells down at me from his "throne" when I've done nothing to deserve that kind of disrespect and he has no right to insult my intelligence. For my part, the church I will give my support to and interest in is the church that regularly exhibits the power and evidence of the Holy Spirit in its meetings and members. That is the one I will try to participate in faithfully every time it meets. I believe that the more everyone takes that attitude, the better chance we will have of the revival lasting. My main interest now, following the publishing of this book, is helping Christians create their own New Testament Home Church and a real relationship with their Lord and Savior, Jesus the Christ, through His Holy Spirit. If we demand real New Testament churches and do not support the Council of Constantinople replacement, we can get what we are entitled to. I really believe that the opportunities will soon be available for everyone who seeks a New Testament Church, which may likely be a "Home Church", to find one.

CHAPTER 7

What About The Condition Of The Church In America Today?

I do not profess to be an authority on the subject, but it doesn't take a rocket scientist to come up with a few conclusions on the subject. The main "thermometer" is the fact that statistics have shown for several years that church membership and participation have been in decline annually in America. Another interesting statistic, however, shows that membership in major denomination churches (the frozen chosen) is declining rather rapidly, whereas membership in Pentecostal and independent churches is increasing. I came across a very informative article in the June 2021 "Levitt Letter" by Lea Marie Ann Klett of ChristianPost.com, quoting Thomas Schirrmachar, secretary-general of the World Evangelistic Alliance. Lea quoted Mr. Schirrmachar as saying "Our biggest problem is that Bible knowledge is fading away. This is the utmost problem we have beyond all theological differences, financial problems, and political questions." Surveys in recent years have revealed a decreasing trend in the depth of key beliefs and habits among church members. Christians are waking up to the weakness of the mainline denominational doctrine. The problem is that when members leave a church for whatever reason, they very often do not find one any better, so they drop out. I know many Christians who have gotten so disgusted or so hurt by a church, that they make no attempt to find a suitable home church. Contrary to popular belief, sitting in church does not make you a Christian, any more than sitting in a garage makes you an automobile. I know many believing Christians who you couldn't get to a church service, no matter how hard you try.

A large poll conducted recently by Gallop and released in July of 2022 does a good job of laying out the status of the Christian church in America today. The first finding is shocking to me but gives an important statistic on why the church appears as weak as it does. The survey revealed that <u>only 20% of Americans now believe that the Bible is the literal word of God! That is about half of what it was in 1980. Conversely, 29% of Americans consider the Bible to simply be a collection of fables, legends, history, and moral precepts recorded by man. In 1980 this precept was believed by only 10% of Americans. I believe those figures tell very graphically the great decline of the Christian Church in America in the past 42 years.</u>

My observation is, that we live in a time in which far too many pastors and teachers, in churches, on TV and on the internet, are more concerned about building up a following than they are about teaching the whole, true gospel. Some people eventually figure them out, others never do. Consequently, the Christian's need to spend daily, quality time studying the Bible with the solicited help of Holy Spirit, is more vital now than ever before. That is one of the main factors that prompted the writing of this book. The apostle Paul warned about these times in his final epistle, shortly before his martyrdom. We read about it in **2 Timothy, 3:1-5 and 4:3-4:**

[1]But know this, that in the last days perilous times will come: [2] For men will be lovers of themselves, lovers of money, boasters, proud, blasphemers, disobedient to parents, unthankful, unholy, [3] unloving, unforgiving, slanderers, without self-control, brutal, despisers of good, [4] traitors, headstrong, haughty, lovers of pleasure rather than lovers of God, [5] having a form of godliness but denying its power. And from such people turn away!

4:3-4 ³ **For the time will come when they will not endure sound doctrine, but according to their own desires,** *because* **they have itching ears, they will heap up for themselves teachers;** ⁴ **and they will turn** *their* **ears away from the truth, and be turned aside to fable**

With all the opportunities available to us on TV and the internet, it becomes very convenient for us to depend on them for our daily "devotional" or "Bible study". Those venues cannot compare to our sitting down with our study Bible and study aids (especially a good exhaustive concordance), and prayerfully studying the Scripture with the Holy Spirit as our coach. The best study Bible I have found has been the *AMG Hebrew/Greek Key Word Study Bible*. With that, I seldom need to go to my concordance because I can usually find the information I need in the back of my Bible. Over one-third of this Bible is study aids. It is available in several different translations. I have used the New American Standard Bible (NASB) and New King James Version (NKJV) for many years. I consider daily Bible study (measured in hours and portions of hours rather than minutes), to be the most important daily activity I do to enrich my knowledge of and relationship with my Savior, and consequently my peace, joy, and happiness. I have observed that most people who consider themselves Christians have no concept of the importance of daily, substantial Bible study, to understand God and have a serious relationship with Him. Many don't even see the need or importance of it.

We have sat back on our blessed assurance and allowed satanic forces through government entities to take the Bible, Bible Study, Lord's Prayer, Ten Commandments, and Pledge of Allegiance out of our schools and public meetings and allowed the history of our nation to be rewritten. Any mention of God is removed from our origin and founding by Christians looking for more religious freedom. The schools instead are teaching our children a lot of immorality (yes, that's my unapologetic opinion,) training them to disregard Biblical teaching. That leaves us with the option of home schools or Christian schools if we are to avoid raising up a generation of heathens. Many of our universities and colleges are trainers of socialists and anti-Christian secularists.

Another problem that we face today lies in the value of words. In the past, I have closed many a deal with simply a handshake or verbal agreement, but today that could be dangerous. I believe the reason is that the value of words has diminished tremendously in the last few years. I blame politicians and the news media for a lot of it, but I am afraid we all have had a hand in it. The current administration in Washington is changing the meaning of simple words regularly to make us think what they are doing is different from what it really is. Recently they authorized armed FBI agents to charge parents protesting unscrupulous school curriculum, to be charged as domestic terrorists. Our words do not carry the same value as they did in the past. That makes us more prone to question the face value of all words. That in turn makes it harder to take God's word at face value. You may very well not agree with my conclusions on this subject, but that is what I believe. After all, we must face up to the fact that some of the Scripture is hard to believe. A story is told about a little boy who was questioned about the Sunday School lesson he had returned home from. He started spinning this tale about a big gang of prisoners that escaped, but their former captors were hot on their trail. When the prisoners got to a river, they quickly built a pontoon bridge and crossed the river. Then when the former captors tried to cross the bridge, they blew it up and killed every one of them! The mother was dumbfounded and asked her son if that was exactly what the teacher taught. His reply was, "well, not exactly, Mom. But if I told it to you the way they told it to me, you would never believe it!". Selah (Go figure).

Another obvious problem is that the church in America is so divided, and that problem goes all the way back to the settling of our country. When the pilgrims first landed in America, the church in Europe only had about six denominations. Not all of those six denominations came ashore in America then. However, that changed very quickly as more and more groups separated themselves from the original. Twenty-five years ago, when I first looked at this, a book I bought on the subject described well over two hundred different denominations in America. My guess is that today there are thousands, and I seriously doubt anyone has attempted to describe all of them. Add to that the fact that there are probably several thousand independent and unaffiliated churches, and you get a picture of what I am talking about. The Bible teaches the unity of the body, so the power that influenced those decisions to separate in most cases obviously came from Satan— "divide and conquer". Usually, most denomination doctrines that separate us are taken from one or two verses of Scripture taken out of context or misinterpreted. In my opinion, those "splits" were caused by church leaders who were somewhat Bible illiterate but influential enough to convince others to agree with them.

John 17:20-23 makes it quite clear what God's will is for us is and spells out the relationship He wants us to have with Him.

[20] I do not pray for these alone ("these alone" referring to the eleven apostles)**, but also for those who will believe in Me through their word; [21] that they all may be one, as You, Father, *are* in Me, and I in You; that they also may be one in Us, that the world may believe that You sent Me. [22] And the glory which You gave Me I have given them, that they may be one just as We are one: [23] I in them, and You in Me; that they may be made perfect in one, and that the world may know that You have sent Me, and have loved them as You have loved Me.**

I have studied that Scripture, as well as all of John chapters 13-17, at least a hundred or more times in the last 15-20 years. I am still mining the depths of them and thank God they are becoming more of a reality in my life. That Scripture clearly says to me that we should all be one together in God. Not only that, but our relationship with God and Jesus should be just as tight as Jesus' relationship with God His Father was when Jesus walked this earth. I believe that Scripture is one of the most important goals that we can pray about and pursue. I know as I personally make progress in that direction, my "comfort level" with God improves, my peace and joy increases, my ability to hear His guidance becomes easier, and my fellowship with Him more constant. As that happens among more and more members of the church in America, the church will become more effective to the individual and the nation.

Many Scriptures like these which I am drawing attention to are Attitudes and Mindsets of our God. Our relationship to God and to each other is many times ignored by teachers and preachers. Imagine what the world would be like if everyone who considers themselves to be a Christian joined God in accepting this opportunity that He clearly makes available to us in **John 17:20-23**. If just every <u>believer</u> in America would adhere to this one Scripture, we could quickly change the world as well as America and the church.

I recently received an open letter from the head of a Bible college who had a very interesting conversation with one of his graduating students. This former student told him she had been extremely liberal when she first came to the school, but now she had become so conservative that many of her friends and family members were bothered by her current attitude. When asked how she could have been a Christian and yet supportive of abortion, homosexuality, and such things as transgenderism. her reply was that when she arrived at the Bible college, she was in love with God but not the Bible. She was Bible illiterate. Bible college changed everything so that she become in love with God's word as well as with God. I had often wondered how some of my Christian friends have such liberal attitudes, and that answers that question. If a Christian gets careless about studying the Bible and depends on preachers and teachers to tell them what it says, they can easily become Bible illiterate. It is obvious we live in a day and time when far too many Christians are Bible illiterate because it sometimes seems very convenient to tune in to a preacher or teacher on the internet than to open your own Bible and study it. Far too many preachers and teachers do not have the courage to teach the whole Gospel of The Kingdom of God, for fear of losing followers and supporters. Most Bible Colleges do a good job and I highly recommend some of them, but if that is not an option for you, serious study of a sound translation of the Bible with an exhaustive concordance and Holy Spirit tutoring you can get the job done very well.

The good news is that there are many indications that many Christians are beginning to wake up and realize we must act quickly. More and more serious Christians are beginning to see that if God doesn't rescue our nation, it is doomed. Many Christians are beginning to realize they do not really know what much of the Bible reveals and are starting to search for answers in the Bible. We are seeing the rumblings and hearing the prophecies indicating that a great outpouring of Holy Spirit is on the way and has already started in some locations. Someone wisely said a long time ago, "The best way to ensure the victory of evil, is for good men (and women) to do nothing". I personally believe that the church in America has proven that statement to be true. However, I believe an army of good Christian men and women who are realizing the depth of the failure of "the church", are looking for ways to turn things around. We can see it in school board meetings across America. Parents are demanding school boards stop approving such evil and ridiculous curriculums for their children or get out of the way and let someone else make those decisions. I am sad to say, that in my long sojourn on this earth, I have witnessed a gradual decline in the success and mission of the church in America, and it is at a low point now. History records that the church is rampant with such low points, but so far has managed to survive them. Let's hope it survives this one and returns to the New Testament Church of the book of Acts, the one Jesus established. I really believe that God has again maintained a small remnant of true believers which He will use to revive His Church.

CHAPTER 8

How We Can Bring In And Sustain The Next Great Revival

A study of the Old Testament and church history teaches us that God sends revival in response to His people's attitudes and cries for help. Sometimes it is a small "remnant" of loyal followers that causes God to respond to the cries of His people. "Hoping" for a revival doesn't cut it; it takes serious prayer coupled with deep faith to cause a real response. History has proven that even a small group of dedicated Christians can foster a local revival, which may or may not spread like wildfire. The Hebrides (Islands off the coast of Scotland) revival in 1949 was started by the prayers of two elderly, devoted sisters.

The book of Acts shows how revivals were started by the early church.

Look at Acts 2 to see how the Holy Spirit fell on the approximately 120 praying church members, causing great excitement when Peter explained what had just happened. Here are a few excerpts from Acts chapter 2, to show what happened. I suggest you study the whole chapter to really get an understanding of the subject.

Acts 2:1-6— ¹When the Day of Pentecost had fully come, they were all with one accord in one place. ² And suddenly there came a sound from heaven, as of a rushing mighty wind, and it filled the whole

house where they were sitting. ³ Then there appeared to them divided tongues, as of fire, and *one* sat upon each of them. ⁴ And they were all filled with the Holy Spirit and began to speak with other tongues, as the Spirit gave them utterance. ⁵ And there were dwelling in Jerusalem Jews, devout men, from every nation under heaven. ⁶ And when this sound occurred, the multitude came together, and were confused, because everyone heard them speak in his own language.

Acts 2:14-18—¹⁴ But Peter, standing up with the eleven, raised his voice and said to them, "Men of Judea and all who dwell in Jerusalem, let this be known to you, and heed my words. ¹⁵ For these are not drunk, as you suppose, since it is *only* [a]the third hour of the day. ¹⁶ But this is what was spoken by the prophet Joel: ¹⁷ 'And it shall come to pass in the last days, says God, That I will pour out of My Spirit on all flesh; Your sons and your daughters shall prophesy, Your young men shall see visions, Your old men shall dream dreams. ¹⁸ And on My menservants and on My maidservants I will pour out My Spirit in those days, And they shall prophesy.

Acts 2:40-42—⁴⁰ And with many other words he testified and exhorted them, saying, "Be saved from this perverse generation." ⁴¹ Then those who gladly received his word were baptized; and that day about three thousand souls were added to them. ⁴² And they continued steadfastly in the apostles' doctrine and fellowship, in the breaking of bread, and in prayers.

History and the book of Acts show that these revivals were started and sustained, not so much by skilled orators, but by men of faith who were so filled with God's Holy Spirit, that they were able to bring forth God's power by their words of faith. Chapters 3 and 4 of the book of Acts show how the new church more than doubled in size when the lame man was healed at the temple gate.

Acts 3:1-16 ¹Now Peter and John went up together to the temple at the hour of prayer, the ninth *hour*. ² And a certain man lame from his mother's womb was carried, whom they laid daily at the gate of the temple which is called Beautiful, to ask alms from those who entered the temple; ³ who, seeing Peter and John about to go into the temple, asked for alms. ⁴ And fixing his eyes on him, with John, Peter said, "Look at us." ⁵ So he gave them his attention, expecting to receive something from them. ⁶ Then Peter said, "Silver and gold I do not have, but what I do have I give you: In the name of Jesus Christ of Nazareth, rise up and walk." ⁷ And he took him by the right hand and lifted *him* up, and immediately his feet and ankle bones received strength. ⁸ So he, leaping up, stood and walked and entered the temple with them—walking, leaping, and praising God. ⁹ And all the people saw him walking and praising God. ¹⁰ Then they knew that it was he who sat begging alms at the Beautiful Gate of the temple, and they were filled with wonder and amazement at what had happened to him.

Now as the lame man who was healed held on to Peter and John, all the people ran together to them in the porch which is called Solomon's, greatly amazed. ¹² So when Peter saw *it*, he responded to the people: "Men of Israel, why do you marvel at this? Or why look so intently at us, as though by our own power or godliness we had made this man walk? ¹³ The God of Abraham, Isaac, and Jacob, the God of our fathers, glorified His Servant Jesus, whom you delivered up and denied in the presence of Pilate, when he was determined to let *Him* go. ¹⁴ But you denied the Holy One and the Just, and asked for a murderer to be granted to you, ¹⁵ and killed the Prince of life, whom God raised from the dead, of which we are witnesses. ¹⁶ And His name, through faith in His name, has made this man strong, whom you see and know. Yes, the faith which *comes* through Him has given him this perfect soundness in the presence of you all.

Acts 4:1-4— ¹Now as they spoke to the people, the priests, the captain of the temple, and the Sadducees came upon them, ² being greatly disturbed that they taught the people and preached in Jesus the resurrection from the dead. ³ And they laid hands on them,

and put *them* in custody until the next day, for it was already evening. ⁴ However, many of those who heard the word believed; and the number of the men came to be about five thousand.

The book of Acts shows how the New Testament church grew because God's power through His Holy Spirit attracted followers, and those followers went forth and the Holy Spirit worked the same miracles through them. Jesus attracted His followers by exercising the power of God, and the apostles followed His example. If the church operated that way today, we should have the same results. Paul describes it best in **I Corinthians chapter 2:1-5—**

¹And I, brethren, when I came to you, did not come with excellence of speech or of wisdom declaring to you the testimony of God. ² For I determined not to know anything among you except Jesus Christ and Him crucified. ³ I was with you in weakness, in fear, and in much trembling. ⁴ And my speech and my preaching *were* not with persuasive words of human wisdom, but in demonstration of the Spirit and of power, ⁵ that your faith should not be in the wisdom of men but in the power of God.

All the revivals that we have had in this country have had the Holy Spirit at the heart of them. Each one, progressively, has been blessed with more and more evidence of God's power exercised through His Holy Spirit with signs and miracles.

That ingredient is what is largely missing in the church today. When was the last time you saw several signs and miracles in a single service? That is what I witnessed over and over during the Charismatic Renewal, in Sunday morning church services as well as week-night home church meetings as well as monthly Full Gospel Businessmen's meetings and Women's Aglow meetings. I believe that is what church looked like in the New Testament gentile church that Chapters 10-28 of Acts and the Epistles describe. The mostly Jewish Church in Jerusalem was different, mainly because it was much bigger than the gentile churches, according to what I read and understand about the New Testament.

The sad fact of the matter is that a large majority of people who consider themselves Christians, do not believe that God's power is even available to us today. The early church was formed on the display of His power. <u>To believe that God's power is not available to us today is to not believe the Bible.</u> I believe that if you eliminated all the references and illustrations of God's power from the Bible, as exercised through His Holy Spirit, there would hardly be enough printed paper left to call it a book.

It is beyond me to grasp why the biggest part of the church and of Christians today <u>just don't get it!</u> I do not understand why something that is so obvious in the Bible and provided repeatedly in different revivals and ministries, is completely ignored by many churches and Christians today. Without the miracles that Jesus and His disciples manifested in the New Testament, we would not have a Christian church today, and it is the absence of those miracles and power that has weakened the church to its current condition, in my opinion. I cannot understand why pastors and teachers do not study the Bible today enough with the Holy Spirit coaching them, to find out how to access this almost untapped power. My perception is that many times when miracles are not seen, it is lack of understanding of God's Word and His plan for our lives. Failure to see a miracle when I pray for one tells me that I may not understand God or the Bible well enough. That nudges me towards studying the Bible and praying more. Maybe that is the key that some have found, but others have not. I also understand that there are other times that an instantaneous miracle is not what God has for me at that moment. Knowing God and His Word helps me to have faith and trust in Him, even when I don't understand why my prayer is not answered the way I expected it to be answered. Too many people give up when they don't receive the answer they expect. To me, determination and walking closely with my friend Jesus helps me to remember to keep asking and listening for understanding of His will for me. Someone has wisely said, "a mistake or failure at least proves someone tried". Selah (go figure). Don't give up!

Jesus paid a horrific price for us to be healed, and we dishonor Him if we don't accept that gift that He so graciously gave us. We need to burn this proven fact into our mind: <u>The Bible is absolute truth and if we don't experience all of the blessings that are provided for us therein, then we need to study the Bible more, ask God to show us His plan for us, and if there is something we are believing or doing that hinders His plan.</u> Perhaps it is time that we took stock of our own Attitudes and Mindsets.

As I mentioned in an earlier chapter, the big difference between the New Testament Church and most churches today, is the absence of the Holy Spirit in the operation and services, thank you, Emperor Constantine. Another big difference, as we saw in 1 Corinthians 12-14 in the previous chapter, is that churches today operate based on a speaker-audience format, whereas the New Testament format utilized a leader-participant format. A third big difference is that the smaller home church was the basic unit (like in the Charismatic Renewal and in the original BSA patrol format), not the Sunday morning services we usually have today. Perhaps a fourth big reason is that for several generations, particularly since World War II when parents neglected the home for a period to participate in the war effort, then changed homelife from one working parent to two, because the higher lifestyle afforded by two incomes became the norm. Teaching children in the home the importance of sound Bible doctrine went out the window in many homes. Perhaps the biggest difference is the fact that the leadership of the New Testament Church was selected based on the Fruit and Gifts of the Holy Spirit operating in their lives rather than today's leadership being selected according to academic achievements and success in building membership and church buildings. <u>Come on, people! Constantine has been dead for 1700 years and we owe him nothing. There is no reason to keep following his plan. It ain't working! Jesus Christ is alive and well on planet earth through the Holy Spirit today, and we owe Him everything.</u> Let's follow His plan that does work—the New Testament plan that Jesus initiated. We are worshiping sacred cows, identified as church buildings and denominations.

One of the differences between the New Testament Church and today's churches is leadership. I had a very interesting conversation recently with a good friend, a businessman in Charlottesville, Virginia. He is a Jewish believer who is filled with the Holy Spirit and an elder in his church. I mentioned this book I am writing, and we got into a deep fruitful discussion about the church in America. We soon realized that our two churches were trying and making some progress towards becoming more like the New Testament Church. His church seems to have been successful in creating functioning home groups, whereas our church has not been able to accomplish this yet. After discussing the difference between the New Testament Church and our two churches, we concluded that one possible solution to bring our churches closer to the New Testament model was to bring the whole community together from all the home churches to worship on Sunday morning and share together. Training and encouraging the leaders of the smaller groups would be included in those coming-together times. What if part of the function of the Sunday morning service was that of training the "home church" leadership and participants in how to make the "home church" concept function like the New Testament Church? Sounds simple enough, but not an easy sell. Sacred Cows do not die easily. It will depend on how well a particular church's leadership sees the need to change and is brave enough to step out and do something about it. Big groups do not offer the opportunity for everyone to participate, small groups give more opportunities to do so.

Since the above conversation with my friend, I have come to some further conclusions. To get from point "A", the way most Christian Churches in America operate today; to point "B", the New Testament Church as described in 1 Corinthians chapters 12-14. We could take the following steps:

1. To give every participant an opportunity to participate in the service as described in chapters 12, 13, and 14 of 1 Corinthians, have home church meetings during the week with well-trained,

Spirit-baptized leadership, with not over a dozen participants in each home church.
2. Consider the home church meetings at the heart of the ministry of the "Sunday or "Mother Church" and reflect this in the Sunday morning services.
3. Have monthly meetings of the home church leaders with the "Mother Church" leadership for training and sharing.
4. Recognize the home churches as the key ministry unit, and the "Mother Church" places a predominant emphasis on supporting and training the leaders of the home churches.

The main principle behind the home church concept is that the home church is made of close friends who fellowship with each other throughout the week as well as in the home church meetings. Everyone in the home church is very close friends. In the presence of only close friends, it is much easier to speak out when the Holy Spirit prompts a member to give a word than it is in a large congregation. In a large congregation, only a small percentage of the participants would have time to give a word, thus the majority of those present are mere spectators rather than participants. I cannot visualize the above Scripture being fulfilled in a large congregation meeting, but it seems completely feasible in a small group of close friends who are filled with the Holy Spirit. That is exactly what we witness during the Charismatic Renewal, so we know from experience that it can work. It is quite clear from the New Testament that "church" should be an all-inclusive participation body/meeting, rather than a spectator body/meeting. That doesn't mean that we do away with the established church, but instead give it a very meaningful role to serve the home churches, which is where "community" takes place. The Sunday services bring all together for a corporate worship gathering time. Our churches, nation, BSA, and family life have all been severely changed from their original concepts by upper-echelon leadership usurping more power than they were originally granted and completely changing those organizations from the concepts that were originally established. Like I said, "give man enough time, and he will mess anything up". We can face up to the reality of that statement and take drastic steps to straighten out our mess, or we can keep our mouths shut, do nothing, and wallow in our sloppy mess. The home, home church, and the BSA patrol have been robbed of their original role and purpose, and until that power shift is recognized and corrected, I see no hope of them getting any better.

The New Testament of the Bible, the Constitution of the United States of America, and the guidelines for leadership in The Scoutmaster's Handbook that was in use when I was a Scoutmaster clearly reflect this type of organization that we have experienced in past years. We can't change history, (although a lot of people are trying to do that now), but we can stop and realize that we have royally messed things up big time. The local working unit of groups has been taken over by the larger, more powerful leaders and their goals. We must stop putting band-aids on problems, figure out where we went wrong, and go back to that point and make major changes. In my humble opinion, every church in America should do like hundreds of denominational churches are doing today and secede from their denomination. Most of the Church leaders who started all those thousands of denominations are now dead, and for the most part, the Bible does not back up their reason for starting a new denomination in the first place. Denominations are in direct opposition to what Jesus prayed to the Father for us the night before He was crucified:

John 17:20-23—20 "I do not pray for these alone, but also for those who will believe in Me through their word; 21 that they all may be one, as You, Father, *are* in Me, and I in You; that they also may be one in Us, that the world may believe that You sent Me. 22 And the glory which You gave Me I have given them, that they may be one just as We are one: 23 I in them, and You in Me; that they may be made perfect in one, and that the world may know that You have sent Me, and have loved them as You have loved Me.

It is obvious that our nation, church, and family is suffering, for the most part, because we have too many people in administration telling us what to do, and too few doing what God has called the church to do. In the

New Testament gentile church, according to the model Paul gives in **1 Corinthians 12:12-31**, every member was a leader and a doer.

1 Corinthians 12:12-31—¹² Just as a body, though one, has many parts, but all its many parts form one body, so it is with Christ. ¹³ For we were all baptized by[a] one Spirit so as to form one body—whether Jews or Gentiles, slave or free—and we were all given the one Spirit to drink. ¹⁴ Even so the body is not made up of one part but of many.

¹⁵ Now if the foot should say, "Because I am not a hand, I do not belong to the body," it would not for that reason stop being part of the body. ¹⁶ And if the ear should say, "Because I am not an eye, I do not belong to the body," it would not for that reason stop being part of the body. ¹⁷ If the whole body were an eye, where would the sense of hearing be? If the whole body were an ear, where would the sense of smell be? ¹⁸ But in fact God has placed the parts in the body, every one of them, just as he wanted them to be. ¹⁹ If they were all one part, where would the body be? ²⁰ As it is, there are many parts, but one body.

²¹ The eye cannot say to the hand, "I don't need you!" And the head cannot say to the feet, "I don't need you!" ²² On the contrary, those parts of the body that seem to be weaker are indispensable, ²³ and the parts that we think are less honorable we treat with special honor. And the parts that are unpresentable are treated with special modesty, ²⁴ while our presentable parts need no special treatment. But God has put the body together, giving greater honor to the parts that lacked it, ²⁵ so that there should be no division in the body, but that its parts should have equal concern for each other. ²⁶ If one part suffers, every part suffers with it; if one part is honored, every part rejoices with it.

²⁷ Now you are the body of Christ, and each one of you is a part of it. ²⁸ And God has placed in the church first of all apostles, second prophets, third teachers, then miracles, then gifts of healing, of

> helping, of guidance, and of different kinds of tongues. ²⁹ **Are all apostles? Are all prophets? Are all teachers? Do all work miracles? ³⁰ Do all have gifts of healing? Do all speak in tongues[b]? Do all interpret? ³¹ Now eagerly desire the greater gifts.**

I cannot visualize how this can work consistently in a large church body, but I can see how it could work in a church body of 3-15. I saw it repeatedly during the Charismatic Renewal. It seems that we have tuned our ears to listening to church leaders more than to Holy Spirit.

As I consider the upcoming great outpouring of the Holy Spirit, I think about the many churches I have been a part of in the past, have visited, or become familiar with, who have no expectation of seeing the power of the Holy Spirit in action in their churches when this great outpouring comes about. Will they recognize what is happening and become part of the movement, or will they still blindly stumble in their ignorance and not even acknowledge what is going on all around them? We need to pray for these churches, that they are caught up in the outpowering and be truly revived.

Another difference between the New Testament Church and today's church is how the leadership was and is selected. According to the book of Acts, and *Eusebius Ecclesiastical History*, up until the time of Constantine, the leadership rose to the top the way cream rises to the top of a bottle of raw milk. Those people who exhibited the stronger attributes of the Fruit of Holy Spirit and exercised the stronger power through the Gifts of the Holy Spirit, naturally become the leaders. The Holy Spirit selected the leaders, not a committee surveying resumes, experiences, and qualifications. The biggest challenge will be to work on raising up home church leaders who are first filled with the Holy Spirit as evidenced by the Fruit and Gifts of the Holy Spirit operating in their lives. Making the home church the basic unit of the church and the big church existing only to support the home church looks to be a better plan to me. In my opinion, only radical changes can turn the American church around and turn it into the church, Jesus, envisioned and tried so hard to establish and did establish. <u>We need to consider honoring Jesus who is alive and well on planet earth instead of a bunch of dead men who let Satan lead them astray. The church should not be a spectator activity, but a participating activity.</u> You know by experience that we learn by doing, more so than listening to someone tell us about it. As we consider the rapid increase in crime and all sorts of immorality and see the church and our beloved nation in decline, why can we not see that any way you look at it, the church is failing in its mission? There are reasons to be concerned and do something different from what we have been doing.

If we broaden our perspective away from our local church to what is going on in our nation and around the world, we can see much reason for hope for the revival of the church. Around the world, particularly in countries with very repressive governments, we can see pockets of many people being converted to Christianity. There is a strong fellowship of churches and ministries in the United States which is moving strongly in Prophecy and seeing many prophecies fulfilled. Also in our United States, we are seeing more and more churches experiencing miracles of healing on a regular basis, and this has been fostered by several ministries which have been training people in this aspect of the gospel for years. If we take time to see what is going on in the church in the rest of the world beyond our own church, we can be encouraged. I trust you will be encouraged to the point of seeing what Jesus the Messiah provided for you 2000 years ago, and "go for it".

Accessing the power of God in our lives is only available if we KNOW it is available to us, and we are willing to spend enough time studying the Scriptures and developing a close personal relationship with Jesus. Having done that, we must maintain faith in what the Scripture and Jesus tell us. Like most things in life, we must put forth the effort to maintain a positive attitude and strong faith in the Word of God to stay in a good-faith position. With all the trash that is going on around us and being spoken constantly over the airways, it is very difficult to maintain that absolute belief in the Bible and absolute faith in God. I have been high, and I have been low, and I can assure you it is worth the effort to stay high. It takes a lot of determination and willpower to stay built up, but it sure is worth the effort. It is hard to absolutely believe the Bible as absolute truth and the word of God in today's environment, but the rewards make it worth the effort.

Even Jesus could do no mighty works in Nazareth, because of their unbelief according to **Matthew 13:54-58— **^{54}**When He had come to His own country, He taught them in their synagogue, so that they were astonished and said, "Where did this** *Man* **get this wisdom and** *these* **mighty works?** ^{55} **Is this not the carpenter's son? Is not His mother called Mary? And His brothers James, Joses, Simon, and Judas?** ^{56} **And His sisters, are they not all with us? Where then did this** *Man* **get all these things?"** ^{57} **So they were offended at Him. But Jesus said to them, "A prophet is not without honor except in his own country and in his own house."** ^{58} **Now He did not do many mighty works there because of their unbelief.**

Mark records in **Mark 8:22-26**, an interesting incident that happened in the city of Bethsaida, one of the cities Jesus later pronounced judgement over for their unbelief—

^{22} **Then He came to Bethsaida; and they brought a blind man to Him, and begged Him to touch him.** ^{23} **So He took the blind man by the hand and led him out of the town. And when He had spit on his eyes and put His hands on him, He asked him if he saw anything.** ^{24} **And he looked up and said, "I see men like trees, walking."** ^{25} **Then He put** *His* **hands on his eyes again and made him look up. And he was restored and saw everyone clearly.** ^{26} **Then He sent him away to his house, saying, "Neither go into the town, nor tell anyone in the town."**

We need to notice several things here:

1. Jesus led the blind man out of town, away from the unbelieving people of that town, to pray for him.

2. Jesus had to pray for him twice to manifest complete healing, perhaps because of the unbelief present in the man.

3. Jesus told him to not go back into the town, where he could be influenced by unbelief.

My opinion is that these Scriptures indicate that an environment of unbelief negates faith so that even Jesus could not use His power to completely overcome it. Hard as it might seem, even almighty God is limited in an atmosphere of unbelief. Certainly, yours will be also.

Basically, we need to start our quest for the next great revival at **2 Chronicles 7:14 – If My people who are called by My name will humble themselves, and pray and seek My face, and turn from their wicked ways, then I will hear from heaven, and will forgive their sin and heal their land.**

That verse has been quoted many times lately, but I don't apologize for using it again here, because it most certainly fits in this discussion. A universal sin of all of us is pride, and it is not easy to look honestly and humbly at our sin without the power of Holy Spirit working in and with us.

In Acts chapters 2 and 4, we see how the early disciples prayed and were filled with/baptized in the Holy Spirit. In the following chapters of this book, I describe how new believers were filled with the Holy Spirit. These verses from Ephesians explain why it could be very important to you: **Ephesians 1:13-14—-**

[13] **In Him you also *trusted*, after you heard the word of truth, the gospel of your salvation; in whom also, having believed, you were sealed with the Holy Spirit of promise,** [14] **who is the guarantee of our inheritance until the redemption of the purchased possession, to the praise of His glory.**

That is one of those important Scriptures that you need to read over several times and spend some time praying and meditating on. I interpret this Scripture to indicate that by being filled with/baptized in the Holy Spirit makes us participants in the Kingdom of God while still in this part of our life. The Holy Spirit here on this side of heaven, is the guarantee, earnest, taste, or sample of what our inheritance waiting for us in heaven is like. We get some of that victory now, including miracles of healing, provision, etc. The catch is it needs to be achieved according to God's directions in His Word. I experienced a great deal of that victory during and after the prime years of the Charismatic Renewal and am still experiencing much of it, so I know we can achieve that degree of victory again. I'm going for it, and I'm going to bring as many of you as I can along with me.

CHAPTER 9

God's Extreme Love For Us Evident Through His Creation

This is one of my favorite subjects, and I cannot remember a time in my life when I did not appreciate those Attitudes and Mindsets of God, that He had when He created the universe as we know it today. I regularly express my appreciation to Him for it. I have several thousand photographs on my computer and on thumb drives that I have taken to try to capture the beauty to be found in His creation and have many etched in my mind that are just as vivid as those on the screen. Another gift that God has given me and many of you is eyes to behold the beauty of that part of His creation that lies in front of us. I appreciate the opportunities I have had in school, Boy Scouting, Florida State Park Service, and my travels, to gain a richer understanding of God's creation.

When I first started writing about God's creation many years ago, I found that scientists had discovered that there were approximately one million species of plants and a half million species of animals known to science. I thought that was amazing. I have continued to read about new discoveries around the world, and I heard someone on television a couple of days ago say that scientists have to date discovered millions of species of animals. Wow!

I feel sorry for folks who have never developed an appreciation of the natural environment, but some even don't have the opportunity to escape from their concrete jungle to see a natural environment. As I sit here on the front porch of the apartment my good friend has made available to us, writing this chapter, looking across the pond into the forest, I consider how appreciating the natural environment is a lot like appreciating God and the Bible. We can merely look at each one and say, "Oh yeah, that's pretty, or interesting, or whatever," or we can look closer, research that particular plant community, and see how so many plants and animals that live there are dependent on each other and serve each other. It is interesting to note that if man doesn't do anything to alter that plant community, it will continue to perpetuate itself indefinitely. The more we search out the workings of that plant community, the more interested we become. And if we realize that it is a creation of God and He designed it so perfectly for our benefit, we see another Attitude and Mindset of God. We gain a new love and respect for The One who created all that and placed us in the middle of it.

Now you know why I don't like to live in the city. It is similar when we look at God and look at the Bible, His Word. We can just give it a casual look and say "yeah, that's good", or we can delve into it more seriously, and seek a better understanding and appreciation of it. As I look at the following scene, I see much more than the deer. I have been in those woods, so I know what trees are in it, including a few scattered pines, several different oaks, maples, hickories etc. That indicates to me that that patch of woods is soon to evolve into a climax hardwood forest. It was probably a pine forest originally, when the first white settlers came here, at least in the early 1800s according to the assumed date of the log cabin on the backside of the property. Of course, it is possible that they were right here on this property even before that. A pine forest is dependent on fire to occasionally remove the deadwood and young hardwood seedlings which the birds had scattered, to maintain it as a pine forest. But, when the early settlers spotted a forest fire caused by lightning, or whatever. they saw it as destructive and immediately rushed in to put the fire out. This allowed the hardwood seedlings to grow and eventually help the pines create a very shady under-story. That was good for the hardwood seedlings but bad for the pine seedlings. So that set up a process of evolution that eventually would turn the pine forest into a hardwood forest. The forest provides cover, acorns, and other food for the deer, squirrels, snakes, birds, and other animals that live there. You could consider the whole forest a living organism, and when you study all that is going on beneath your feet, even the ground itself can be considered a living organism. I am often amused by God's sense of humor, not only with His dealings with man and me but also with His creation. We have guinea fowl on the farm here, who do a good job of controlling ticks. They are also both entertaining and aggravating. They are funny-looking creatures to start with. But they have such a small brain that they can do so many weird things; they can be fun to observe. But, if they hang around close to your abode, their loud, obnoxious calling can be irritating.

Evolution is obvious at many levels in nature, including in animals, as I found out some years ago when I raised rabbits. By selecting only the rabbits with the features I wanted my baby rabbits to have in order to be better breeders, within a couple of years I had greatly improved my stock. The weight of my mature rabbits increased by several pounds. But the scientific community has known for many years that one species cannot evolve into another. Can anyone tell me why we still allow our school systems to use books and teachers to teach that stupid lie that all animal life "evolved" from one form, in our schools, and on television? Selah (go figure). I remember as a boy when the teacher started talking that trash to my class in school, I sat there giggling and wondered if she was really that stupid, or did she think that we students were that stupid. I guess some of the kids might have swallowed it, but most of us just considered it a joke. A phenomenon that we see more and more today is the scientist who has come to embrace the "intelligent design" concept rather than the "evolution theory". And more and more of them are becoming Christians. This trend has been picking up more steam yearly for several years now. One of my best friends and disciple of Jesus is a nuclear engineer with a doctor's degree.

Please do not take what I have said that I consider a deeper study of nature as important as a deeper study of God and the Bible. I don't believe that at all. Nothing can benefit you more than a deeper study of God and the Bible. However, a deeper study of nature will show you more of the love of God.

The deeper we dig, the more blessed we become, and the more we want to dig deeper. As a teacher once told us, "You only get out of something as much as you put into it." I regret it took me so long to realize she was right. I do believe from what I have observed that the great majority of Christians never understand this, and thereby deny themselves of much of the blessings of experiencing a closer fellowship with their creator God, who would like to be a close friend and counselor.

In consideration of what has been said here, I believe a reread of Genesis chapter one is in order. You may even want to read the first six chapters.

Genesis 1:1-31: **[1]In the beginning God created the heavens and the earth. [2]The earth was without form, and void; and darkness *was* on the face of the deep. And the Spirit of God was hovering over the face of the waters. [3]Then God said, "Let there be light"; and there was light. [4]And God saw the light, that *it was* good; and God divided the light from the darkness. [5]God called the light Day, and the darkness He called Night. So the evening and the morning were the first day.**

[6]Then God said, "Let there be a firmament in the midst of the waters, and let it divide the waters from the waters." [7]Thus God made the firmament, and divided the waters which *were* under the firmament from the waters which *were* above the firmament; and it

was so. ⁸ And God called the firmament Heaven. So the evening and the morning were the second day.

⁹ Then God said, "Let the waters under the heavens be gathered together into one place, and let the dry *land* appear"; and it was so. ¹⁰ And God called the dry *land* Earth, and the gathering together of the waters He called Seas. And God saw that *it was* good. ¹¹ Then God said, "Let the earth bring forth grass, the herb *that* yields seed, *and* the fruit tree *that* yields fruit according to its kind, whose seed *is* in itself, on the earth"; and it was so. ¹² And the earth brought forth grass, the herb *that* yields seed according to its kind, and the tree *that* yields fruit, whose seed *is* in itself according to its kind. And God saw that *it was* good. ¹³ So the evening and the morning were the third day.

¹⁴ Then God said, "Let there be lights in the firmament of the heavens to divide the day from the night; and let them be for signs and seasons, and for days and years; ¹⁵ and let them be for lights in the firmament of the heavens to give light on the earth"; and it was so. ¹⁶ Then God made two great lights: the greater light to rule the day, and the lesser light to rule the night. *He made* the stars also. ¹⁷ God set them in the firmament of the heavens to give light on the earth, ¹⁸ and to rule over the day and over the night, and to divide the light from the darkness. And God saw that *it was* good. ¹⁹ So the evening and the morning were the fourth day.

²⁰ Then God said, "Let the waters abound with an abundance of living creatures, and let birds fly above the earth across the face of the firmament of the heavens." ²¹ So God created great sea creatures and every living thing that moves, with which the waters abounded, according to their kind, and every winged bird according to its kind. And God saw that *it was* good. ²² And God blessed them, saying, "Be fruitful and multiply, and fill the waters in the seas, and let birds multiply on the earth." ²³ So the evening and the morning were the fifth day.

24 Then God said, "Let the earth bring forth the living creature according to its kind: cattle and creeping thing and beast of the earth, *each* according to its kind"; and it was so. 25 And God made the beast of the earth according to its kind, cattle according to its kind, and everything that creeps on the earth according to its kind. And God saw that *it was* good. 26 Then God said, "Let Us make man in Our image, according to Our likeness; let them have dominion over the fish of the sea, over the birds of the air, and over the cattle, over all the earth and over every creeping thing that creeps on the earth." 27 So God created man in His *own* image; in the image of God He created him; male and female He created them. 28 Then God blessed them, and God said to them, "Be fruitful and multiply; fill the earth and subdue it; have dominion over the fish of the sea, over the birds of the air, and over every living thing that moves on the earth."29 And God said, "See, I have given you every herb *that* yields seed which *is* on the face of all the earth, and every tree whose fruit yields seed; to you it be for food. 30 Also, to every beast of the earth, to every bird of the air, and to everything that creeps on the earth, in which *there is* life, *I have given* every green herb for food"; and it was so. 31 Then God saw everything that He had made, and indeed *it was* very good. So the evening and the morning were the sixth day.

I thank God often and feel so blessed to have had the many opportunities I have had to enjoy and appreciate our natural environment and have always had an appreciation of it, and the God who created it for us. Growing up in the mountains of East Tennessee with parents who had a strong appreciation of the natural environment and the God who created it, gave me a head start on most folks in gaining that appreciation early on in life. That early start materialized into a continuous search for opportunities to observe His creation. That caused my early interest in Boy Scouting, kayaking, being a Florida State Park Ranger, and so many other pursuits. About three years into my second marriage, after losing my first wife to cancer, my bride and I were discussing how taking care of our house and yard was interfering with our time for ministering and doing things we wanted to do. After a month or two of praying and considering the matter, we decided to sell our house and move into an RV. We spent several years parked at a private RV park, taking various side trips to enjoy God's nature. In 2017 we took off in our motor home and spent five months out west, had a ball. We got tired of paying lot rent for a spot we were only occupying about six months a year, so we started taking jobs in different parks to cover our site rent, just traveling from park to park doing that. We spent the winters in Florida and South Georgia and the summers in North Carolina. Yes, we were living a dream life, and many people along the way told us we were living their dream. I don't mind telling you that if you reach a time in your life you can afford to do that, it is a great life. Most of the other "resident volunteers" we worked with were younger than we were. The beauty of it was that we worked in many different natural beauty spots, and fellowshipped with so many like-minded, travelers. It is such a great life for a Christian who appreciates the beauty of their Creator Lord's provision for us. We heartily recommend it for like-minded souls. Our ongoing ministry was not as convenient under those circumstances, so we now feel we should settle down here in our "home base", the Raleigh, N.C. area, to the ministries God has called us to in this next chapter of our lives. The time we spent traveling was not wasted on self-satisfying entertainment, because it greatly enhanced our love for our Creator Lord, and we still found many opportunities for ministry along the way.

The reason I share these personal experiences with you is to share the ways that are available to strengthen your relationship with our Lord and Savior and have a very happy, satisfying life along the way. Granted, everyone for various reasons cannot do what Patricia and I did, but we simply suggest to you that if you can do it, it can be an opportunity to strengthen your relationship with your Creator God while thoroughly enjoying the adventure.

I thank God for all the many opportunities God has given me to enjoy and appreciate His love for us as expressed through His creation. I realized that I have been blessed with more opportunities than most folks have had, and I am very thankful for every one of them. However, some of those opportunities were not just something that happened to me, but opportunities that I chose to take advantage of. I think a lot of it goes back to that night in 1955 when God interrupted my Sunday School lesson preparation to enlighten me on **Matthew 6:19-34** (see chapter 1) and caused me to try to make pleasing Him the main motivation behind everything I did. I chose to serve God, not mammon. Jesus spoke about what he first said as recorded in **Matthew 6:19-34** many times in His short ministry. Another reference to this wisdom can be found **in Matthew 16:26-27—**

26 For what profit is it to a man if he gains the whole world, and loses his own soul? Or what will a man give in exchange for his soul? 27 For the Son of Man will come in the glory of His Father with His angels, and then He will reward each according to his works.

I have not acquired a lot of earthly possessions, but I have acquired a lot of joy and satisfaction. As **Matthew 6:19-34** suggests I have stored my treasures in heaven, rather than here on earth. At the ripe old age of 91, I can tell you for a fact, that making those choices 65 years ago has proven to me that I made the right choices. The best is yet to come because I have not gotten to heaven yet, where my treasure is stored. I only get a sample of it here, as we read about earlier in the book of Ephesians. I can also tell you, that I am enjoying what I am doing here and now, with my wife, and the co-laborers I minister with, so much, that I am not chomping at the bit to graduate to my heavenly reward. Please do not take this to indicate that I have lived a perfect life since making that important decision. I certainly have not. I have sinned many times but repented and have been forgiven. I have made a lot of mistakes when I made decisions without consulting with my helper, Holy Spirit. My family and others suffered the consequences with me. I have hurt people unintentionally, and I have gone through some rough times and rough situations, but God delivered me from them all. But altogether I have lived a very blessed life and look forward to much more of it. The important thing is that because of that commitment I made 65 years ago, God has walked with me through the good, bad, and ugly, and brought me through all of them victoriously.

DISCOVERING THE ATTITUDES AND MINDSETS OF GOD

Some years ago, I was sitting in my office, looking out at the trees in my backyard, and meditating on God's love for us through His creation, I was moved to pray a prayer of thanksgiving for the way He had blessed us with His Creation. I also felt moved to write it down, and here it is:

Father God, I love You.
I praise You and I worship You.
I thank You for Your unfathomed love for us, Your children,
    Whom You created, wooed, and blessed beyond measure or understanding.
I thank You for Your patience, Your forgiveness, and Your love for me,
    Which You have heaped upon me without measure.
I thank You for giving me eyes to behold Your love, wisdom, and sense of humor,
    Which you expressed to Your creation, man, through all that You have created,
    From the individual expanse, my eyes can behold,
    To the tiny plants, animals, and minerals that I have to search out to see.
Thank You for the great variety, simplicity, magnificence, and uniqueness
    Of the individual plants, animals, and celestial bodies which You created,
    Just to provide for our well-being and joy.
I thank You for the beauty, perfection, inter-relation, and inter-dependence
    Of all that You created.
I thank You for each opportunity you have given me to help others see Your love for them,
    That You express through all that You created,
    Love expressed to us originally when You created our environment,
    And love expressed to us as we behold the particular minute part of Your creation
    That we see, feel, and hear at a particular moment.
I thank You for Your great love for us,
    That is far greater than we can ever fully understand.
Amen

                                                              Ron Ely 2002

CHAPTER 10

The Love And Wrath Of God

God's Attitude and Mindset about His purpose for sending His Son to earth can be found in **Luke 4:16-21**, where Jesus announced in His hometown His purpose for coming to earth. This incident fulfilled the prophecy in **Isaiah 61:1-2**.

Luke 4:16-21— *16*So He came to Nazareth, where He had been brought up. And as His custom was, He went into the synagogue on the Sabbath day, and stood up to read. *17*And He was handed the book of the prophet Isaiah. And when He had opened the book, He found the place where it was written: *18* "The Spirit of the Lord *is* upon Me,
Because He has anointed Me
To preach the gospel to *the* poor;
He has sent Me to heal the brokenhearted,
To proclaim liberty to *the* captives
And recovery of sight to *the* blind,
To set at liberty those who are oppressed;
19 To proclaim the acceptable year of the Lord."
20 Then He closed the book, and gave *it* back to the attendant and sat down. And the eyes of all who were in the synagogue were fixed on Him. *21* And He began to say to them, "Today this Scripture is fulfilled in your hearing."

As Jesus was finishing up His time here on earth, He explained to His disciples how they would carry on the work He had started, in **Mark 16:15-20—** **[15]And He said to them, "Go into all the world and preach the gospel to every creature. [16] He who believes and is baptized will be saved; but he who does not believe will be condemned. [17] And these signs will follow those who believe: In My name they will cast out demons; they will speak with new tongues; [18] they will take up serpents; and if they drink anything deadly, it will by no means hurt them; they will lay hands on the sick, and they will recover." [19] So then, after the Lord had spoken to them, He was received up into heaven, and sat down at the right hand of God. [20] And they went out and preached everywhere, the Lord working with *them* and confirming the word through the accompanying signs. Amen.**

When people make the comment that God in the Old Testament is a God of wrath, but God in the New Testament is a God of Love, they are simply admitting that they really have not studied the Bible very well. God's love and wrath are very evident in both, the Old and New Testaments, but a brief, casual reading might give one an impression of a different attitude between the two. Look at verse 16 above. That looks straightforward and a little harsh, doesn't it? Verse 16 would indicate to me that God had little patience with a person who heard the gospel but refused to accept it. That doesn't indicate a lot of patience to me. The first fifteen books of the Old Testament are primarily History and reflect God's effort to create a people for Himself and settle them in their own land—a land occupied at that time by heathen idol worshippers. He warned the Israelites that if they did not annihilate all the idol worshippers who were occupying the land, but moved into the land and lived among them, they would pick up their bad habits. God told them that the people they let live would be a "thorn in their flesh". The Israelites did not obey and paid a high price.

Then look in the New Testament, at **Romans 1:18-2:11—[18] For the wrath of God is revealed from heaven against all ungodliness and unrighteousness of men, who suppress the truth in unrighteousness, [19] because what may be known of God is manifest** in them, for God has shown *it* to them. ²⁰ For since the creation of the world His invisible *attributes* are clearly seen, being understood by the things that are made, *even* His eternal power and Godhead, so that they are without excuse. ²¹ because, although they knew God, they did not glorify *Him* as God, nor were thankful, but became futile in their thoughts, and their foolish hearts were darkened. ²² Professing to be wise, they became fools, ²³ and changed the glory of the incorruptible God into an image made like corruptible man—and birds and four-footed animals and creeping things.

²⁴ Therefore God also gave them up to uncleanness, in the lusts of their hearts, to dishonor their bodies among themselves, ²⁵ who exchanged the truth of God for the lie, and worshiped and served the creature rather than the Creator, who is blessed forever. Amen.

²⁶ For this reason God gave them up to vile passions. For even their women exchanged the natural use for what is against nature. ²⁷ Likewise also the men, leaving the natural use of the woman, burned in their lust for one another, men with men committing what is shameful, and receiving in themselves the penalty of their error which was due.

²⁸ And even as they did not like to retain God in *their* knowledge, God gave them over to a debased mind, to do those things which are not fitting; ²⁹ being filled with all unrighteousness, sexual immorality, wickedness, covetousness, maliciousness; full of envy, murder, strife, deceit, evil-mindedness; *they are* whisperers, ³⁰ backbiters, haters of God, violent, proud, boasters, inventors of evil things, disobedient to parents, ³¹ undiscerning, untrustworthy, unloving, unforgiving, unmerciful; ³² who, knowing the righteous judgment of God, that those who practice such things are deserving of death, not only do the same but also approve of those who practice them.

2: ¹ Therefore you are inexcusable, O man, whoever you are who judge, for in whatever you judge another you condemn yourself;

for you who judge practice the same things. ² But we know that the judgment of God is according to truth against those who practice such things. ³ And do you think this, O man, you who judge those practicing such things, and doing the same, that you will escape the judgment of God? ⁴ Or do you despise the riches of His goodness, forbearance, and longsuffering, not knowing that the goodness of God leads you to repentance? ⁵ But in accordance with your hardness and your impenitent heart you are treasuring up for yourself wrath in the day of wrath and revelation of the righteous judgment of God, ⁶ who "will render to each one according to his deeds": ⁷ eternal life to those who by patient continuance in doing good seek for glory, honor, and immortality; ⁸ but to those who are self-seeking and do not obey the truth, but obey unrighteousness—indignation and wrath, ⁹ tribulation and anguish, on every soul of man who does evil, of the Jew first and also of the Greek; ¹⁰ but glory, honor, and peace to everyone who works what is good, to the Jew first and also to the Greek. ¹¹ For there is no partiality with God.

Look at this Scripture. **Malachi 3:6—**

"For I *am* the LORD, I do not change;
Therefore you are not consumed, O sons of Jacob.
And in the New Testament, **Hebrews 13:8—**
Jesus Christ *is* the same yesterday, today, and forever.

Remember, The Bible makes it clear Jesus was in the beginning and equal with God, is God.

Considering what is going on around the world today, particularly in the U S. I have some strong opinions about homosexuality and the promotion of it while demeaning Christian principles in most of the media and government, but I will not elaborate on them at this point. However, I would like to throw out some things for you to consider. Think about the prevalence of homosexuality, and the open dialogue about it, compared to thirty years ago. Selah- (go figure). Think about our government's, and media's, attitude towards Christianity today compared to thirty years ago. Selah- (go figure) Think about the way socialism is rapidly being crammed down our throats by our government, schools, and most of the media. Selah. (Go figure). Now, ask ourselves, what we have done and are doing about these situations. We have allowed these things to take over our country, by doing nothing to stop them. If every one of us does not rise and start making our voices heard where it counts, we will very shortly be another socialist country. Are you prepared to live under those conditions? If that happens to us, will you blame God? I really hope not. We will have no one to blame but ourselves.

The love and the wrath of God are very evident in Jesus' interactions with the Pharisees and other religious leaders He encountered. As you consider God's love for them, understand that Jesus knew all along that they were going to have Him arrested, brutalized, and crucified. Look at **Matthew 22:34-40**—

34 But when the Pharisees heard that He had silenced the Sadducees, they gathered together. 35 Then one of them, a lawyer, asked Him a question, testing Him, and saying, 36 "Teacher, which is the great commandment in the law?" 37 Jesus said to him, "'You shall love the Lord your God with all your heart, with all your soul, and with all your mind.' 38 This is the first and great commandment. 39 And the second is like it: 'You shall love your neighbor as yourself.' 40 On these two commandments hang all the Law and the Prophets."

Now, let's look at **Matthew 23:1-36-**

1 Then Jesus spoke to the multitudes and to His disciples, 2 saying: "The scribes and the Pharisees sit in Moses' seat. 3 Therefore whatever they tell you to observe, that observe and do, but do not do according to their works; for they say, and do not do. 4 For they bind heavy burdens, hard to bear, and lay them on men's shoulders; but they themselves will not move them with one of their fingers. 5 But all their works they do to be seen by men. They make their phylacteries broad and enlarge the borders of their garments. ⁶ They love the best places at feasts, the best seats in the synagogues, ⁷ greetings in the marketplaces, and to be called by men, 'Rabbi, Rabbi.' ⁸ But you, do not be called 'Rabbi'; for One is your Teacher, the Christ, and you are all brethren. ⁹ Do not call anyone on earth your father; for One is your Father, He who is in heaven. ¹⁰ And do not be called teachers; for One is your Teacher, the Christ. ¹¹ But he who is greatest among you shall be your servant. ¹² And whoever exalts himself will be humbled, and he who humbles himself will be exalted. ¹³ "But woe to you, scribes and Pharisees, hypocrites! For you shut up the kingdom of heaven against men; for you neither go in *yourselves,* nor do you allow those who are entering to go in. ¹⁴ Woe to you, scribes and Pharisees, hypocrites! For you devour widows' houses, and for a pretense make long prayers. Therefore you will receive greater condemnation. ¹⁵ "Woe to you, scribes and Pharisees, hypocrites! For you travel land and sea to win one proselyte, and when he is won, you make him twice as much a son of hell as yourselves. ¹⁶ "Woe to you, blind guides, who say, 'Whoever swears by the temple, it is nothing; but whoever swears by the gold of the temple, he is obliged *to perform it.*' ¹⁷ Fools and blind! For which is greater, the gold or the temple that [i]sanctifies the gold? ¹⁸ And, 'Whoever swears by the altar, it is nothing; but whoever swears by the gift that is on it, he is obliged *to perform it.*' ¹⁹ Fools and blind! For which is greater, the gift or the altar that sanctifies the gift? ²⁰ Therefore he who swears by the altar, swears by it and by all things on it. ²¹ He who swears by the temple, swears by it and by Him who dwells in it. ²² And he who swears by heaven, swears by the throne of God and by Him who sits on it.

²³ "Woe to you, scribes and Pharisees, hypocrites! For you pay tithe of mint and anise and cummin, and have neglected the weightier *matters* of the law: justice and mercy and faith. These you ought to have done, without leaving the others undone. ²⁴ Blind guides, who strain out a gnat and swallow a camel!

[25] "Woe to you, scribes and Pharisees, hypocrites! For you cleanse the outside of the cup and dish, but inside they are full of extortion and self-indulgence. [26] Blind Pharisee, first cleanse the inside of the cup and dish, that the outside of them may be clean also.

[27] "Woe to you, scribes and Pharisees, hypocrites! For you are like whitewashed tombs which indeed appear beautiful outwardly, but inside are full of dead *men's* bones and all uncleanness. [28] Even so you also outwardly appear righteous to men, but inside you are full of hypocrisy and lawlessness.

[29] "Woe to you, scribes and Pharisees, hypocrites! Because you build the tombs of the prophets and adorn the monuments of the righteous, [30] and say, 'If we had lived in the days of our fathers, we would not have been partakers with them in the blood of the prophets.'

[31] "Therefore you are witnesses against yourselves that you are sons of those who murdered the prophets. [32] Fill up, then, the measure of your fathers' *guilt*. [33] Serpents, brood of vipers! How can you escape the condemnation of hell? [34] Therefore, indeed, I send you prophets, wise men, and scribes: *some* of them you will kill and crucify, and *some* of them you will scourge in your synagogues and persecute from city to city, [35] that on you may come all the righteous blood shed on the earth, from the blood of righteous Abel to the blood of Zechariah, son of Berechiah, whom you murdered between the temple and the altar. [36] Assuredly, I say to you, all these things will come upon this generation.

Jesus offered those Jews who did believe in Him, hope. Look **at John 8:31-32**—

Then Jesus said to those Jews who believed Him, "If you abide in My word, you are My disciples indeed. [32] And you shall know the truth, and the truth shall make you free."

Question: How can you abide in Jesus' word if you don't know His word?

Let's look at Jesus' interaction with Nicodemus, because that reveals much about Jesus' love for this Pharisee who first was intrigued by Jesus, and after interacting with Him, came to love Him.

John 3:1-21—¹There was a man of the Pharisees named Nicodemus, a ruler of the Jews. ² This man came to Jesus by night and said to Him, "Rabbi, we know that You are a teacher come from God; for no one can do these signs that You do unless God is with him."³ Jesus answered and said to him, "Most assuredly, I say to you, unless one is born again, he cannot see the kingdom of God." ⁴ Nicodemus said to Him, "How can a man be born when he is old? Can he enter a second time into his mother's womb and be born?"

⁵ Jesus answered, "Most assuredly, I say to you, unless one is born of water and the Spirit, he cannot enter the kingdom of God. ⁶ That which is born of the flesh is flesh, and that which is born of the Spirit is spirit. ⁷ Do not marvel that I said to you, 'You must be born again.' ⁸ The wind blows where it wishes, and you hear the sound of it, but cannot tell where it comes from and where it goes. So is everyone who is born of the Spirit." ⁹ Nicodemus answered and said to Him, "How can these things be?"

¹⁰ Jesus answered and said to him, "Are you the teacher of Israel, and do not know these things? ¹¹ Most assuredly, I say to you, We speak what We know and testify what We have seen, and you do not receive Our witness. ¹² If I have told you earthly things and you do not believe, how will you believe if I tell you heavenly things? ¹³ No one has ascended to heaven but He who came down from heaven, *that is,* the Son of Man who is in heaven. ¹⁴ And as Moses lifted up the serpent in the wilderness, even so must the Son of Man be lifted up, ¹⁵ that whoever believes in Him should not perish but have eternal life. ¹⁶ For God so loved the world that He gave His only begotten Son, that whoever believes in Him should not perish but have everlasting

life. ¹⁷ For God did not send His Son into the world to condemn the world, but that the world through Him might be saved.

¹⁸ "He who believes in Him is not condemned; but he who does not believe is condemned already, because he has not believed in the name of the only begotten Son of God. ¹⁹ And this is the condemnation, that the light has come into the world, and men loved darkness rather than light, because their deeds were evil. ²⁰ For everyone practicing evil hates the light and does not come to the light, lest his deeds should be exposed. ²¹ But he who does the truth comes to the light, that his deeds may be clearly seen, that they have been done in God."

John 7:40-52— ⁴⁰Therefore many from the crowd, when they heard this saying, said, "Truly this is the Prophet." ⁴¹ Others said, "This is the Christ." But some said, "Will the Christ come out of Galilee? ⁴² Has not the Scripture said that the Christ comes from the seed of David and from the town of Bethlehem, where David was?" ⁴³ So there was a division among the people because of Him. ⁴⁴ Now some of them wanted to take Him, but no one laid hands on Him.

⁴⁵ Then the officers came to the chief priests and Pharisees, who said to them, "Why have you not brought Him?"⁴⁶ The officers answered, "No man ever spoke like this Man!"⁴⁷ Then the Pharisees answered them, "Are you also deceived? ⁴⁸ Have any of the rulers or the Pharisees believed in Him? ⁴⁹ But this crowd that does not know the law is accursed."

⁵⁰ Nicodemus (he who came to Jesus by night, being one of them) said to them, ⁵¹ "Does our law judge a man before it hears him and knows what he is doing?"⁵² They answered and said to him, "Are you also from Galilee? Search and look, for no prophet has arisen out of Galilee."

John 19:38-42 ³⁸After this, Joseph of Arimathea, being a disciple of Jesus, but secretly, for fear of the Jews, asked Pilate that he might take away the body of Jesus; and Pilate gave *him* permission. So he came and took the body of Jesus. ³⁹ And Nicodemus, who at first came to Jesus by night, also came, bringing a mixture of myrrh and aloes, about a hundred pounds. ⁴⁰ Then they took the body of Jesus, and bound it in strips of linen with the spices, as the custom of the Jews is to bury. ⁴¹ Now in the place where He was crucified there was a garden, and in the garden a new tomb in which no one had yet been laid. ⁴² So there they laid Jesus, because of the Jews' Preparation *Day,* for the tomb was nearby.

Let's look at another Attitude and Mindset of God. Look— at **Hebrews 12:1-11**

¹Therefore we also, since we are surrounded by so great a cloud of witnesses, let us lay aside every weight, and the sin which so easily ensnares *us,* and let us run with endurance the race that is set before us, ² looking unto Jesus, the author and finisher of *our* faith, who for the joy that was set before Him endured the cross, despising the shame, and has sat down at the right hand of the throne of God. ³ For consider Him who endured such hostility from sinners against Himself, lest you become weary and discouraged in your souls. ⁴ You have not yet resisted to bloodshed, striving against sin. ⁵ And you have forgotten the exhortation which speaks to you as to sons:

"My son, do not despise the chastening of the LORD,
Nor be discouraged when you are rebuked by Him;
⁶ For whom the LORD loves He chastens,
And scourges every son whom He receives."

⁷ If you endure chastening, God deals with you as with sons; for what son is there whom a father does not chasten? ⁸ But if you are without chastening, of which all have become partakers, then you are illegitimate and not sons. ⁹ Furthermore, we have had human fathers who corrected *us,* and we paid *them* respect. Shall we not much more readily be in subjection to the Father of spirits and

live? ¹⁰ For they indeed for a few days chastened *us* as seemed *best* to them, but He for *our* profit, that *we* may be partakers of His holiness. ¹¹ Now no chastening seems to be joyful for the present, but painful; nevertheless, afterward it yields the peaceable fruit of righteousness to those who have been trained by it.

I grew up in a time and place when parents considered it necessary to physically punish a child for disobeying rules. My first wife and I raised two sons under the same understanding. There is no doubt in my mind whatsoever that my parents and my wife and I sometimes meted out punishment that could possibly have been not the best thing for the situation. I still loved my parents (although there were a lot of times, I did not like my dad), and my sons both still love my departed wife and me. Neither my sons nor my brothers nor I turned out warped or troubled guys. Self-discipline is one of my better character traits, even to this day. The Bible makes it clear in many Scriptures that good parents need to exercise discipline and control over their children. Our Heavenly Father makes it perfectly clear that He will discipline us if we need it, so it might also be a good practice for us to treat our children that way. Which shows more love—Don't punish a child and leave him to face the world with no compass, or love him enough to instill in him a "compass"? I think God got it right. I know that I am not smarter than He is.

By contrast, we see a generation of young people with many of them confused, frustrated, and some of them completely lost. Where were the church and the millions of "Christians" in the U. S. while they were being raised? We have allowed our education system to be a training ground for atheism and socialism. Again, the Christian community, the Church, can either get up off its "blessed assurance" and investigate how to take steps to fight the downward trend, or we can continue to sit idly by and watch our country go to hell.

A big Attitude and Mindset of God is reflected in how much He values and respects our freedom of choice. We have the privilege of being just as good or just as mean as we want to be. He makes it perfectly clear what the reward of each is. When you look at it, you must wonder why anyone would want to go to Hell. One might say, "but if no Christian leads him to Christ, is that altogether his fault?" The Scripture above in **Romans 1 & 2** shoots that theory down. But God is such a perfect gentleman that He will not impose Himself or His will on anyone. **Revelation 3:19-21**

[19]As many as I love, I rebuke and chasten. Therefore be zealous and repent. [20] Behold, I stand at the door and knock. If anyone hears My voice and opens the door, I will come in to him and dine with him, and he with Me. [21] To him who overcomes I will grant to sit with Me on My throne, as I also overcame and sat down with My Father on His throne.

In my opinion, that Scripture makes a couple of things very clear:

1...Jesus, God's representative, absolutely loves us too much to infringe on our free will which He willingly granted us, by causing us to do something that we don't specifically ask Him to do; and

2...He loves us too much as a son or daughter not to "rebuke or chasten" us as a means of correction, to teach us what is best for us. Any parent can certainly benefit from the example our Heavenly Father sets for us.

The fact that this was a message to a particular church 2000 years ago and recorded in the Bible, does not make it one iota less applicable to us today.

Matthew 10:28—And do not fear those who kill the body but cannot kill the soul. But rather fear Him who is able to destroy both soul and body in hell.

Like it or not, that is another Attitude and Mindset of God. The fear of God is a definite Attitude and Mindset that God specifically advises us to have throughout the Bible. In this Scripture and most of the other references, the Hebrew or Greek word translated as "fear", means "fear"! The Greek Dictionary in my AMG Hebrew-Greek Key Word Study Bible translates the word 'fear" in this instance (phobeo) as "transitively, to fear someone". As you study and meditate on this Scripture, you cannot fail to understand that the word "fear" means "fear", pure and simple.

Matthew 10:24-27 [24]**"A disciple is not above *his* teacher, nor a servant above his master.** [25] **It is enough for a disciple that he be like his teacher, and a servant like his master. If they have called the master of the house Beelzebub, how much more *will they call* those of his household!** [26] **Therefore do not fear them. For there is nothing covered that will not be revealed, and hidden that will not be known.** [27] **"Whatever I tell you in the dark, speak in the light; and what you hear in the ear, preach on the housetops.** [28] **And do not fear those who kill the body but cannot kill the soul. But rather fear Him who is able to destroy both soul and body in hell.**

God is the only one with the power to do that—not Satan.

The various concordances in some cases indicate that in a few cases the Greek or Hebrew word translated as fear can also indicate respect or reverence. I see that as no excuse for pastors and teachers to often dance around the word "fear" and say it only means "respect" or "reverence". To do so in my opinion is very deceptive and disrespectful, to word it as softly as I can. Most of the references in the Old and New Testaments (there are more in the New Testament than most folks realize) that use the word "fear", simply means "fear". Why is it so hard to understand the above verse as it is written? If you don't fear the one person with the authority and power to decide whether you will spend eternity in heaven or hell, who else would you fear?

Let's look at another Attitude and Mindset of God that a lot of folks stumble over:

Matthew 13:10-17—[10] **And the disciples came and said to Him, "Why do You speak to them in parables?"** [11] **He answered and said to them, "Because it has been given to you to know the mysteries**

of the kingdom of heaven, but to them it has not been given. ¹² For whoever has, to him more will be given, and he will have abundance; but whoever does not have, even what he has will be taken away from him. ¹³ Therefore I speak to them in parables, because seeing they do not see, and hearing they do not hear, nor do they understand. ¹⁴ And in them the prophecy of Isaiah is fulfilled, which says:

'Hearing you will hear and shall not understand,
And seeing you will see and not perceive;
¹⁵ For the hearts of this people have grown dull.
Their ears are hard of hearing,
And their eyes they have closed,
Lest they should see with *their* eyes and hear with *their* ears,
Lest they should understand with *their* hearts and turn,
So that I should heal them.' ¹⁶ But blessed *are* your eyes for they see, and your ears for they hear; ¹⁷ for assuredly, I say to you that many prophets and righteous *men* desired to see what you see, and did not see *it,* and to hear what you hear, and did not hear *it.*

This same prophecy is referred to in **Mark 4:12, Luke 8:10, John 12:40, Acts 28:6, and Romans 11:8**. That factor alone tells us that it must be very important, and that we should really study to find out why it is repeated so many times. It seems to me that Jesus is saying that if you are not serious about entering the Kingdom of God, you probably will not. If you think about that and think of other Scriptures that seem to imply the same thought, you probably conclude that is another Attitude and Mindset of God.

Look at **2 Peter 1:2-4—²Grace and peace be multiplied to you in the knowledge of God and of Jesus our Lord, ³ as His divine power has given to us all things that** *pertain* **to life and godliness, through the knowledge of Him who called us by glory and virtue, ⁴ by which have been given to us exceedingly great and precious promises, that through these you may be partakers of the divine nature, having escaped the corruption** *that is* **in the world through lust.**

Also—**2 Peter 3:9— The Lord is not slack concerning *His* promise, as some count slackness, but is longsuffering toward us, not willing that any should perish but that all should come to repentance**

Then, compare this with **Matthew 7:13-14— ¹³"Enter by the narrow gate; for wide *is* the gate and broad *is* the way that leads to destruction, and there are many who go in by it. ¹⁴ Because narrow *is* the gate and difficult *is* the way which leads to life, and there are few who find it.**

So, when we compare these Scriptures that we have looked at in this chapter, I personally draw the conclusion that Jesus offered to share His divine nature with us as we enter the Kingdom of God. Although His desire is for all of us to enter, He knows that many will not because they make choices to follow the world's way rather than His way. I admit that all sounds difficult, but I didn't say it, God did in His Word.

I believe chapters 13-17 of John, which will be covered in chapter 24, does more to explain the passionate desire God has to fellowship and bless all His followers who graciously accept and follow His instructions for us to have the best life possible.

CHAPTER 11

"...Be Holy, For I Am Holy"
-1 Peter 1:16

The Old Testament and the New Testament make it very clear, that God in the Old Testament and Jesus in the New Testament emphasized that it is God's will that all His followers be holy. Sometimes, the word "holy" carries such an extreme understanding that it can seem unpleasantly extreme. If that is the case for you, simply use in its place the words Jesus often used to represent "holy" or "holiness": Jesus more often referred to "obey" or "obedience". "Obey" and "obedience" sound more palatable to me, personally. The New Testament makes it very clear that if we repent (change our mind and purpose) and ask for forgiveness, He will quickly forgive us of our sin/disobedience. **Acts 26:20b— "that they should repent, turn to God, and do works befitting repentance,"**

God's intolerance of sin in His chosen followers (**"For many are called, but few are chosen". Matthew 22:14),** is quite evident from Genesis through Revelation.

Chapter 6 of Genesis is one of the saddest scriptures in the Bible, in my opinion. Look at **Genesis 6:5-8— ⁵Then the LORD saw that the wickedness of man *was* great in the earth, and *that* every intent of the thoughts of his heart *was* only evil continually. ⁶And the LORD**

<u>was sorry that He had made man on the earth, and He was grieved in His heart. ⁷ So the Lord said, "I will destroy man whom I have created from the face of the earth, both man and beast, creeping thing and birds of the air, for I am sorry that I have made them." ⁸ But Noah found grace in the eyes of the Lord.</u> (emphasis mine)

When God led the children of Israel out of Egypt to the promised land, He gave them the Ten Commandments and other laws, statutes, and judgments that included holiness.

Deuteronomy 6:5-7— ⁵You shall love the Lord your God with all your heart, with all your soul, and with all your strength. ⁶ "And these words which I command you today shall be in your heart. ⁷ You shall teach them diligently to your children, and shall talk of them when you sit in your house, when you walk by the way, when you lie down, and when you rise up.

The New Testament did not do away with the Law and the Ten Commandments, as some believe, but it taught us how to fulfill them without having to remember all the laws, statutes, and judgments that God had put the Israelites under in the Old Testament. Check these Scriptures out.

Matthew 5:17 "Do not think that I came to destroy the Law or the Prophets. I did not come to destroy but to fulfill.

Jesus lived His entire life in complete fulfillment of all the commandments, statutes, and judgements found in the book of Deuteronomy. He did, however, chide the religious leaders of His day for adding to, twisting, and replacing some of them with their own interpretation of them, which He refused to obey.

Matthew 22:36-40- ³⁶"Teacher, which is the great commandment in the law?" ³⁷ Jesus said to him, "'You shall love the Lord your God with all your heart, with all your soul, and with all your mind.' ³⁸ This is the first and great commandment. **³⁹ And the second *is* like it: 'You shall love your neighbor as yourself.' ⁴⁰ On these two commandments hang all the Law and the Prophets."**

That does not sound to me like He is canceling the Ten Commandments or any part of the Old Testament law. So, in the New Testament, Jesus taught us that rather than trying to keep up with all the hundreds of laws, statutes, and judgments listed in the Old Testament, if we simply kept these first two laws, which are very clear, we would fulfill all the others. How simple is that?

"The Sermon on the Mount", recorded in **Matthew chapters 5-7**, could be called an explanation of the above Scripture. Together, these Scriptures explain holiness. Check **Matthew 6:48— Therefore you shall be perfect, just as your Father in heaven is perfect.**

Being that some people seem to consider "holiness" a hard word, use "obedience" if that is more comfortable for you. Mankind seems to tend to look for "an easy way out", particularly when it comes to these Scriptures. We hear the expression, "I'm just a sinner saved by grace." Really? If you have repented and been forgiven, you should no longer consider yourself to have the label of a sinner. If you keep on sinning, according to what I read in the Bible, you are not saved by grace until you repent of your sin and receive God's forgiveness. It appears to me that these cliches are used to shirk responsibility for our own behavior and put that responsibility on Jesus. I understand that He agrees to help us by giving us Holy Spirit to live inside us, but I have not found anything to indicate He is going to do it for us. The book of 1 John has a lot to say about this, so it is worth studying. Another cliché is "I'm not righteous, my only righteousness is Jesus in me." I have not found that in the Bible. The Bible teaches us that God's Holy Spirit living within us enables us to be holy, but it is our responsibility to exercise that power to be holy.

1 John 1:9-2:3- ⁹If we confess our sins, He is faithful and just to forgive us *our* sins and to cleanse us from all unrighteousness. ¹⁰ If we

say that we have not sinned, we make Him a liar, and His word is not in us. 2: ¹My little children, these things I write to you, so that you may not sin. And if anyone sins, we have an Advocate with the Father, Jesus Christ the righteous. ² And He Himself is the propitiation for our sins, and not for ours only but also for the whole world. ³ Now by this we know that we know Him, if we keep His commandments.

Please note: a chapter change does not necessarily mean a change in the intent of the narrative, because the chapter and verse numbers were not in the original Scriptures but were inserted by a printer in the 1500s to facilitate referencing a particular Scripture.

James, a half-brother of Jesus, gives some precise instructions on Christian conversation in **James 5:12- But above all, my brethren, do not swear, either by heaven or by earth or with any other oath. But let your "Yes" be "Yes," and** *your* **"No," "No," lest you fall into judgment.**

Look very carefully at **Matthew 12:34-37—³⁴ Brood of vipers! How can you, being evil, speak good things? For out of the abundance of the heart the mouth speaks. ³⁵ A good man out of the good treasure of his heart brings forth good things, and an evil man out of the evil treasure brings forth evil things. ³⁶ But I say to you that for every idle word men may speak, they will give account of it in the day of judgment. ³⁷ <u>For by your words you will be justified, and by your words you will be condemned.</u>"(emphasis mine)**

Matthew 15:10-11— ¹⁰When He had called the multitude to *Himself,* **He said to them, "Hear and understand: ¹¹ Not what goes into the mouth defiles a man; but what comes out of the mouth, this defiles a man."**

The book of Romans is also a good book to study in this regard. Let's look at **Romans 8:5-8—⁵For those who live according to the flesh set their minds on the things of the flesh, but those** *who live* **according to the Spirit, the things of the Spirit. ⁶ For to be carnally minded** *is* death, but to be spiritually minded *is* life and peace. ⁷ Because the carnal mind *is* enmity against God; for it is not subject to the law of God, nor indeed can be. ⁸ So then, those who are in the flesh cannot please God.

Also, **Romans 8:12-16**—Therefore, brethren, we are debtors—not to the flesh, to live according to the flesh. ¹³ For if you live according to the flesh you will die; but if by the Spirit you put to death the deeds of the body, you will live. ¹⁴ For as many as are led by the Spirit of God, these are sons of God. ¹⁵ For you did not receive the spirit of bondage again to fear, but you received the Spirit of adoption by whom we cry out, "Abba, Father." ¹⁶ The Spirit Himself bears witness with our spirit that we are children of God,

The Bible teaches that there is a lot more to being a Christian and being "saved" than just repeating "the sinner's prayer". It involves how we really believe in our heart, and how we live after we repeat that prayer. It is easy to take Scripture out of context to support anything you want to, and it is done often. The command to be holy is repeated throughout the Bible. Jesus told His disciples the night before he was arrested: - ¹⁵**"If you love Me, keep My commandments. ¹⁶ And I will pray the Father, and He will give you another Helper, that He may abide with you forever"**.— John 14:15-16.

Jesus repeated this same admonition in **John 14:21, 23-24, and 15:10, 14**. Repeating basically the same thing so many times certainly indicates Jesus considered it very important for us to understand the importance of loving God so much that we want to keep His Commandments. Again, that phrase the teacher gave me so long ago that I regretfully ignored for years: "the more you put into something, the more you get out of it", is so, so true. I know that from experience, by first ignoring it but later repenting and putting more into my relationship with God and getting so much more out of it.

After receiving Jesus as my Lord and Savior, I remember discussing salvation with my buddies and saying, "well, I don't expect to be the best person to get into heaven, but I think I will barely qualify". I look back at that now and wonder how ignorant and stupid could I be. I don't know where I got such ideas, but they sure did not come from the Bible. The problem was that like many people, I was thinking only about heaven when I die, and not about how I would function between then and heaven. The sad truth is most people think of heaven as their goal, instead of thinking about living until then. They are convinced by over-zealous people that is what Christianity is all about, so I get this free ticket and do not have to be concerned about it anymore. That is not what the Bible says, but you can snatch a verse out here and there and make it say anything you want to. Thank God, I did not take "my free ticket" and run but continued to seek more of God the best way I knew how. Jesus realized this type of thing would happen, so He addressed it from time to time as in The Sermon on the Mount in **Matthew 7:21-23— "Not everyone who says to Me, 'Lord, Lord,' shall enter the kingdom of heaven, but he who does the will of My Father in heaven. 22 Many will say to Me in that day, 'Lord, Lord, have we not prophesied in Your name, cast out demons in Your name, and done many wonders in Your name?' 23 And then I will declare to them, 'I never knew you; depart from Me, you who practice lawlessness!'**

When I think about how the Christian is instructed to live, I always think about my father, who, as far as I know, may have been burning in hell for the last thirty-five years. Every time I tried to talk to him about accepting Jesus as his Lord and Savior, he cussed me out. He would tell me, "The preacher baptized me with his wet hand when I was a baby, so I know I am going to heaven, and that's that. I don't want to hear any more of that Jesus stuff." Although he did continue to go to church off and on, he lived a very sinful life in many ways. He got drunk often, abused his family, cursed terribly, and got into drunken brawls. According to his own account he beat a man to death in a bar. I would certainly be thrilled when I get to heaven if I found out he got his heart right before he passed away, and he was there to greet me upon my arrival.

<u>The important thing is to have an attitude of not wanting to displease God in any way, because we love and respect Him so much for the extreme love He has given us.</u> One of the best ways to acquire that attitude is to spend time daily studying the Bible so that you can see and somewhat understand His extreme love for you. As you are studying and listening for God's interpretation of His Word, your relationship with Him grows. Someone has wisely said, "Someone who is all wrapped up in themselves creates a mighty small package". You can take that in several ways, but as Paul points out in the Book of Romans, life simply comes down to living for God (and others) or living for self and die. Romans 8 is a very good chapter of the Bible to be very familiar with. Believe me, I have tried it both ways, and living for God is better by far if peace, joy, and happiness mean anything at all to you.

The importance of holiness is often neglected by preachers who are more concerned about building up their following than teaching the whole gospel. Although that description does not apply to all pastors, it describes far more of them than we want to admit. Consequently, most church members hear very little about holiness. All too often, Holy and Holiness are treated like dirty words in the church. Christians use so many catchphrases that devalue the importance of being holy, such as "I'm not righteous, except for Jesus in me" (or some various facsimile of that), so that they are sometimes discouraged from making any effort to be holy. The letters of the New Testament and church history in the Old Testament paint a dismal picture of how the lack of sufficient teaching on this important subject from the beginning of the church up to the present time, has been a major cause of weakness in the church and weakness in the Christian. *Eusebius Ecclesiastical History* shows how a lack of holiness accompanied a lack of evidence of the power of the Holy Spirit in the church. That observation should drive us to search the Scriptures on the subject to see how much we need to study and consider it. A good start would be to pick up an exhaustive concordance and check out all the references to "holy" and "holiness" in both the Old Testament and the New Testament. It will take you more than a few minutes to do that, but it would be worth your time. I promise you it will cause a big change in your attitude about the importance of those two words. My personal experience, as well as my study of the Bible and church history, convinces me that if you want all God has already made available to you, you will have to give God all that He asks of you. I have heard a lot of teaching completely contrary to that belief, but I ignore it. Too many church members are willing to sit in church and take for granted everything they hear from the pulpit is Biblical, but that is not always the case.

The book, *Eusebius Ecclesiastical History* charts how the struggling New Testament Church tried to offset the pressure of persecution by the Roman Empire and the Jewish religious leaders, up to the year 321 when Emperor Constantine stopped the persecution and established the Christian religion as the official religion of the Roman Empire. That same book (Eusebius lived from approximately 280-360) tells how the gradual deterioration of holiness in the church corresponded with the gradual lessening of occurrences of the miraculous power of the Holy Spirit. After that, as recorded by Eusebius, Emperor Constantine accelerated this downward trend by building church buildings with throne type pulpits, established salaries for church staff, and introduced business and political practices into the church. These actions drew all kinds of people into the church and some for reasons of greed rather than seeking a relationship with God.

We turn to the book, *2000 Years of Charismatic Christianity* (page 26) by Eddie L. Hyatt, to see "the rest of the story". Montanus, was born in the first half or the second century and may have served as a bishop. Around 172 he started trying to revive the charismatic nature of the church and became well known for working signs and miracles. The qualifying factor for leadership in the church was the possession of spiritual gifts rather than by appointment to ecclesiastic office, according to Montanus. This was apparently the case of the New Testament church, according to the New Testament, beginning with the book of Acts. Montanus was probably responsible for the first charismatic renewal. At the Council of Constantinople in 381 the followers of his doctrine were declared pagan and kicked out of the church, thus ending that early renewal, and you might say, officially kicking the Holy Spirit out of the church. You can continue reading *2000 years of Charismatic Christianity* and other accounts to see how the New Testament church continued to exist, usually outside of "the church". Most historians of church history completely ignore the existence of this small but important part of church history. It wasn't until the Azusa Street Revival at the beginning of the 20th century that this remnant of the New Testament Church was recognized as part of the Christian Church. I personally believe that it is time for serious Christians to quit playing church by worshiping sacred cows, and seriously endeavor to follow the Bible pattern for the church. It seems to me that 1600 years is enough to realize that what we have, for the most part, is not the intended outcome when compared with the New Testament Church in the Bible.

It is only by understanding God enough to see what a loving, intelligent heavenly Father He is that we can begin to see how much He loves us. He has done that to give us peace, joy, and victory as we prepare for heaven. He does not give us instructions just to satisfy Himself but to give us a better life. It is next to impossible to reach that understanding by simply listening to someone else. We need to study His word and fellowship with Him via His Holy Spirit as we do so.

CHAPTER 12

The Kingdom Of God

In Matthew, chapter 6, the disciples asked Jesus to teach them to pray, and He introduced them to what has been called The Lord's Prayer. I prefer to refer to it as the Model Prayer and John 17 as the Lord's Prayer. In **Matthew 6:10** He prayed to Father God, **"Your kingdom come. Your will be done on earth as it is in heaven."** Thus, Jesus called down the Kingdom of God from heaven to earth. Earlier, John the Baptist prophesied that Jesus would introduce the Kingdom of God on earth, in **Matthew 3:1-2—In those days John the Baptist came preaching in the wilderness of Judea, [2] and saying, "Repent, for the kingdom of heaven is at hand!"**

Although the New Testament has a lot to say about The Kingdom of God, you may not hear it mentioned very often from the pulpit of your church, or by most of the preachers on television. There is a good reason for that. In my studies, it appears to me that The Kingdom of God is associated with the baptism/infilling with the Holy Spirit, with the evidence of power. **Luke 17:20, 21: [20] Now when He was asked by the Pharisees when the kingdom of God would come, He answered them and said, "The kingdom of God does not come with observation; [21] nor will they say, 'See here!' or 'See there!' For indeed, the kingdom of God is within you."** Sadly, talking about the infilling of the Holy Spirit is taboo in many churches today, and billions of Christians are left in the dark when it comes to The Kingdom of God. Many people assume that The Kingdom of God only refers to what we experience when we leave this life and enter heaven. A thorough study of the New Testament convinces me that The Kingdom of God is available to believers here and now, even though not completed until we get to heaven. I think Jesus fully expected all His followers to be a part of it while walking this planet. The New Testament has much to say about it, and you can study it for yourself to find out whatever you want to know about it. In this chapter, I hope to convince you why it should be important to you now, and help you understand what it is all about. I need to point out at this point that Matthew in his gospel seldom referred to The Kingdom of God, but instead referred to The Kingdom of Heaven. By comparing the 4 gospels' references to similar events, we can conclude the two terms refer to the same thing.

As I mentioned earlier, the New Testament Church as described in the book of Acts, obviously expected new church members to believe that Jesus was the Son of God, that He died for their sins and rose from the grave to make eternal life available to them, and they, in turn, repent of their sinful nature and be converted to God's nature. After that, they would be baptized in water (complete immersion) to signify outwardly their death to their old way of believing and their sins being washed away and rising from the death to self and "being born again" to a new life in union with Jesus the Christ. Then they were to be filled with the Holy Spirit with evidence of the newly acquired power. I listed Scripture in an earlier chapter to justify that conclusion. (Restudy Acts: 2-10) The Bible, and billions, of other Christians' experiences, justify that conclusion as well. If there is no evidence of the <u>power</u> of the Holy Spirit and <u>fruit</u> of the Holy Spirit in a Christian's life, then we cannot be sure that person has been filled with the Holy Spirit.

Galatians 5:22-25- ²²But the fruit of the Spirit is love, joy, peace, longsuffering, kindness, goodness, faithfulness, ²³ gentleness, self-control. Against such there is no law. ²⁴ And those *who are* Christ's

have crucified the flesh with its passions and desires. ²⁵ If we live in the Spirit, let us also walk in the Spirit.

Most Christians look forward to being a participant in The Kingdom of God when they graduate from this life to heaven. But many Christians are not aware of the fact that God loves us so much that He made it possible for us to have a wonderful taste of The Kingdom of God while living for Him while we are still in this life. That is just one of the many Attitudes and Mindsets of God. There are many Scriptures that indicate we "sample" The Kingdom of God while on this earth. Here are a few of the more obvious ones:

Ephesians 1:13, 14: ¹³ In Him you also *trusted*, after you heard the word of truth, the gospel of your salvation; in whom also, having believed, you were sealed with the Holy Spirit of promise, ¹⁴ who is the guarantee of our inheritance until the redemption of the purchased possession, to the praise of His glory.

Mark 1:14– Now after John was put in prison, Jesus came to Galilee, preaching the gospel of the kingdom of God.

As Jesus continued to preach the gospel of The Kingdom of God, He demonstrated The Kingdom of God with His power to heal the sick and lame, raise the dead, etc.

When Jesus sent the twelve and the seventy out, He obviously anointed them with the baptism in the Holy Spirit, because He instructed them to heal the sick, cast out demons.

In **Luke 9:1-6**, where Jesus sent out the 12, **verse 2** reads **He sent them to preach the kingdom of God and to heal the sick.**

In **Luke 10:1-12**, where Jesus sent out the 70, **verse 9** reads **Luke 10:9— And heal the sick there, and say to them, 'The kingdom of God has come near to you.'**

Dr. Luke records in **Luke 24:9** and **Acts 1:8**, Jesus telling His disciples, shortly before His ascension back to His throne in heaven, that they will receive <u>power</u> when they are filled with the Holy Spirit.

Luke 24:9—"Behold, I send the Promise of My Father upon you; but tarry in the city of Jerusalem until you are endued with power from on high."

Acts 1:8—"But you shall receive power when the Holy Spirit has come upon you; and you shall be witnesses to Me in Jerusalem, and in all Judea and Samaria, and to the end of the earth."

Those Scriptures I have quoted so far make it clear that John the Baptist and Jesus were indicating that The Kingdom of God was being introduced to people on earth and was going to be available to everyone who chose it. They never indicated you had to die to receive it. Jesus made it clear from the beginning that The Kingdom of God was the main thing He came to introduce, and it was soon to be available.

Early on in His ministry, Jesus laid out the "code of conduct" or His description of the old Jewish law in the Sermon on the Mount. (**Matthew 5-7.**) that His followers would need to adhere to, to have The Kingdom of God in each life, as well as in the community of believers. He introduced it to the Jews first, because they were God's chosen people, but He made it clear that it would not be limited to the Jews. **John chapters 13-17**, explain how The Kingdom of God becomes a reality. The baptism of the Holy Spirit and The Kingdom of God is identified with power and holiness, involving the fruit of the Spirit and the gifts of the Spirit. This was what His ministry was all about. He was preparing us to learn to live according to His standard to create The Kingdom of God, a type of paradise, with God's Holy Spirit within each of us, enabling God's power, glory, and virtue to flow through God's people. The main characteristic that made The Kingdom of God different from the way that people had been functioning, was that they would experience the indwelling Holy

Spirit of God so deeply and powerfully that they would desire to live to please God and their fellow man rather than living to please themselves.

We will talk more about Satan's influence in the lives of people in a later chapter, but for now, I will simply say that the Bible and church history clearly show how Satanic forces always jump in to try to thwart the advancement of the Kingdom of God. If we are ignorant of that fact, we are prone to ignore the advances, not actively fight them, and become victims of them. That is the only explanation I can offer for why all Christians are not living in The Kingdom of God today. **John Chapters 13-17** has opened my eyes to The Kingdom of God as much as any Scripture. I believe that this is the only place in the Bible where living with the Holy Spirit within you is explained in much detail. When the Holy Spirit fell on the 120 praying believers in the upper room (Acts 2), and Peter stood up with the others and explained to the multitude that had gathered the meaning of what had just happened, the door swung open to all who chose to enter The Kingdom of God. The rest of the book of Acts shows how it began.

Matthew 16:13-20— When Jesus came into the region of Caesarea Philippi, He asked His disciples, saying, "Who do men say that I, the Son of Man, am?" [14] So they said, "Some *say* John the Baptist, some Elijah, and others Jeremiah or one of the prophets." [15] He said to them, "But who do you say that I am?" [16] Simon Peter answered and said, "You are the Christ, the Son of the living God."

[17] Jesus answered and said to him, "Blessed are you, Simon Bar-Jonah, for flesh and blood has not revealed *this* to you, but My Father who is in heaven. [18] And I also say to you that you are Peter, and on this rock I will build My church, and the gates of Hades shall not prevail against it. [19] And I will give you the keys of the kingdom of heaven, and whatever you bind on earth will be bound in heaven, and whatever you loose on earth will be loosed in heaven." [20] Then He commanded His disciples that they should tell no one that He was Jesus the Christ.

Nowhere in the Bible do I see anything to indicate that the Apostle Peter was ever considered the official head of the church. I see him as one of the 12, an elder in the church in Jerusalem, and an evangelist who was very instrumental in establishing the church in Jerusalem, and possibly Caesarea. *Eusebius Ecclesiastical History* indicates that he evangelized several other areas. Both the book of Acts and *Eusebius Ecclesiastical History* indicate that James, the half-brother of Jesus, became the leader of the church in Jerusalem. What I do see, is that the Apostle Peter did in fact fulfill the prophecy Jesus made about him in the above Scripture, primarily by his actions in **Acts 2-4.**

When the Apostle Paul visited the churches on his missionary trips, he also demonstrated The Kingdom of God as Jesus did. We have too few pastors and evangelists today, following the examples of Jesus, Peter, Paul, and the other disciples. Check out what Paul told the Corinthian Church in **1 Corinthians 2:1-5—**

¹And I, brethren, when I came to you, did not come with excellence of speech or of wisdom declaring to you the testimony of God. ² For I determined not to know anything among you except Jesus Christ and Him crucified. ³ I was with you in weakness, in fear, and in much trembling. ⁴ And my speech and my preaching *were* not with persuasive words of human wisdom, but in demonstration of the Spirit and of power, ⁵ that your faith should not be in the wisdom of men but in the power of God.

A study of the books of **1 Corinthians and Ephesians** will give you the best introduction to what living in The Kingdom of God is like as we prepare for graduation into our heavenly reward. Here are a few more excerpts from **1 Corinthians:**

2:9—But as it is written: "Eye has not seen, nor ear heard, Nor have entered into the heart of man the things which God has prepared for those who love Him."

2:12-13— ¹²Now we have received, not the spirit of the world, but the Spirit who is from God, that we might know the things that have been freely given to us by God. ¹³ These things we also speak, not in words which man's wisdom teaches but which the Holy Spirit teaches, comparing spiritual things with spiritual.

4:20— For the kingdom of God *is* not in word but in power.

Paul explained to the Ephesus Church the reality of their repenting of their sins, accepting Jesus as their Lord and Savior, being baptized in water, and being baptized in the Holy Spirit, thus entering The Kingdom of God.

Ephesians 1:13-14- ¹³**In Him you also** *trusted,* **after you heard the word of truth, the gospel of your salvation; in whom also, having believed, you were sealed with the Holy Spirit of promise,** ¹⁴**who is the guarantee of our inheritance until the redemption of the purchased possession, to the praise of His glory.**

In all but a couple of instances, Matthew refers to The Kingdom of Heaven, instead of The Kingdom of God. Being that many of his references are obviously of the same event as reported in Mark and Luke, where they refer to The Kingdom of God, I personally assume the two terms mean the same thing.

Here are some more references which I believe tell us that we can live in a degree of The Kingdom of God here and now.

In **Luke 10:1-12**, where Jesus sent out the 70, verse 9 reads **Luke 10:9— And heal the sick there, and say to them, 'The kingdom of God has come near to you.'**

Luke 18:16-17— But Jesus called them to *Him* **and said, "Let the little children come to Me, and do not forbid them; for of such is the kingdom of God.** ¹⁷ **Assuredly, I say to you, whoever does not receive the kingdom of God as a little child will by no means enter it."**

John 3:5—Jesus answered, "Most assuredly, I say to you, unless one is born of water and the Spirit, he cannot enter the kingdom of God. (Speaking to Nicodemus)

Mark 1:14-15— Now after John was put in prison, Jesus came to Galilee, preaching the gospel of the kingdom of God, [15] and saying, "The time is fulfilled, and the kingdom of God is at hand. Repent, and believe in the gospel."

We can find more references to The Kingdom of Heaven and The Kingdom of God in the book of Matthew than anywhere, and he records many quotations of Jesus giving examples of different things to compare to The Kingdom. Here are a few. **Matthew 13:44-45**—

[44] "Again, the kingdom of heaven is like treasure hidden in a field, which a man found and hid; and for joy over it he goes and sells all that he has and buys that field. [45] "Again, the kingdom of heaven is like a merchant seeking beautiful pearls, [46] who, when he had found one pearl of great price, went and sold all that he had and bought it.

Mark and Luke also record several descriptions Jesus gave to describe The Kingdom of God. I have not listed all of them here, but I hope it is enough to help you get a reasonably clear picture of The Kingdom of God.

Mark 4:30-32—[30] Then He said, "To what shall we liken the kingdom of God? Or with what parable shall we picture it? [31] *It is* like a mustard seed which, when it is sown on the ground, is smaller than all the seeds on earth; [32] but when it is sown, it grows up and becomes greater than all herbs, and shoots out large branches, so that the birds of the air may nest under its shade."

Luke 17:20-21:— [20]Now when He was asked by the Pharisees when the kingdom of God would come, He answered them and said, "The kingdom of God does not come with observation; [21] nor will they say,

'See here!' or 'See there!' For indeed, the kingdom of God is within you."

Mark 9:1— And He said to them, "Assuredly, I say to you that there are some standing here who will not taste death till they see the kingdom of God present with power."

It is hard to fathom that a great number of Christians today have no concept of living in The Kingdom of God while still in this life phase. Most of the teaching seems to talk about being good today so you can go to heaven, and be in The Kingdom of God when this life phase is over. So much of what Jesus did for you and suffered for you, He did so that you would have a better life while still in this earthly life phase. Please, do not dishonor and disrespect Him by ignoring much of His great sacrifice. To miss that is to ignore most of the New Testament. How miserable my life would have been if I had not discovered this 53 years ago, as a result of my personal Bible study following an encounter with God's Holy Spirit; not solely from listening to the preaching and teaching of the church. If nothing else results from producing this book, if it motivates you to start seriously studying the Bible for yourself, all the efforts that have gone into producing it will be very well worthwhile. My ministry has always been motivated by a hunger to open the eyes of the believers to the blessings that Jesus paid so dearly for you to have NOW, in addition to what is waiting for you in heaven. Thank God, there are a few churches around that do a good job of preaching and teaching what I call The Full Gospel, and that includes the one I am currently a member of. From what I have observed and experienced, they are a definite minority. For the sake of the time you have left in this phase of life, if you are part of a dead church, that offers you little help for living your current life, but only assurance of heaven when you die, flee for your life—you owe them nothing. Go find one that will enhance your understanding of The Kingdom of God.

After Jesus was resurrected and before He ascended to the Father, He reassured His disciples of what He had explained to them before He was arrested. He emphasized that they would receive the power they would need to do what He commissioned them to do.

Luke 24:49— Behold, I send the Promise of My Father upon you; but tarry in the city of Jerusalem until you are endued with power from on high."

Acts 1:8—But you shall receive power when the Holy Spirit has come upon you; and you shall be witnesses to Me in Jerusalem, and in all Judea and Samaria, and to the end of the earth."

Notice Jesus' references to "power" in the above Scriptures. I trust that you will read over the above different descriptions that Jesus gave of The Kingdom of God, until you feel satisfied in your spirit, with confirmation from the Holy Spirit, that you have a clear understanding.

I realize that when we start talking about baptism in the Holy Spirit, we can offend people and turn them off easily. I am very anxious not to do that. But, at the same time, I must be careful not to misinterpret the Bible. I remind you of what I related earlier, that I spent the first thirty-seven years of my life in the Presbyterian church, then many years jumping from church to church (Presbyterian, Southern Baptist, Independent Baptist, Bible Baptist, Pentecostal, Free Will Baptist, Methodist, Christian Missionary Alliance, Christian, Church of God, Assembly of God, Apostolic, Charismatic, Independent, etc.), all done to try to find a church that doctrinally reflected what I was reading in the Bible. Believe me, when I say that I have seen it all, I have seen it all. I tell you this to let you know that I can understand where you are coming from. So, I will endeavor not to offend you or misinterpret the Bible.

After 65 years of Bible study, plus some study of church history, I have concluded that most denominational doctrines were established by church leaders years ago who started these various denominations when they stumbled over certain Scriptures, failed to succeed in making them work in their lives or come to an accurate understanding of them, and took Scripture verses out of context and twisted them to justify their own belief. It is bad enough to pervert the Scripture for one's own benefit, but it becomes a major crime when some of it ends up misguiding <u>billions</u> of followers to the point that they are denied the benefit of being filled with the Holy Spirit and experiencing The Kingdom of God while walking the earth. Ever since I was baptized in the Holy Spirit, my heart has ached for those billions of fine Christians, many of whom are dear friends and relatives, who have become convinced that Baptism in the Holy Spirit and the power available through that, is not available to them today, all because of the false (doctrine of man) doctrine that they have been fed. One of the greatest outcomes of the recent Charismatic Renewal was that probably millions of denominational Christians overcame the false doctrine they had spent many years under and were baptized in the Holy Spirit. In fact, I was one of that number. That is one of the reasons we had a profusion of non-denominational churches spring up during that time. Many participants in the Charismatic Renewal came to realize how incomplete their understanding of the Bible had been, and how much their church had failed them. Many of those individuals left the dead churches they had been a member of and got together and started their own non-denominal or independent church. That all helps to explain why for many years in this country and around the world, major denominations lose membership annually, whereby Pentecostal, and non-denominational churches collectively have been gaining membership.

It seems that people can get hung up on references to the Baptism in the Holy Spirit. Depending on which version of the Bible you use, we frequently see the terms. "Baptism in or by the Holy Spirit", "Filled with the Holy Spirit" or "Received the Holy Spirit". The King James (1611) Version, and perhaps a few others, use the term "Holy Ghost" instead of "Holy Spirit". My studies indicate to me that basically, they all refer to the same experience when referenced in the Bible. Many Christians can point to the time they were filled with the Holy Spirit, just as they can point to the time that they repented of their sinful nature and received Jesus as their Lord and Savior. Can you reference the time you were filled with the Holy Spirit?

I realize that many denominations believe that the power and gifts of the Holy Spirit ended with the death of the last of the twelve Apostles. I assert that the Bible does not support this theory, but in fact refutes it:

Romans 11:29 For the gifts and the calling of God *are* irrevocable.

The justification I have heard for such a theory is based on taking a verse or two out of context and then twisting it to support a predetermined theory. That is not a suitable method of Bible interpretation. A study of Bible history reveals that ever since that original major outpouring of the Holy Spirit recorded in Acts chapter 2, there has always been a remnant of believers who were experiencing the power and gifts of the Holy Spirit, while at the same time there were elements yielding to demonic forces and trying to change the doctrine. We certainly see believers and ministries today all over the world who are experiencing the power and gifts of the Holy Spirit. I personally have experienced them hundreds of times, and I know many other Christians who have experienced the power and gifts of the Holy Spirit often. I cannot picture a loving heavenly Father who would give His children gifts for a short period of time and then take them away. So, consider how much of the New Testament talks about or is written in the context of people filled with the Holy Spirit. Why would that portion even be recorded if it had no application to the readers following the death of the writer? I would encourage you to stick with this study and see what the Bible teaches on the subject. A great deal of denominational theology is the doctrine of man, and the doctrine of demons in my opinion, and often is not really supported by the Bible. You owe your denomination nothing except what you obligate yourself to, but you owe God everything. You have the responsibility to believe the correct source of information rather than say "that just doesn't work for me today", or "that is not what my church believes". You are the one who is ultimately totally responsible for your salvation, not the church, so take that responsibility seriously. I suggest that you study the Bible and find out why it doesn't work for you as well as you want it to if that is what you have experienced. Hopefully, we will be able to shine some light on the subject for you in this study.

I believe that The Kingdom of God (involving Power) is alive and available to all believers today, through their being filled with the Holy Spirit. We will look at Scripture as we go through this study that forms the basis for my belief.

As I read Scripture, it becomes obvious to me that Jesus imparted the Holy Spirit and The Kingdom of God to His apostles and disciples when He sent them out ahead of Him to prepare the way for Him. Otherwise, how would they get the power they obviously utilized?

Luke 9: 1-6 ¹Then He called His twelve disciples together and gave them power and authority over all demons, and to cure diseases. ² He sent them to preach the kingdom of God and to heal the sick. ³ And He said to them, "Take nothing for the journey, neither staffs nor bag nor bread nor money; and do not have two tunics apiece. ⁴ Whatever house you enter, stay there, and from there depart. ⁵ And whoever will not receive you, when you go out of that city, shake off the very dust from your feet as a testimony against them." ⁶ So they departed and went through the towns, preaching the gospel and healing everywhere.

Why do we see little evidence of the power of the Holy Spirit in the Apostles' lives from then until after Pentecost? That question has puzzled me for years. Because **Romans 11:29** reads:

For the gifts and the calling of God are irrevocable.

As I pondered and researched this, I found the answer that at least satisfied me. It was right after the return of the twelve and the seventy that Jesus fed the 5,000 and the 4000, and evidently the 12 apostles and probably the 70 participated in those miracles. As you follow the Scriptures from the time Jesus sent the twelve out to evangelize and fed the thousands, until the time of Pentecost, Jesus chided the Apostles repeatedly for their lack of faith.

Matthew 14:25-31— ²⁵ Now in the fourth watch of the night Jesus went to them, walking on the sea. ²⁶ And when the disciples saw Him walking on the sea, they were troubled, saying, "It is a ghost!" And they cried out for fear. ²⁷ But immediately Jesus spoke to them, saying, "Be of good cheer! It is I; do not be afraid." ²⁸ And Peter answered Him and said, "Lord, if it is You, command me to come to You on the water." ²⁹ So He said, "Come." And when Peter had come down out of the boat, he walked on the water to go to Jesus. ³⁰ But when he saw that the wind *was* boisterous, he was afraid; and beginning to sink he cried out, saying, "Lord, save me!" ³¹ And immediately Jesus stretched out *His* hand and caught him, and said to him, "O you of little faith, why did you doubt?"

Matthew 16:5-12— ⁵Now when His disciples had come to the other side, they had forgotten to take bread. ⁶ Then Jesus said to them, "Take heed and beware of the leaven of the Pharisees and the Sadducees." ⁷ And they reasoned among themselves, saying, *"It is* because we have taken no bread." ⁸ But Jesus, being aware of *it,* said to them, "O you of little faith, why do you reason among yourselves because you have brought no bread? ⁹ Do you not yet understand, or remember the five loaves of the five thousand and how many baskets you took up? ¹⁰ Nor the seven loaves of the four thousand and how many large baskets you took up? ¹¹ How is it you do not understand that I did not speak to you concerning bread?—*but* to beware of the leaven of the Pharisees and Sadducees." ¹² Then they understood that He did not tell *them* to beware of the leaven of bread, but of the doctrine of the Pharisees and Sadducees.

Matthew 17:14-20— ¹⁴ And when they had come to the multitude, a man came to Him, kneeling down to Him and saying, ¹⁵ "Lord, have mercy on my son, for he is [a]an epileptic and suffers severely; for he often falls into the fire and often into the water. ¹⁶ So I brought him to Your disciples, but they could not cure him." ¹⁷ Then Jesus answered and said, "O faithless and perverse generation, how long shall I be with you? How long shall I bear with you? Bring him here to Me." ¹⁸ And Jesus rebuked the demon, and it came out of him; and the child was cured from that very hour. ¹⁹ Then the disciples came to Jesus privately and said, "Why could we not cast it out?" ²⁰ So Jesus said to them, "Because of your unbelief; for assuredly, I say to you, if you have faith as a mustard seed, you will say to this mountain, 'Move from here to there,' and it will move; and nothing will be impossible for you.

It appears to me that Jesus expected His 12 Apostles to exercise far more faith and power than they did because He had endowed them with the power of the indwelling Holy Spirit when He sent them out on their initial mission trip. However, the Apostles were content to be completely dependent on Jesus for the miracles. It also convinces me, when considering my own experience, that the adage, "use it or lose it" strongly applies here. Also, I have observed that once we receive the Holy Spirit, we often "leak" down and become less victorious if we don't continue to operate in the power of the Holy Spirit and seriously make it a prerogative to maintain our intimate relationship with God.

The Scripture reveals that at least some of these twelve men received the Holy Spirit possibly four different times. The first we just read about in **Luke 9:1-6**.

The second time is recorded in **John 20:21-22-** ²¹ **So Jesus said to them again, "Peace to you! As the Father has sent Me, I also send you."** ²² **And when He had said this, He breathed on *them*, and said to them, "Receive the Holy Spirit.-**

The third time was on the day of Pentecost.

Acts 2:1-4 ¹**When the Day of Pentecost had fully come, they were all with one accord in one place.** ² **And suddenly there came a sound from heaven, as of a rushing mighty wind, and it filled the whole house where they were sitting.** ³ **Then there appeared to them divided tongues, as of fire, and one sat upon each of them.** ⁴ **And they were all**

filled with the Holy Spirit and began to speak with other tongues, as the Spirit gave them utterance.

The fourth time came a day or two later.

Acts 4:29-31 ²⁹ Now, Lord, look on their threats, and grant to Your servants that with all boldness they may speak Your word, ³⁰ by stretching out Your hand to heal, and that signs and wonders may be done through the name of Your Holy Servant Jesus. ³¹ And when they had prayed, the place where they were assembled together was shaken; and they were all filled with the Holy Spirit, and they spoke the word of God with boldness.

So, if the twelve apostles, even while walking with Jesus, could become needful of being filled with the Holy Spirit repeatedly, why should we be surprised that we do? Some people suggest we leak down like an old rusty bucket. Others repeat the adage "use it or lose it", like a muscle that doesn't get enough exercise. Speaking from experience, I would suggest the latter.

The Bible indicates to me that we receive The Kingdom of God within ourselves when we receive the Holy Spirit.

Luke 17:20-21 ²⁰Now when He was asked by the Pharisees when the kingdom of God would come, He answered them and said, "The kingdom of God does not come with observations 21 nor will they say, 'See here!' or 'See there!' For indeed, the kingdom of God is within you."

So, the question becomes, "Why do we see so little evidence of The Kingdom of God evident in so many Christians and churches today?" Why? Well, I have an opinion about that, and I would like to share it with you. First, I will say that there is no doubt in my mind that The Kingdom of God is present in the world today because I have seen and continue to see so much evidence of it. I have personally experienced it and have many friends who have. There are many scattered ministries around the world today, some big and some small, in which they regularly see prayers answered miraculously, and other evidence of The Kingdom of God when they pray. I believe that Jesus did everything that needs to be done nearly 2000 years ago to enable us to participate in The Kingdom of God now, while on earth. I do not believe that we should be waiting for God to send a "special anointing" or let "His Spirit fall". I think we should be seriously studying His Word, particularly the New Testament, and living out our lives in an intimate relationship with Him, freely walking in what He provided for us. I believe the ball is in our court now, so it is up to us to seek and find what has been purchased for us at such a heavy price by Jesus. If we want God to send a special anointing, we have the responsibility and privilege of creating the "womb" for the birthing of that anointing.

It appears to me that the original Christians and the original church fully expected all new converts to be filled with the Holy Spirit (often speaking in tongues) soon after being converted and baptized in water, then start living in The Kingdom of God.

Acts 8:4-8 ⁴Therefore those who were scattered went everywhere preaching the word. ⁵ Then Philip went down to the city of Samaria and preached Christ to them. ⁶ And the multitudes with one accord heeded the things spoken by Philip, hearing and seeing the miracles which he did. ⁷ For unclean spirits, crying with a loud voice, came out of many who were possessed; and many who were paralyzed and lame were healed. ⁸ And there was great joy in that city.

Acts 8:14-17 ¹⁴ Now when the apostles who were at Jerusalem heard that Samaria had received the word of God, they sent Peter and John to them, ¹⁵ who, when they had come down, prayed for them that they might receive the Holy Spirit. ¹⁶ For as yet He had fallen upon none of them. They had only been baptized in the name of the Lord Jesus. ¹⁷ Then they laid hands on them, and they received the Holy Spirit.

Acts 10:44-48 **⁴⁴While Peter was still speaking these words, the Holy Spirit fell upon all those who heard the word. ⁴⁵ And those of the circumcision who believed were astonished, as many as came with Peter, because the gift of the Holy Spirit had been poured out on the Gentiles also. ⁴⁶ For they heard them speak with tongues and magnify God. Then Peter answered, ⁴⁷ Can anyone forbid water, that these should not be baptized who have received the Holy Spirit just as we *have?"* ⁴⁸ And he commanded them to be baptized in the name of the Lord. Then they asked him to stay a few days.**

When I was filled with the Holy Spirit in 1967, I almost immediately started experiencing what it is like to live in The Kingdom of God. Prior to that time, I had been studying the Bible for two hours every morning for at least twelve years. I was very frustrated by seeing what the Bible said should be happening in my life, was not actually happening. I was also troubled by the fact that no one else I had contact with, including my pastor, really believed that the power and victory the Bible described were relevant to our life on earth today. But, when I found a small group of believers meeting in a home for prayer and Bible study who believed the Bible to be true, observably had The Kingdom of God functioning within them, and were experiencing the victory, power, and miracles the Bible said they should be experiencing, I figured I had found somebody with the answers I had been searching for all those many years. I asked God in Jesus' name to fill me with His Holy Spirit because I saw for the first time why I had not been living in The Kingdom of God like the Bible indicated that I, as a believer, could be living. For the first time in my life, I saw that the Scriptures made it clear that Jesus intended for all His followers to receive His Holy Spirit so that we could experience The Kingdom of God, and the love, grace, victory, and power He promised us in His Word.

The New Testament speaks of holiness (or obedience) quite often. In John chapters 13-17 (which we will cover in chapter 24), Jesus connected obedience with the infilling of the Holy Spirit often. As you study the

New Testament, you will see that Jesus taught holiness. Remember The Beatitudes in **Matthew 5.**

Paul also spoke of holiness often as in **Romans 12:1-2— I beseech you therefore, brethren, by the mercies of God, that you present your bodies a living sacrifice, holy, acceptable to God, *which is* your reasonable service. ² And do not be conformed to this world, but be transformed by the renewing of your mind, that you may prove what *is* that good and acceptable and perfect will.**

Holiness is further spelled out in **Galatians 5:22-26—² But the fruit of the Spirit is love, joy, peace, longsuffering, kindness, goodness, faithfulness, ²³ gentleness, self-control. Against such there is no law. ²⁴ And those *who are* Christ's have crucified the flesh with its passions and desires. ²⁵ If we live in the Spirit, let us also walk in the Spirit. ²⁶ Let us not become conceited, provoking one another, envying one another.**

Most Christians are familiar with the Great Commission as recorded in **Matthew 28:16-20**, although they seldom hear it in total. Jesus also gave another great commission, about the same time, in **Mark 16:14-20—¹⁴ Later He appeared to the eleven as they sat at the table; and He rebuked their unbelief and hardness of heart, because they did not believe those who had seen Him after He had risen. ¹⁵ And He said to them, "Go into all the world and preach the gospel to every creature. ¹⁶ He who believes and is baptized will be saved; but he who does not believe will be condemned. ¹⁷ And these signs will follow those who believe: In My name they will cast out demons; they will speak with new tongues; ¹⁸ they will take up serpents; and if they drink anything deadly, it will by no means hurt them; they will lay hands on the sick, and they will recover." ¹⁹So then, after the Lord had spoken to them, He was received up into heaven, and sat down at the right hand of God. ²⁰ And they went out and preached everywhere, the Lord working with them and confirming the word through the accompanying signs. Amen**

Jesus very obviously commissioned His disciples to do the works He had been doing. History tells us that the disciples of Jesus carried out that commission and spread the gospel of The Kingdom of God throughout the Middle East and Europe in 300 years.

Matthew 11:12 is a verse to ponder and meditate on. **And from the days of John the Baptist until now the kingdom of heaven suffers violence, and the violent take it by force.** You need to read all of chapter 11 to start to understand what Jesus was talking about here. We won't print the whole chapter but just a few more verses—We do suggest you read the whole chapter, however. Take a close look at verses 20-24—

Matthew 11:20-24— ²⁰Then He began to rebuke the cities in which most of His mighty works had been done, because they did not repent: ²¹ "Woe to you, Chorazin! Woe to you, Bethsaida! For if the mighty works which were done in you had been done in Tyre and Sidon, they would have repented long ago in sackcloth and ashes.²² But I say to you, it will be more tolerable for Tyre and Sidon in the day of judgment than for you. ²³ And you, Capernaum, who are exalted to heaven, will be brought down to Hades; for if the mighty works which were done in you had been done in Sodom, it would have remained until this day. ²⁴ But I say to you that it shall be more tolerable for the land of Sodom in the day of judgment than for you."

It appears to me that Jesus is pointing out the great warfare that has already taken place up to this point, from the times of John the Baptist when The Kingdom of God was first mentioned. The Kingdom of God was introduced in all these cities by the many mighty works that Jesus did, but very few people in those cities believed Him to be the Son of God or believed that The Kingdom of God had been introduced on the earth. Remember the blind man from Bethsaida, whom Jesus led all the way out of the city, (possibly to get away from the atmosphere of unbelief,) to pray for him, then told him not to return to the city. **Mark 8:22-26**.

I personally believe the "take it by force" statement in **Matthew 11:12** refers to both the Christian who is trying to enter The Kingdom of God and the satanic forces that are trying to prevent it from happening. It appears to me that **Matthew 11:12** is one of those many Scriptures that the Apostle John talks about at the close of his Gospel:

John: 21:24-25— [24]This is the disciple who testifies of these things, and wrote these things; and we know that his testimony is true. [25] And there are also many other things that Jesus did, which if they were written one by one, I suppose that even the world itself could not contain the books that would be written. Amen.

When do we enter The Kingdom of God? According to how I understand the New Testament, particularly the Scriptures I quoted in this chapter, I believe that when we are filled with the Holy Spirit, we've opened the door to The Kingdom of God. Our relationship with Holy Spirit enables us to experience God's power for miracles, signs, and wonders, and so much more. We also understand that The Kingdom of God we experience won't be to the full degree until we graduate from this life. But there is even more.

John 17:20-23— [20]"I do not pray for these alone, but also for those who will believe in Me through their word; [21] that they all may be one, as You, Father, *are* in Me, and I in You; that they also may be one in Us, that the world may believe that You sent Me. [22] And the glory which You gave Me I have given them, that they may be one just as We are one: [23] I in them, and You in Me; that they may be made perfect in one, and that the world may know that You have sent Me, and have loved them as You have loved Me.

We will spend chapter 24 discussing this powerful Scripture, but for now, focus on verse 22. That tells me that God's **glory** is also available to us so that it is possible for Christians to agree in one body and be as intimate with God the Father and Jesus His Son, as the two of them were when Jesus walked the earth! WOW! So, we also gain access to Jesus' glory when we are filled with His Holy Spirit. My experience has been that we have access to Jesus' power and glory, but we only have them when we recognize them and take advantage of them. It seems to me that we are experiencing The Kingdom of God when we have been filled with/baptized in His Holy Spirit, exercising His power and glory, walking in constant fellowship with God and Jesus, through His Holy Spirit.

If you have not been studying the Bible, I would like to suggest to you a "fast track" schedule of Bible study to help you achieve a better understanding of the Bible. These are scriptures that I have found very helpful in my walk. Feel free to alter the list any time along the way and ask the Holy Spirit to direct you. Start with **Isaiah chapters 7-14 and 25-66**, which are loaded with prophecies about the coming Messiah, Jesus. Then go to **Matthew**, particularly **chapters 3-12**. Then **Mark**, particularly **chapters 11-16**. After that go directly to **John**, particularly **chapters 3 and 10-17. Then all of Acts and the first 8 chapters of Romans.** After that pickup **1 Corinthians** and **Ephesians**. From that point simply ask the Holy Spirit for guidance. All the Bible is important and none of it should be rejected but studying it according to your needs and interest is much more fulfilling than simply starting at the beginning and reading through.

Eusebius' Ecclesiastic History makes it clear that as holiness declined in the church, so did the miracles. I believe that sends a very powerful message. We continue that discussion in the following chapters.

CHAPTER 13

God's Provision For The Healing Of Our Bodies

Many in the body of Christ completely missed something important that took place in the latter chapters of all four gospels. That important "something" is that Jesus atoned for our pain and sickness as well as the forgiveness of our sins that day He hung on that cross and died. I discovered this one day many years ago, when I was studying the book of Isaiah in the Old Testament.

Isaiah 53:1-5—
Who has believed our report?
And to whom has the arm of the LORD been revealed?
² For He shall grow up before Him as a tender plant,
And as a root out of dry ground.
He has no form or comeliness;
And when we see Him,
There is **no beauty that we should desire Him.**
³ He is despised and rejected by men,
A Man of sorrows and acquainted with grief.
And we hid, as it were, ***our*** **faces from Him;**
He was despised, and we did not esteem Him.

**⁴ Surely He has borne our griefs
And carried our sorrows;
Yet we esteemed Him stricken,
Smitten by God, and afflicted.
⁵ But He *was* wounded for our transgressions,
He was bruised for our iniquities;
The chastisement for our peace *was* upon Him,
And by His stripes we are healed.**

As I studied this and read the notes in my study Bible, I found that this Scripture was specifically confirmed twice in the New Testament:

Matthew 8:16-17—¹⁶ When evening had come, they brought to Him many who were demon-possessed. And He cast out the spirits with a word, and healed all who were sick, ¹⁷ that it might be fulfilled which was spoken by Isaiah the prophet, saying: "He Himself took our infirmities And bore *our* sicknesses."

Also in 1 Peter 2:24—who Himself bore our sins in His own body on the tree, that we, having died to sins, might live for righteousness— by whose stripes you were healed.

As I meditated on those verses, I received the revelation that yes, Jesus did atone for our pain and suffering as He suffered during His trial and execution. But I didn't really get a full picture of how much He suffered until further research led me to a couple of verses in the preceding chapter of Isaiah 53.

Isaiah 52:13-14—Behold, My Servant shall deal prudently; He shall be exalted and extolled and be very high. Just as many were astonished at you, So His visage was marred more than any man, And His form more than the sons of men.

I remembered something I had read in Isaiah 50 and looked it up. **Isaiah 50:4-7**

> [4]"The Lord G<small>OD</small> has given Me
> The tongue of the learned,
> That I should know how to speak
> A word in season to *him who is* weary.
> He awakens Me morning by morning,
> He awakens My ear
> To hear as the learned.
> [5] The Lord G<small>OD</small> has opened My ear;
> And I was not rebellious,
> Nor did I turn away.
> [6] I gave My back to those who struck *Me,*
> And My cheeks to those who plucked out the beard;
> I did not hide My face from shame and spitting.
> [7] "For the Lord G<small>OD</small> will help Me;
> Therefore I will not be disgraced;
> Therefore I have set My face like a flint,
> And I know that I will not be ashamed.

Having worn a full beard for many years and had a few babies grab a handful and pull, I cringed at that one reference to pulling the beard, and that was just a minor part of the torture He endured that day.

As I meditated on the above Scriptures together, before I fully grasped the reality of it, and was literally talking to God about it, a beautiful new understanding and appreciation of Jesus' extreme sacrifice to atone for our pain and sickness enveloped me. I even questioned God as to how He could bear to watch His only begotten Son be tortured beyond recognition, more than any other man had ever been before, and lived when it had nothing to do with the forgiveness of sin. I considered the 39 lashes rule that the Roman army had established because they did not want to kill a man with 40 lashes before they had a chance to nail him on the cross to hang in agony. I probably spent an hour or two in meditation and talking to God about these Scriptures. Then I considered the fact that nowhere in the Old Testament is there any mention of any sacrificial lamb ever being tortured before it was sacrificed. It was never done. I am told that the sacrificial lamb was selected ahead of time and placed in a special place to receive special care in preparation of being sacrificed. Those factors also indicated that Jesus' horrendous suffering had nothing to do with forgiveness of sin, but everything to do with atoning for our pain and suffering. As I questioned Father God about how He could bear to watch His only begotten Son suffer such horrendous torture when it was not needed to atone for sin. He let me know that I had concluded correctly and told me Jesus' torture had everything to do with atonement for our pain and sickness. We accept healing for our bodies the same way we accept forgiveness for our sins—we accept it by faith in what Jesus did for us on the cross.

To confirm everything God taught me during that blessed time together, He took me to **Matthew *26:26-28*— [26]And as they were eating, Jesus took bread, blessed and broke it, and gave it to the disciples and said, "Take, eat; this is My body."[27] Then He took the cup, and gave thanks, and gave it to them, saying, "Drink from it, all of you. [28] For this is My blood of the new covenant, which is shed for many for the remission of sins.**

Dr. Luke records it similarly. **Luke 22.19-20— [19]And He took bread, gave thanks and broke it, and gave it to them, saying, "This is My body which is given for you; do this in remembrance of Me."[20] Likewise He also took the cup after supper, saying, "This cup is the new covenant in My blood, which *is shed for you.***

God pointed out to me that when He instituted the Lord's supper, He specifically used two elements—Bread, which represented His body which was given to pay the price for all of the pain that we could ever have, and the wine or grape juice, to represent His blood "the life is in the Blood", which was given to pay for our sins. Just as the torture on the cross did not have anything to do with the forgiveness of our sins, the bread did not have anything to do with the forgiveness of our sins. I realize that very few pastors and teachers teach this (I have found a few who do), but I am convinced it is the truth because God told me so and the Bible backs Him up.

Sadly, nearly all the teaching I had heard on the above-quoted Scriptures, had ascribed them to simply "emotional" or "spiritual healing". That is contradictory to what a study of the original Hebrew words of that Scripture reveals. The original Hebrew language that the Scripture was originally written in clearly indicates physical healing. **Isaiah 61:1-3** and the reference to it in **Luke 3:18-19** does clearly bring out Jesus' ministry to the spiritually and emotionally wounded.

¹⁸"The Spirit of the LORD *is* upon Me, Because He has anointed Me To preach the gospel to *the* poor; He has sent Me to heal the brokenhearted, To proclaim liberty to *the* captives And recovery of sight to *the* blind, *To* set at liberty those who are oppressed; ¹⁹ To proclaim the acceptable year of the LORD."

I would suggest you read **Isaiah 52: through 53:12** to gain a clearer understanding of what the prophet Isaiah had to say about Jesus' life and suffering.

It seems it is harder for us to accept Jesus's atonement for our healing than it is to accept atonement for the forgiveness of our sins. There are several reasons for this, but the major difference is that atonement for salvation is taught far more than atonement for our pain and suffering. We can believe that God heard our petition to forgive and save our soul because we do not need a physical manifestation that God has heard and answered our prayer. It isn't that easy to believe God has healed you if you are still in pain. The New Testament lays out many instructions on how to have faith for healing. A very important instruction can be found in

Mark 11:22-25—²² So Jesus answered and said to them, "Have faith in God. ²³ For assuredly, I say to you, whoever says to this mountain, 'Be removed and be cast into the sea,' and does not doubt in his

heart, but believes that those things he says will be done, he will have whatever he says. ²⁴ Therefore I say to you, whatever things you ask when you pray, believe that you receive *them,* and you will have *them.* ²⁵ "And whenever you stand praying, if you have anything against anyone, forgive him, that your Father in heaven may also forgive you your trespasses."

I have heard some teachers paraphrase verse 24: "You must believe you have what you pray for in order to receive it."

I will remind you of an incident I told you about earlier in this book. One Friday afternoon about 15 years ago, I accidentally had the four knuckles on my right hand crushed and had a 20-penny nail go through my wrist. My hand was very painful, swollen, and discolored. I chose to pray for God to heal it and trust Him for complete healing. When I returned home and was eating dinner, the pain got so bad I was starting to get nauseated. I rose from the table and sat down in my recliner, to pray. I started my prayer, "Lord, I know You know how much my hand hurts," and He immediately replied, "Yes, son, I do know exactly how much your hand hurts right now, but what I want you to understand is, that when I hung on that cross atoning for your healing, every joint in my body, including between every vertebra of my back, hurt just as much as your hand is hurting right now". Wow, what a revelation. I count that as one of the highlights of my life. Our conversation continued for a few minutes, the pain eased up, and I finished dinner. By Wednesday my hand and wrist were completely healed with no visible evidence or physical evidence I had ever suffered the injury. I have never had any repercussions from the injury. The important point is that I continued to believe God had healed my hand, even though my hand still hurt. There is no reason to believe that four obviously crushed knuckles will naturally heal in five days, with no repercussions 15 years later. Add to that the big puncture wound that I had no antibiotics for.

During the recent Charismatic Renewal, it seemed that miracles of healing, provision, etc., were somewhat commonplace. It is much easier to have faith for miracles when you see them happening all around you. It is also easier to have faith if you are in a community of believers. Even Jesus had trouble getting people healed in the company of doubters.

Look at **Matthew 13.54-58—**⁵⁴ **When He had come to His own country, He taught them in their synagogue, so that they were astonished and said, "Where did this** *Man* **get this wisdom and** *these* **mighty works?** ⁵⁵ **Is this not the carpenter's son? Is not His mother called Mary? And His brothers James, Joses, Simon, and Judas?** ⁵⁶ **And His sisters, are they not all with us? Where then did this** *Man* **get all these things?"** ⁵⁷ **So they were offended at Him. But Jesus said to them, "A prophet is not without honor except in his own country and in his own house."** ⁵⁸ **Now He did not do many mighty works there because of their unbelief.**

Mark 8 also records such an incident—**Mark 8.22-25**—²² **Then He came to Bethsaida; and they brought a blind man to Him, and begged Him to touch him.** ²³ **So He took the blind man by the hand and led him out of the town. And when He had spit on his eyes and put His hands on him, He asked him if he saw anything.** ²⁴ **And he looked up and said, "I see men like trees, walking."** ²⁵ **Then He put** *His* **hands on his eyes again and made him look up. And he was restored and saw everyone clearly.** ²⁶ **Then He sent him away to his house, saying, "Neither go into the town, nor tell anyone in the town."**

Jesus later commented on the unbelief He had encountered in Bethesda. **(Matthew 11:21, Luke 10:13.)** I believe that is possibly why He took the time to walk the man all the way out of town to pray for him, then warned him not to go back into the town or talk to anyone from there. We have already pointed out how an atmosphere of doubt obviously negatively affects faith. See the above scripture, **Matthew 13:58.**

There is much more that can be said about praying for healing, that we will cover in subsequent chapters. I suggest that you read this chapter over several times, talk to Holy Spirit about it and read the Scripture in your personal Bible. Do it until you really get a handle on God's provision for the healing of your body.

There is still another provision God made for the healing of our bodies when He created Adam. I stumbled across this provision a couple of years ago, while waiting in a lobby to have some bloodwork done. Being bored, I picked up a National Geographic Magazine, thumbed through it, and stumbled across a very interesting article titled *Unlocking the Healing Power of You*. The link to information on it is https://www.insidehook.com/article/health-and-fitness/healing-power-faith. What I found when I read the article blew my mind. This investigative reporter uncovered research that proves we can heal our bodies through faith. With several pages of photographs of brain scans and information from researchers, he showed how scientific researchers proved graphically how several people were healed by no other method than faith. They showed brain scans that revealed how the brain functions when faith is activated, to cause the body to heal itself. These examples did not illustrate faith in God necessarily, but faith for whatever reason. They were simply confident they would be healed. What that investigative reporter uncovered is a fact that I have not found in the Bible. The fact is that when God created the human body, He designed it so that it could heal itself. We can see this in plants and wild animals, so it is completely reasonable that He would also design the human body to heal itself. I heartily recommend that you use the link above and check this out for yourself. It absolutely blows my mind to see that scientific research can prove how God designed our body so that we can heal it simply by our faith. Several pages of brain scans in that article graphically show how the brain reacts when we speak with faith.

CHAPTER 14

Praying For A Miracle

I have found that for me a key component to receiving a miracle of healing from God, is to place my faith in God first for my healing before I consider doctors or medicine. I went many years without seeing a doctor for anything or taking any medicine, not even aspirin. That is not to say that I went that long without getting sick or even having a headache. I simply prayed immediately for God to heal me and believed He would do it, and He did. Don't expect a miracle of healing from God if your first response is to call the doctor or go to the medicine cabinet. If I don't receive a timely response, I pray differently, rebuke the evil spirit, or ask God what He wants me to know about not healing me. Sometimes He tells me He is taking care of the problem; in which case I am forced to simply trust His word and wait ever how long I must before I am healed. There have been instances where I have not been healed; we will talk about that below. The more often I am healed by trusting God, the easier it is to have the faith needed to get healed.

For many church members today, much of the New Testament reads like a fairy tale. They have trouble really believing that the principles outlined in the Bible can relate to us today. Believing that the miracles that the Bible documents really happened, or that those same miracles can happen today, is simply beyond the ability of some people to believe. If you have never really seen a miracle or known someone who has, it really is hard to believe they happened. I remember hearing a Sunday School teacher years ago before I found out I didn't have to attend a dead church, say "there really is no such thing as a miracle; things simply happen that we are unable to explain". The sad thing about that is, I was the only adult in the class who disagreed. I knew better because I had experienced hearing Holy Spirit tell me that my wife was not going to be crippled within seven years as the doctor predicted. Within three years she was completely healed of rheumatoid arthritis and had no symptoms that she had ever had that dreadful disease. That teacher and other members of that class obviously did not study the Bible for themselves and have Holy Spirit help them to understand the Scripture, and I know for a fact they never heard the message of the gospel of The Kingdom of God from the pastor or Sunday School teacher.

The promises of the Bible must be considered in the context of the whole Bible, which reflects the Attitudes and Mindsets of God. For instance, The New Testament particularly makes it very clear that we are stewards of our physical body, which is the temple of God where His Holy Spirit resides. The Apostle Paul makes that very clear in **1 Corinthians 6:19-20— Or do you not know that your body is the temple of the Holy Spirit *who is* in you, whom you have from God, and you are not your own? ²⁰ For you were bought at a price; therefore glorify God in your body and in your spirit, which are God's.**

Maybe, just maybe, we have desecrated that temple (carelessly or out of ignorance) and might have even caused the physical problem we are praying for. So, have we repented, changed direction, in our poor stewardship of that temple? It may be that our poor stewardship of that temple is what caused that physical problem. Also, we must keep in mind another pair of Scriptures that are very important to remember when considering any Scriptures.

Isaiah 55:11—So shall My word be that goes forth from My mouth; It shall not return to Me void, But it shall accomplish what I please,

And it shall prosper *in the thing* for which I sent it.

Romans 11:29—For the gifts and the calling of God *are* irrevocable.

I quickly admit that I do not receive a miraculous healing every time I pray for one. That does not cause me to doubt one word of Scripture, and it does not cause me to feel shame. I have received and prayed for many miraculous healings, and I thank God for every one of them. I realize I am not God, but I do have the Holy Spirit of God within me that gives me access to His power. What the failure causes me to do is to search the Scripture and find out how I missed God's provision and pray about it until I find the answer. God's promises generally do not come with a time schedule, so if I don't get the answer immediately it doesn't necessarily mean that it is not coming. You could say that it takes more faith to believe in the healing miracle when it doesn't happen immediately, than when it does.

God is the one who made the promises, so He has the right to fulfill them at the time He considers best. We hope He answers our prayer immediately, but if He chooses to do it later, we need to respect His wisdom and be patient. The closer we draw to Him and develop our relationship with God and His Son through His Holy Spirit, the easier it is to discuss situations with Him and get responses. I recommend you keep a journal of your prayer requests with room to record the date and method the prayer is answered. This will build your faith because it will show you that God answers more of your prayers than you give Him credit for, since sometimes by the time He answers, you have forgotten your prayer.

Recently, I realized that my lifestyle had been slowly becoming more sedentary and was beginning to slowly stiffen my body up more and more. That is dangerous, because as activities become harder and harder to do, we do less and less. When I realized what I was doing to my body, the temple of God, I got busy with a daily exercise routine. Even after only a few days, I could tell my body parts were freeing up. It has been a delightful experience.

I recently had prayers answered that I prayed three years ago. Holy Spirit told me at that time that all the petitions, which included major healing of my wife's and my bodies, were being met. But He did not say when these big miracles would happen. As I was praying a couple of days ago, Holy Spirit told me that the process of answering all those petitions had begun and He said He was giving me a sign to confirm His statement. I looked down at my feet, and my right foot which had been turned out about 30 degrees, was now perfectly straight like the other one. I had been stricken a few years ago with a neurological disease that had caused the problem and made the act of simply walking very difficult. By not losing faith that God would answer my prayers, I am now seeing one miracle after another of answered prayers. Several serious physical problems which I prayed about three years ago are now gradually being healed. Walking is becoming more natural and easier; a couple of serious digestive problems are going away, and my constant fellowship with the Holy Spirit has greatly improved. I understand why these miraculous healings were delayed. I am writing this book at a very critical time in the history of the United States of America, and a very critical time in the church in America. I believe things are about to change dramatically.

It is thrilling to see an instant miracle, but a miracle is a miracle, whether it is done on our time schedule or on God's time schedule—I figure His time schedule is better than mine. If we give up on one word of the Bible being accurate, whether we understand it or not, we can destroy our own faith. I have seen several people do that to themselves. It goes back to what I said earlier. God's love for us is much stronger than we can possibly understand, but that is what the Bible teaches. Our heavenly Father is not Santa Claus, but a much more loving and intelligent Heavenly Father than we can imagine.

Romans 8:28—And we know that all things work together for good to those who love God, to those who are the called according to *His* purpose.

When we pray about a particular thing, be sure to consider the whole Bible, all The Attitudes and Mindsets of God.

What is most important is that we remember that God's word is always true, and we can count on it. So, if we are not healed it's not because his Word is not true, or God has not fulfilled His Word. It is possibly because we have misinterpreted or mishandled God's word. Maybe we didn't have enough faith, or maybe we didn't pray according to Scripture. Maybe our heart wasn't in the right place, or we had unforgiveness over something we had difficulty dealing with. Perhaps God has a different way of answering our prayers than the way we thought He would. If we pray "according to God's will" He will answer. Can any of us completely understand God's will; I know that I cannot. There can be many reasons why our prayer is not answered, but we must understand that the reason is not that God's Word is not true. If we doubt the validity of God's Word, we waste our time praying, in my opinion. If we don't have that, we don't have anything. I believe that is absolutely the most important thing that we must keep in mind and hang on to.

I have been guilty of making people feel I was shaming them by not being clear enough on that subject. I don't mean to throw the guilt on anyone, but I do intend to make it clear that if our prayer is not answered in the way that we prayed there must be a reason. We know that God does not change, and His Word is true. We could be in error in the way we are praying or the way we are understanding the Scripture. Or God could just have a better way in mind that we don't understand; that's where trust and faith are exercised. We may not completely understand particular Scriptures, so we have to dig in and find out what there is about it that we do not understand. Sometimes, it simply takes a lot of Bible study to really understand some of the Scriptures, and some of it we may not ever understand.

The bottom line is, that just as I pointed out earlier, Jesus paid a horrendous price to provide for our physical healing while we are still on this earth. Please, please don't waste it and cause Him to have paid that terrible price to no avail in your case. Think about how much He loved you when He did that for you. These are things that you may not have known about if you had not studied the whole Bible for yourself, even though you might have attended church regularly most of your life. I hope it causes you to understand how much of God's provisions for your life on this earth you can miss by not studying the Bible for yourself. If God wants to heal you in a different way than you expected, just remember that He is a lot smarter than you and loves you more than you love yourself.

A Scripture that is relevant, **is Matthew 7:7-11—⁷ "Ask, and it will be given to you; seek, and you will find; knock, and it will be opened to you. ⁸ For everyone who asks receives, and he who seeks finds, and to him who knocks it will be opened. ⁹ Or what man is there among you who, if his son asks for bread, will give him a stone? ¹⁰ Or if he asks for a fish, will he give him a serpent? ¹¹ If you then, being evil, know how to give good gifts to your children, how much more will your Father who is in heaven give good things to those who ask Him!**

Dr Luke records that last verse a little different in his account—**Luke 11:13- If you then, being evil, know how to give good gifts to your children, how much more will *your* heavenly Father give the Holy Spirit to those who ask Him!"-**

There is some disagreement on the meaning of that Scripture (**Matthew 7:7-11**). Some theologians say that the words used in the original Aramaic and Greek texts indicate that the meaning was ask and keep on asking, seek and keep on seeking, knock and keep on knocking. I researched that in the exhaustive concordance and could not find that concept. But understand that I am not a Greek scholar nor theologian. The disagreement comes in that some Bible teachers say that when we pray, we should have enough faith in that prayer that it does not need repeating. I personally, try not to pray the same prayer over again if I don't receive an answer right away, but pray differently in case I prayed in error the first time. I will leave it up to you as to how you interpret that Scripture, because I don't profess to be a theologian.

Let's look at a few Scriptures that offer us some direction on how to pray for a miracle. The first one is **Luke 8:43-48 ⁴³Now a woman, having a flow of blood for twelve years, who had spent all her livelihood on physicians and could not be healed by any, ⁴⁴ came from behind and touched the border of His garment. And immediately her flow of blood stopped. ⁴⁵ And Jesus said, "Who touched Me?" When all denied it, Peter and those with him said, "Master, the multitudes throng and press You, and You say, 'Who touched Me?' "⁴⁶ But Jesus said, "Somebody touched Me, for I perceived power going out from Me." ⁴⁷ Now when the woman saw that she was not hidden, she came trembling; and falling down before Him, she declared to Him in the presence of all the people the reason she had touched Him and how she was healed immediately.**

⁴⁸ And He said to her, "Daughter, be of good cheer; your faith has made you well. Go in peace."

It is very important to note here, that Jesus did not make a conscious decision to heal this woman. She had faith that the power to heal was in and on Him and that she only had to touch His clothing to access that power to be healed of that affliction of 12 years. Jesus told her that <u>her faith </u>had made her whole. Jesus stated the same thing to several other people that He healed.

This brings up another circumstance to consider when it comes to receiving a miracle. As Jesus went about the countryside healing no telling how many people, people would become convinced that He could heal them also. This Scripture makes it clear that it was possible to get miraculous healing from Him without Him even knowing it. In other words, it did not need a decision from Jesus for this woman to be healed. From observing Him in action, she had concluded that there was power in Him to miraculously heal her, and He didn't have to do anything about it. She had simple faith, seeing His healing of others, that she too could be healed. Seeing miracles can give you more faith for your own healing. Another point is that you don't have to wait for God to decide whether to heal you or not. <u>God made the decision to heal your body 2000 years ago through the atonement for your healing that Jesus willfully made when He took your suffering in His own body in His trial, 39 lashes, and hanging naked on that cross for hours.</u> I have already shown you that with different Scriptures, particularly **Isaiah 53:1-5**, in Chapter 12.

It is amazing how much easier it is to pray for and receive a miracle when you see others around you receiving a miracle. That is what happened during the Charismatic Renewal and that is what we are going to see in this great outpouring of the Holy Spirit that is getting underway now. Rather than just wait for that outpouring to come to you, I urge you to study your Bible, build up your faith, and help pray in this great outpouring. The value of this great outpouring of the Holy Spirit is that it creates a community and an atmosphere of answered prayer, and just like when Jesus walked through a town and people saw what He was doing, it was easier to believe that He could heal you also. That is what went on during the Charismatic Renewal.

Another thing that will help you receive a miracle is to adjust your attitude about how to get healed. From 1968 till 2011 I <u>primarily depended on God to heal me and seldom consulted a doctor or my medicine cabinet.</u> For many years I took no medicine of any kind, not even aspirin, and went years without seeing any doctor except a dentist. I won't take time here to explain what happened to me in 2011 but will try to explain that in the final chapter of this book. Now, at the age of 91 I take one prescription, which is to help my thyroid gland do its job. My suggestion is to <u>make the doctor and medicine cabinet your last resort, rather than first.</u> Developing that Attitude and Mindset makes a world of difference in your success in praying for your sickness and afflictions. The more your first response is to consult doctors and medicines, the harder it will be to have faith in God for healing. God uses doctors many times, in many peoples' healings, including my own. My point is it is God who is responsible for your healing, no matter the way He chooses to do it. That's my firm belief and I'm sticking to it!

Jesus demonstrated and taught several different ways for us to pray for a miracle. The main thing he taught His disciples in the last days of His earthly sojourn, was that all authority in heaven and on earth had been given to Him by the Father, and He was passing along that authority to His followers. If you study the following verses, you will see that Jesus granted you a "power of attorney" to use His name to access all that authority. Prayerfully consider these Scriptures:

Matthew 28:18—[8] **And Jesus came and spoke to them, saying, "All authority has been given to Me in heaven and on earth."**

John 16:23-24—And in that day you will ask Me nothing. Most assuredly, I say to you, whatever you ask the Father in My name He will give you. [24] **Until now you have asked nothing in My name. Ask, and you will receive, that your joy may be full.**

So that is the main Attitude and Mindset we work with when we pray—we pray with all the authority that Jesus has when we pray in His name. To put it another way, we pray with the understanding that when we pray in Jesus' name, we access the power of authority He has granted us to use.

This Scripture should be considered part of the great commission. Jesus gave it just before His ascension. **Mark 16: 15-20— And He said to them, "Go into all the world and preach the gospel to every creature.** [16] **He who believes and is baptized will be saved; but he who does not believe will be condemned.** [17] **And these signs will follow those who believe: In My name they will cast out demons; they will speak with new tongues;** [18] **they will take up serpents; and if they drink anything deadly, it will by no means hurt them; they will lay hands on the sick, and they will recover."** [9] **So then, after the Lord had spoken to them, He was received up into heaven, and sat**

down at the right hand of God. [20] And they went out and preached everywhere, the Lord working with *them* and confirming the word through the accompanying signs. Amen.

We can command demons to leave in the name of Jesus, and they must leave just as they did in the Scripture when Jesus commanded them to leave. When we command an infirmity to be gone, healed, or restored, in Jesus' name, it should happen just as it did when Jesus prayed that way in the Scriptures. That all sounds simple enough, and you probably think there must be a "catch" to it. Well, there is, and it is found in **Mark 11:23-25—For assuredly, I say to you, whoever says to this mountain, 'Be removed and be cast into the sea,' and does not doubt in his heart, but believes that those things he says will be done, he will have whatever he says. [24] Therefore I say to you, whatever things you ask when you pray, believe that you receive *them*, and you will have *them*.**

I believe you could paraphrase the message of that Scripture this way: "You have to believe you already have 'it' if you are going to get 'it' when you pray for 'it'.

Here is another Scripture that somewhat conveys the same message:

1 John 5:14-15—Now this is the confidence that we have in Him, that if we ask anything according to His will, He hears us. [15] And if we know that He hears us, whatever we ask, we know that we have the petitions that we have asked of Him.

This scripture indicates to me that we can know God's will before we pray. How? By knowing Him and His Word and hearing His voice. If you can really believe those Scriptures to the point of having complete faith in them as being God's promises to you, it will revolutionize your prayer life. If you can do that, it will more than make all the effort I put in to writing this book, and you put into procuring and reading it, more than worth the effort.

It does not hurt to add a "back-up" —**Matthew 18:19-20**—**"Again I say to you that if two of you agree on earth concerning anything that they ask, it will be done for them by My Father in heaven. [20] For where two or three are gathered together in My name, I am there in the midst of them."**

Patricia's thoughts on praying for a miracle: "I look at this praying for miracles from a bit different perspective and I don't completely agree with several of these premises, based on my experience of interaction with people over the years. I absolutely believe that God's intention for each of us is the best, including healing of all kinds, physical, mental, emotional, and spiritual. I particularly lean on these two Scriptures:

John 10:10— The thief does not come except to steal, and to kill, and to destroy. I have come that they may have life, and that they may have *it* more abundantly.

Romans 8:28—And we know that all things work together for good to those who love God, to those who are the called according to *His* purpose.

I come at the subject of miracles from a bit different angle. My passion for many years has been to see people experience full health: physically, emotionally, and spiritually. As part of that passion, God has led me to be involved in the Isaiah 61 Healing Ministry at our church. While wholeheartedly agreeing with Ron in most of his precepts, my experience in working with some, is that they are unable to "pursue or seek" because of soul blockages. These might be in the form of lies believed about themselves, depression, PTSD, anxiety, fear, or other traumatic challenges to their pursuit of truly experiencing God in all His fullness. They want to be a part of the fullness of the Kingdom but may not have the full capacity to seek it. My thought and experience tell me that those are the ones who need people that are walking strongly in The Kingdom of God, to come alongside and walk with them. This needs to be a gentle walk of support, prayer, and safe ministry so that they can eventually get to the place to go after God's love with all their being. And that is a real miracle in their lives!

Ron and I are wired somewhat differently and that might be one of the primary reasons God put us together. Being a part of The Kingdom of God and experiencing all that God has for me and others, including miracles, is absolutely my heart's desire. Ron has taught me so much about walking in the power of the Holy Spirit and experiencing the miracles that Jesus provided for us over 2000 years ago. Jesus has given me a passion to encourage others to do the same. Whereas Ron primarily operates in the gift of teaching, I primarily operate in the gift of encouragement. His passion for teaching and understanding the Word is a life-long calling. My life-long passion is that I, and those I encounter, can love Jesus with all their heart and walk fully: spiritually, emotionally, and physically in His Kingdom. So, along with the suggestions he gives above, which are also helpful for me, I experience The Kingdom of God more fully as I help others to do the same. As they experience His healing it so encourages me. Each of us is unique, and as we say, these are suggestions. Ask God how He wants you to grow more in love with Him and experience His Kingdom and His miracles."

Ron: Here is another Scripture that shows another prospective on how to pray for a miracle:

Acts 3:1-9- ¹Now Peter and John went up together to the temple at the hour of prayer, the ninth *hour*. ² And a certain man lame from his mother's womb was carried, whom they laid daily at the gate of the temple which is called Beautiful, to ask alms from those who entered the temple; ³ who, seeing Peter and John about to go into the temple, asked for alms. ⁴ And fixing his eyes on him, with John, Peter said, "Look at us." ⁵ So he gave them his attention, expecting to receive something from them. ⁶ Then Peter said, "Silver and gold I do not have, but what I do have I give you: In the name of Jesus Christ of Nazareth, rise up and walk." ⁷ And he took him by the right hand and lifted *him* up, and immediately his feet and ankle bones

received strength. ⁸ **So he, leaping up, stood and walked and entered the temple with them—walking, leaping, and praising God. ⁹ And all the people saw him walking and praising God.**

Peter simply told the man "In the name of Jesus Christ of Nazareth rise up and walk," and the man did. Jesus healed people several times by simply telling them to do something. So that is one way to pray for someone. By praying in the name of Jesus we can ask God to heal, or we can command the sickness to be gone, command the person to be healed, or demand the demon to leave. A study of the 4 gospels and the book of Acts will show you the various ways the disciples prayed for miracles. You have the same authority they had to pray the same way.

The above incident created quite an uproar, which put the disciples in trouble with the Jewish religious leaders while proving to be a major factor in the growth of the first church. Look at what Peter told those bewildered religious leaders in **Acts 4:8-10— Then Peter, filled with the Holy Spirit, said to them, "Rulers of the people and elders of Israel: ⁹ If we this day are judged for a good deed *done* to a helpless man, by what means he has been made well, ¹⁰ let it be known to you all, and to all the people of Israel, that by the name of Jesus Christ of Nazareth, whom you crucified, whom God raised from the dead, by Him this man stands here before you whole.**

There is another way of praying for the sick as discussed in the book of James: **James 5:14-15—¹⁴ Is anyone among you sick? Let him call for the elders of the church, and let them pray over him, anointing him with oil in the name of the Lord. ¹⁵ And the prayer of faith will save the sick, and the Lord will raise him up. And if he has committed sins, he will be forgiven.**

That is the only time anointing with oil is mentioned in the New Testament as it relates to praying for healing. While we are in the book of James, we will look at another Scripture related to healing: verse 16 of the same chapter offers another aspect of prayer:

James 5:16—Confess *your* trespasses to one another, and pray for one another, that you may be healed. The effective, fervent prayer of a righteous man avails much.

As we look at Jesus' ministry of healing people, notice that more than one time He indicated that their sin had brought on their physical problem. Check out **Mark 2:4-5 &9-12**—[4] And when they could not come near Him because of the crowd, they uncovered the roof where He was. So when they had broken through, they let down the bed on which the paralytic was lying. [5] When Jesus saw their faith, He said to the paralytic, "Son, your sins are forgiven you. [9] Which is easier, to say to the paralytic, '*Your* sins are forgiven you,' or to say, 'Arise, take up your bed and walk'? [10] But that you may know that the Son of Man has power on earth to forgive sins"—He said to the paralytic, [11] "I say to you, arise, take up your bed, and go to your house." [12] Immediately he arose, took up the bed, and went out in the presence of them all, so that all were amazed and glorified God, saying, "We never saw *anything* like this!"

It seems somewhat radical to some people, to pray to God the Father in the name of Jesus and ask Him for a miracle; even more so to speak to a body, sickness, or demon in the name of Jesus, and demand the body to be healed or the demon or sickness to leave. But, bottom line, that is what the New Testament of the Bible clearly tells us to do. I have seen hundreds of miracles come to pass just that simply, so I know that is one way for me to pray. If I don't see a satisfactory answer, I discuss it with Holy Spirit and keep praying.

I sometimes hear people end their prayers with "if it be thy will". The Bible does not teach that at all. They base that habit on what Jesus said in the Garden of Gethsemane the night before He was crucified. **Matthew 26:39— He went a little farther and fell on His face, and prayed, saying, "O My Father, if it is possible, let this cup pass from Me; nevertheless, not as I will, but as You *will*."**

The important thing to understand about this verse is that Jesus had the choice of whether to go through with the ordeal His Father had asked Him to endure. Knowing the horror of what He was about to face, He asked Father if there was any other way to accomplish what He was about to accomplish, but He was willing to do as Father had asked of Him because He loved Father and you and me enough to do it, even though He was aware of the price. Nowhere in the Bible are we instructed to finish a prayer with "if it be thy will". The Bible does make it perfectly clear what God's will is in many matters, particularly so with healing, as I have previously shown you with Scripture. Therefore, we can know what His will is before we pray. We can only have faith to believe God will do what we ask of Him if we know His will on that matter.

The more we understand what the New Testament has to say about what Jesus so lovingly provided for us to experience in this life and how to access it, the more successful we will be in getting prayers answered and experiencing the fullness of The Kingdom of God that is always available to us if we know it and believe it.

CHAPTER 15

If God Loves Me So Much, Why Did He Let That Happen To Me?

This is a heart-wrenching question we hear all too often; a question not easy to answer. As I write this, it is Saturday, August 28, 2021, and literally millions of Christians around the world are probably crying out that question. August 15, after U.S. and other NATO forces started withdrawing from Afghanistan, the Taliban quickly overran the country and captured Kabul. the capitol. That left thousands in fear of their lives and asking that question. A few days later two suicide bombers killed 167 Afghan civilians and 13 U.S. servicemen at the gate to the airport in Kabul, where the crowd was gathered in hopes of catching a flight out of the chaos. A huge hurricane is heading into New Orleans and East Texas, due to make landfall on the anniversary of the deadly landfall of Hurricane Katrina several years ago. Thousands of people around the world are being sickened and dying from the deadly Covid virus, which we thought a few months ago we had under control. A few weeks ago, a major earthquake struck southeast Haiti, killing and injuring hundreds, destroying churches, homes, and leaving thousands homeless. All this is going on while the United States is spinning down out of control. Yes, millions of Christians around the world are crying out today, "If God loves me so much, why did He let this happen to me".

I hear the expressions many times "God is in charge", or "God is in control". I have not found any Scripture to confirm those statements. I doubt those millions of Christians who are crying out "Why" today would believe those statements. So how do we answer them? It is not easy. Let's look at **Luke 13:1-5—**

¹ There were present at that season some who told Him about the Galileans whose blood Pilate had mingled with their sacrifices. ² And Jesus answered and said to them, "Do you suppose that these Galileans were worse sinners than all *other* Galileans, because they suffered such things? ³ I tell you, no; but unless you repent you will all likewise perish. ⁴ Or those eighteen on whom the tower in Siloam fell and killed them, do you think that they were worse sinners than all *other* men who dwelt in Jerusalem? ⁵ I tell you, no; but unless you repent you will all likewise perish."

I personally conclude two things from Jesus' response to these two incidents: First, their sin or lack of sin had nothing to do with their being victims of the tragedies; and second, unless you repent of your sins you will likewise perish. Personally, I think His answer left more questions unanswered than answered. I think the main point He made is that the two incidents had nothing to do with the victim's sin or lack thereof. In the first incident, a heathen who did not respect God made the decision to commit the atrocity, and in the second, it appears to be an engineering error.

The main idea I want to point out is that God gave every man and woman a free choice to do as he or she pleases, and He will never over-ride the free will of anyone. He proved that in the Garden of Eden when He did not interfere with Adam and Eve eating from the tree of knowledge of good and evil after He had specifically told them not to do it. He proved that at His trial and execution. Let's look at **Psalm 115:16—The heaven,**

***even* the heavens, *are* the LORD's; But the earth He has given to the children of men.**

This Scripture refers to the first several chapters of the book of Genesis. It seems like God has granted free rein of what takes place on earth to mankind and does not interfere with what man does with it, unless God's people cry out to Him for help. This was demonstrated in the Old Testament several times when He was initially establishing the nation of Israel. We see evidence of God's people crying out when England, probably the most powerful military power in the world at that time, tried to prevent the new nation, The United States of America, from becoming independent from them. We whipped them twice. And again, we see God's intervention in the early years of the re-establishing of the nation of Israel starting at its birth in 1948. Three times the tiny new nation was attacked by all the powerful Arab nations around it, and three times the tiny new nation defeated the much larger, stronger, and better-equipped aggressors. The only reasonable explanation of how these events could have happened is that God performed miracle after miracle to save the U.S.A., and the tiny Jewish nation of Israel by answering the prayers of His people. The many books and documentaries on these wars make it clear God was a major player in all those wars. There is no other way of explaining why the U.S.A. and the nation of Israel still exist. As we witness the destruction of our once-great nation by our "elected" leadership, we best cry out to God for help before we bottom out. Consider how such a small number of pioneers striving to establish the new nation on the American continent in roughly 150 years of the first pilgrims landing, were able to defeat the strongest nation in the world at that time and completely run them off the continent. If we fail to succeed in petitioning God to rescue us now from our own government, we could all wind up in similar positions to those who are crying out "Why did God let this happen to us?"

Free will is something we all cherish, but if our choices are influenced more by evil forces than God, it can be quite destructive. It is the bad choices certain people have made with that free will has put the world and our nation in the chaotic situation we are in now. It is that free will of ungodly men that causes so many of the situations that so many blame God for. God did not cause the problems, but He allowed men to create the problems by giving them free will and respecting it. The free will we have, enjoy, and appreciate so much is a wonderful gift, used with Holy Spirit's guidance and principles.

I do not completely understand what people mean when they say, "God is in control", or "God is in charge". Yes, He is sovereign! I do not see Him in control of all the things going on in the world now. I know He has the power and authority to be, but as I look at what I see going on in the world, it appears to me that God has granted control to man, and many of the men in power now are under the influence of satanic forces instead of God. There are a few "bright spots" around, but they are few and far between. That behooves us to pray as never before for God to intercede and show us the way out of this mess. It has become obvious that we are not capable of doing it by ourselves.

I do not believe that the Bible teaches us that God causes bad things to happen to His followers, although as pointed out earlier, as our loving heavenly Father, He will discipline us if He feels it is needed for our own good. I do not think He causes horrible things to happen to us, but His Word teaches us that when they do happen, He can cause good to come out of it. This is spelled out in the following two Scriptures:

Romans 8:28- And we know that all things work together for good to those who love God, to those who are the called according to *His* purpose-

2 Corinthians 1:3-4 ³Blessed *be* the God and Father of our Lord Jesus Christ, the Father of mercies and God of all comfort, ⁴ who comforts us in all our tribulation, that we may be able to comfort those who are in any, with the comfort with which we ourselves are comforted by God.

I have seen both of those Scriptures play out in my life repeatedly when I had to go through rough situations. We have seen instances in our lives where God has used what we looked at as tragedies, to give us wisdom to minister to others in similar situations at a future time. There are other times when we have absolutely no idea why something tragic happens, but because we know God and His Attitude and Mindset, we can trust Him in the tragedy. The bottom line is, if we love God and are called according to His purposes, all things will work together for good!

"Why did God let this happen to me", can be explained by choices and for reasons we don't know or understand. For example, many of the sicknesses we have can be caused by the manipulation of our food sources and the chemicals that are used to produce the food that we ingest. This can cause all sorts of harm to our bodies, unknown to us until health deteriorates. It comes back to the free will to make choices to manipulate God's food sources. You become the victim of those who chose to make decisions based on Satan's principles rather than God's principles. The place where we choose or are forced to live may put us in harm's way.

There are instances where believing Christians have been alerted by the Holy Spirit just in time to avoid a tragedy. I have heard about and read several. My friend, Tom related an incident that happened to him. He was on duty one night as a deputy sheriff, when he was chasing a dangerous criminal in a rural area. The culprit suddenly ditched his car and ran into the woods. Tom stopped his patrol car and pursued the guy on foot. In his pursuit in the dark, he came upon an old barn, and as he considered entering it, the Holy Spirit warned him not to do it, so he gave up the chase and returned to his patrol car. A few days later he saw the man on a downtown street and arrested him without an incident. He asked the criminal about that night, and he admitted that he was waiting to club him if he came through the door.

My friend Eugene, whom we worked with at Peacock Springs State Park in Florida, related a similar story. He said he was driving over an overpass into Jacksonville, Florida one day in very heavy traffic. He was traveling in the right lane, and the Holy Spirit told him three times to move into the left lane before he realized it was the Holy Spirit speaking to him. He obeyed and changed lanes as he was topping the overpass. It was then that he discovered a large car stopped in the right lane a short distance in front of him with several people of different ages scrambling to retrieve a mattress that had blown off the top of the car. If he had not obeyed Holy Spirit when He did, he would not have been able to prevent slamming into them.

I read in a book by Dr. John D. Lake of Spokane, Washington, of a similar experience when he was driving up a steep mountain road. He related that as he was approaching a blind left curve in the road, Holy Spirit told him to pull over to the left and stop. After he did that, a big truck out of control barreled down the mountain in the right lane, which would have obliterated him if he had continued to travel in that lane, the natural thing to do. My personal explanation for these incidents is that these men were obviously in such a close relationship with God at those times, that they were sensitive to "that still small voice" of the Holy Spirit that probably saved lives.

Some years ago, I was kayaking through the "flats" between the Inter-Coastal Waterway and the barrier islands in Southwest Florida returning home alone, at night, and during a storm. The "flats" were shallow and overgrown with seagrass which made paddling more difficult, but I chose that route to avoid the powerboats in the Inter-Coastal Waterway. I had forgotten that the area was also frequented by drug runners. I suddenly realized a large motorboat with a muffled motor and no lights were bearing down on me. I quickly turned on my spotlight and saw this 25-foot boat less than 50 feet away, speeding straight at me, wide open. The captain quickly killed his motor and spun the wheel, coming to rest two feet from me, after almost rolling over on top of me. As I regained my senses and paddled on by them, I looked up into four ashen faces with mouths open. We were all shocked and speechless. For some reason, every time I hear the phrase, "like two ships passing in the night" I relive that incident and see those faces. I believe God alerted me through His

Holy Spirit over the noise of the wind and the rain and waves beating on my vinyl-covered kayak.

FAITH and TRUST are the keys, but that faith and trust need to be built on a knowledge of the Scriptures and an understanding of what faith looks like. The most important key is to have an ever-deepening relationship with the One in whom we put our faith and trust. That is one of the many factors that I feel makes this book so important for this time in our nation. We live in a time when the general attitude about the meaning of words is so weak that it becomes very difficult to have the real faith necessary to access the promises the Bible lists for us.

CHAPTER 16

Dealing With Satanic Forces

Matthew 11:12— And from the days of John the Baptist until now the kingdom of heaven suffers violence, and the violent take it by force.

It is not going to be easy to fight off demonic attacks, because Satan realizes the power we have over him if we use the power available to us to defeat his forces. You can rest assured he will fight you with tooth and toenail every step of the way. I believe that "violence" in the above scripture refers to both demonic and Holy Spirit power violence. "The violent take it (the Kingdom of God, the treasure, the pearl of great price) by force". God is not holding The Kingdom of God back from us, He paid a dear price for us to have it. But Satan is aware of what it will cost him if we use that power available to us. Can you imagine that kind of power being manifested in a church full of people walking in all the power Jesus made available to them, and how much those outside of the church would want what we have? The church today, especially the western church has been losing ground, but the New Testament church spread the gospel to almost all of the then-known world in less than 300 years. They did it the same way Jesus did, by utilizing the power available to them through Holy Spirit.

The Bible and my own experience taught me that anytime I try to do something that will glorify God, I will have to battle satanic forces to do it. It is easy not to recognize these deterrents as satanic assaults. After all, that is Satan's character! The above Scripture convinces me that if I am going to constantly live in the Kingdom of God now, I am going to have to be very forceful and determined to achieve it. Let me point out that I am a work in progress, and do not mean to imply that I have achieved total victory. I also hasten to point out that I have a lot of "battle scars" from my many skirmishes with demonic forces. I watched my first wife get miraculously healed by God of rheumatoid arthritis three times, only to have satanic forces put the same symptoms back on her. I am not constantly bombarded with evil thoughts, but when I run into a deterrent, I stop and discern whether it is from God, natural circumstances, or satanic interference. Then I must deal with it accordingly. My first mission trip would never have happened, had I not been aware of demonic interference and fought forcibly through one battle after another. I worked with Norvel Hayes for a while back in the 1970's He was a famous teacher on Spiritual Warfare, particularly during the charismatic renewal. He often said that every time God miraculously heals you, Satan will come along and try to steal it. If you don't resist him, you will lose your healing. I have seen that happen repeatedly to myself and others. I believe that God miraculously heals His children much more often than we give Him credit for. Remember these verses from Mark's account of the "great commission" in **Mark 16:17-18 [17]And these signs will follow those who believe: In My name they will cast out demons; they will speak with new tongues; [18] they will take up serpents; and if they drink anything deadly, it will by no means hurt them; they will lay hands on the sick, and they will recover."**

Some years ago, I did a survey of all the healing miracles in the four gospels and the book of Acts. I listed them in several different categories, according to the wording of the prayer that wrought the miracle. When I finished and analyzed the results, I was amazed to realize that nearly a third of those miracles were wrought by casting out demons.

James 4:7-8 *⁷Therefore submit to God. Resist the devil and he will flee from you. ⁸ Draw near to God and He will draw near to you. Cleanse *your* hands, *you* sinners; and purify *your* hearts, *you* double-minded.

I find that all too often, people do not realize they have to resist demonic forces, or they will be controlled by them. If they are not aware of their activity and learning to resist it, they will be victims of it. I have heard people say, "Oh, I don't want to mess with that spooky stuff". Well, you jolly well better learn how to mess with that "spooky stuff", because if you are going to serve God, "that spooky stuff" is surely going to try to mess with you. If you attempt to serve God, Scripture and experience make it clear that "spooky stuff" will mess with you. If you don't fight it, it can defeat you.

I have been involved in many miraculous healings, only to see them be stolen by demonic activity. For many years I suffered from severe headaches for about half of my waking hours because of allergies and deteriorating bone disease. This was during the Charismatic Renewal when I was praying for myself and others and seeing miraculous healings. I finally realized that God had answered my prayers and healed me several times, but demonic forces would bring back the same symptoms so quickly that I would assume that I had not been healed. When I finally realized what had been going on, I repented of my lack of faith, promised God that if He would heal me one more time, I would stay alert to satanic activity and not let it steal my healing again. God healed me again, and I finally got free of the affliction. But it was not easy. I spent nearly all the next day rebuking the demonic forces while having a very active day in my job as a Florida State Park Ranger. From time to time all week I would have flare-ups that had to be dealt with. I finally convinced the demonic forces that my support team was stronger than theirs, so they gave up and left me alone. That incident is confirmation of the above Scripture. Ignoring satanic activity in your life is simply submitting to it. If you are serving God, you are going to be attacked by demonic forces. Look at **2 Corinthians 10:3-6—³ For though we walk in the flesh, we do not war according to the flesh. ⁴ For the weapons**

of our warfare are not carnal but mighty in God for pulling down strongholds, ⁵ casting down arguments and every high thing that exalts itself against the knowledge of God, bringing every thought into captivity to the obedience of Christ, ⁶ and being ready to punish all disobedience when your obedience is fulfilled.

According to the Bible, sin and temptation can be classified into three categories. This is pointed out in **1 John 2:16— For all that is in the world—the lust of the flesh, the lust of the eyes, and the pride of life—is not of the Father but is of the world.**

It seems amazing that sin is that simple. But, when you check the temptation of Adam and Eve in the garden and Jesus in the wilderness, you can see that Satan threw everything he had at them, but those three temptations were all he had. Rest assured that Satan will attempt to tempt you with the same three tools.

Peter gives somewhat the same advice that we saw from James, about being alert and resisting. Look at **1 Peter 5:6-9—⁶ Therefore humble yourselves under the mighty hand of God, that He may exalt you in due time, ⁷ casting all your care upon Him, for He cares for you. ⁸ Be [sober, be vigilant; because your adversary the devil walks about like a roaring lion, seeking whom he may devour. ⁹ Resist him, steadfast in the faith, knowing that the same sufferings are experienced by your brotherhood in the world.**

Satanic forces can affect you in many ways, including clouding your thinking with trivial ideas to keep you from being in fellowship with God, or feeding you lies about yourself, others, and God. Rest assured that if you are seriously serving God and trying hard to do something you feel God has called you to do, Satan will send his demons to try to distract you and derail your efforts. When I start encountering a lot of satanic interference in my effort to do something I feel God wants me to do, I know I am on the right track. I deal with demonic forces with renewed zeal, knowing they disapprove of what I am doing encourages me. Satanic interference encourages me because it simply confirms that I am ticking him off and am pleasing God, so I am on the right track. I have the confidence that by using the name of Jesus and all the power associated with Him, I can overcome anything he throws at me.

CHAPTER 17

How Do We Maintain A Growing Relationship With God?

We know that developing human close relationships requires time and effort. It seems to me that developing my relationship with my Lord is even more important, so it will take time and effort on my part. Your relationship with God, I believe, can be compared to paddling a kayak upstream. The harder you paddle, the more progress you make. But, if you quit paddling, the current will take you back downstream. That is the way it has seemed to work for me, anyway. So, how do we work at it?

Remember **Matthew 6:33—"But seek first the kingdom of God and His righteousness, and all these things shall be added to you.**

Making your life goal seeking God and His Kingdom is as good a life goal that you can set for yourself. I can attest to that, because that is what I decided to do 65 years ago, and I have and am enjoying a great life. I don't possess a pot full of money, but I am blessed with enough to have everything I need and more. I have enjoyed a great, well-lived life, and look forward to many more years of it. I am and have been loved by many, and I am expecting more. I have had to go through many very tough experiences and have made a lot of mistakes along the way, but like Paul, I praise God for delivering me from them.

2 Corinthians 1:8-11— **[8]For we do not want you to be ignorant, brethren, of our trouble which came to us in Asia: that we were burdened beyond measure, above strength, so that we despaired even of life. [9]Yes, we had the sentence of death in ourselves, that we should not trust in ourselves but in God who raises the dead, [10]who delivered us from so great a death, and does deliver us; in whom we trust that He will still deliver *us*, [11] you also helping together in prayer for us, that thanks may be given by many persons on our behalf for the gift *granted* to us through many.**

The next thing I would suggest, which I have alluded to several times earlier, is to develop a habit of daily Bible study. After all, isn't your relationship with God the most important thing you need to do with your time? What could be more important than that? If you really place value on your relationship with God as the most important use of your time, you will find time in your daily schedule for daily Bible study. I suggest that you pray about it and ask Holy Spirit to guide you in choosing your course of study. Commentaries can be helpful if you are aware that they are one person's conclusions. Study guides that someone else developed can be helpful if they align with where you are and where you want to go in your relationship with God. I know that when Holy Spirit interrupted me in a Sunday school lesson preparation that night in 1955 and opened the Bible to me, it was one of if not **the**, most important thing(s) that ever happened to me. I thank God for that experience often. You are responsible for your life, and you are the one who will have to live it and answer for it when you stand before your Maker, so don't allow someone else to determine your destiny for you. Test what you experience being taught from the pulpit or in study guides; do the teachings line up with God's Word?

Choosing your friends, and particularly your mate is very important. These are the people who will have the most effect on your decisions and direction. Choose close friends who help you stay on the right road, rather than those who would lead you astray. Ask God to help you find those friends. Many a soul has been challenged by someone befriending a person traveling the wrong road to try to help them. They can be sucked down that wrong road by the one they were trying to help. Know your own limitations before taking on such a task. God may call you to this type of ministry and if so, He will equip you to do it. "Don't bite off more than you can chew." Or perhaps we might say, don't bite off more than God wants you to chew.

Never feel obligated to associate with a particular church for any reason, other than being a part of a body of believers that is listening, following, and dedicated to Jesus, and His Word. Why waste your time at a church that doesn't do this, when there are those around that do. There is no doubt in my mind that I have wasted many hours in dead churches that could better have been spent at home doing my own Bible study. The fact that your family has always attended that church does not obligate you to go there. If the teaching and ministry of a church do not draw you closer to your Lord and Savior, then leave and go find one that does. Feeling obligated to a particular church has hurt many a soul. It took me over thirty years to realize I was wasting my time and throwing my life away by feeling I could only go to the church of the denomination my family had always gone to. Realizing that was one of the most liberating experiences I ever had. "You can't soar with eagles if you spend most of your time hanging out with turkeys". If a church doesn't help you draw nearer to God, don't waste your time and money there. You owe them nothing.

CHAPTER 18

What Does The Bible Teach About Predestination?

I spent the first 33 years of my life attending a Presbyterian church, so I heard a lot about predestination. Not so much since then. If you have been attending any other church except Presbyterian, you may not have heard much about it, either. The Bible talks about it, and I have heard a lot of man's doctrine about it, so I decided it was worth talking about here. Paul talks about it in several places in the Bible, so we will start with him.

We will start with **Ephesians 1:1-14—**¹**Paul, an apostle of Jesus Christ by the will of God, To the saints who are in Ephesus, and faithful in Christ Jesus: ² Grace to you and peace from God our Father and the Lord Jesus Christ. Blessed** *be* **the God and Father of our Lord Jesus Christ, who has blessed us with every spiritual blessing in the heavenly** *places* **in Christ, ⁴ just as He chose us in Him before the foundation of the world, that we should be holy and without blame before Him in love, ⁵ having predestined us to adoption as sons by Jesus Christ to Himself, according to the good pleasure of His will, ⁶ to the praise of the glory of His grace, by which He** [a]**made us accepted in the Beloved.**

⁷ In Him we have redemption through His blood, the forgiveness of sins, according to the riches of His grace ⁸ which He made to abound toward us in all wisdom and [b]prudence, ⁹ having made known to us the mystery of His will, according to His good pleasure which He purposed in Himself, ¹⁰ that in the dispensation of the fullness of the times He might gather together in one all things in Christ, [c] both which are in heaven and which are on earth—in Him. ¹¹ In Him also we have obtained an inheritance, being predestined according to the purpose of Him who works all things according to the counsel of His will, ¹² that we who first trusted in Christ should be to the praise of His glory. ¹³ In Him you also *trusted*, after you heard the word of truth, the gospel of your salvation; in whom also, having believed, you were sealed with the Holy Spirit of promise, ¹⁴ who is the guarantee of our inheritance until the redemption of the purchased possession, to the praise of His glory.

There is much to talk about in this very important Scripture, some of which we have already discussed. I quote this whole section to place it in context for better understanding. We primarily just want to look at the references to predestination here, so we start with verses 3-6.

³ Blessed *be* the God and Father of our Lord Jesus Christ, who has blessed us with every spiritual blessing in the heavenly *places* in Christ, ⁴ just as He chose us in Him before the foundation of the world, that we should be holy and without blame before Him in love, ⁵ having predestined us to adoption as sons by Jesus Christ to Himself, according to the good pleasure of His will, ⁶ to the praise of the glory of His grace, by which He made us accepted in the Beloved.

I personally understand that Scripture to indicate that "chose us" (predestined or called) refers to at the least, all who would choose to accept His offer of salvation. The question comes then, did God only call or predestine those that made the choice to follow Him, or did He predestine others and only some of those choose to accept His offer? Having studied the Bible for many years, I am inclined to believe that

God is so loving of man, His creation, that He would offer the gift of salvation to everybody that would repent and follow (try to become like Him) Him. Look at **2 Peter 3:9- The Lord is not slack concerning *His* promise, as some count slackness, but is longsuffering toward us, not willing that any should perish but that all should come to repentance.**

Jesus often spoke through parables and comparisons in an obvious attempt to cause His listeners to seriously consider if they really wanted to be His disciple. The following Scriptures illustrate this**: John 6:47-65—**

[47]Most assuredly, I say to you, he who believes]in Me has everlasting life. [48] I am the bread of life. [49] Your fathers ate the manna in the wilderness, and are dead. [50] This is the bread which comes down from heaven, that one may eat of it and not die. [51] I am the living bread which came down from heaven. If anyone eats of this bread, he will live forever; and the bread that I shall give is My flesh, which I shall give for the life of the world." [52] The Jews therefore quarreled among themselves, saying, "How can this Man give us *His* flesh to eat?" [53] Then Jesus said to them, "Most assuredly, I say to you, unless you eat the flesh of the Son of Man and drink His blood, you have no life in you. [54] Whoever eats My flesh and drinks My blood has eternal life, and I will raise him up at the last day. [55] For My flesh is food indeed, and My blood is drink indeed. [56] He who eats My flesh and drinks My blood abides in Me, and I in him. [57] As the living Father sent Me, and I live because of the Father, so he who feeds on Me will live because of Me. [58] This is the bread which came down from heaven—not as your fathers ate the manna, and are dead. He who eats this bread will live forever."

[59] These things He said in the synagogue as He taught in Capernaum. [60] Therefore many of His disciples, when they heard *this,* said, "This is a hard saying; who can understand it?" [61] When Jesus knew in Himself that His disciples complained about this, He said to them, "Does this offend you? [62] What then if you should see the Son

of Man ascend where He was before? ⁶³ It is the Spirit who gives life; the flesh profits nothing. The words that I speak to you are spirit, and they are life. ⁶⁴ But there are some of you who do not believe." For Jesus knew from the beginning who they were who did not believe, and who would betray Him. ⁶⁵ And He said, "Therefore I have said to you that no one can come to Me unless it has been granted to him by My Father."**

I would like for you to particularly notice verse 65, above.

Remember what we read previously in another chapter concerning this- **Matthew 7:13-14—¹³"Enter by the narrow gate; for wide *is* the gate and broad *is* the way that leads to destruction, and there are many who go in by it. ¹⁴ Because narrow *is* the gate and difficult *is* the way which leads to life, and there are few who find it.**

That Scripture tells us that Jesus knew more people would turn down His offer than would accept it.

Let's finish looking at the last part of **Ephesians 1:4—…."that we should be holy and without blame before Him in love."** That says that this is the reason He chose us, isn't it? Now we are back to holiness. That begs the question, "are we saved by works or by grace." That takes us to **Ephesians 2:8-10-⁸ For by grace you have been saved through faith, and that not of yourselves; *it is* the gift of God, ⁹ not of works, lest anyone should boast. ¹⁰ For we are His workmanship, created in Christ Jesus for good works, which God prepared beforehand that we should walk in them.**

I paraphrase those verses to say, "We are saved through our God given faith in God's grace towards us for the purpose of doing the good works which He prepared for us to do for The Kingdom of God. To put it another way, "we do the good works because of our appreciation of what He has done for us, not to save our soul from hell." If we really understand what God has made available to us through His Son, Jesus the Christ,

Messiah, we will want to do everything within our power to experience and please Him.

But here is the problem: You can listen to preachers and teachers for hours without ever really, truly understanding the depth of God's Love. It is by studying the Bible for yourself, with the help of the Holy Spirit that you really get to the truth of the matter. Yep! I'm right back to that same old theme, which you may be tired of hearing. But take it from an old man who has struggled most of his life to find out what the ultimate relationship with God is all about. And I am telling you, it is very unlikely that you will find it by listening to other people. You need the fellowship of a loving, supportive Christian community. But it is not practical to depend on someone else to mold your understanding of and relationship to God. Don't try to tell me that you are too busy. You are not spending any time on anything more important than your relationship with your creator, God. We are not just talking about where you will spend eternity when you breathe your last breath, but we are talking also about all the time you have left here in this life. Excuse me, I will leave preaching and get back to our Bible study.

Ephesians 1: 5-6 (above) tells me that we are predestined to be adopted as sons of God through the grace of His Son, our brother, Jesus, who made us acceptable to Father God. God predestined us, but He also granted us a free-will that makes it possible for us to choose whether we would accept His precious gift that He paid for with a horrible price. **Verses 7-12** speaks of Jesus sacrifice with His own blood according to His own will to offer this great salvation.

Let's look at another Scripture which seems to me to spell out God's predestination for us.

Romans 8:28-30— ²⁸ And we know that all things work together for good to those who love God, to those who are the called according to *His* purpose. ²⁹ For whom He foreknew, He also predestined *to be* conformed to the image of His Son, that He might be the firstborn

among many brethren. **³⁰ Moreover whom He predestined, these He also called; whom He called, these He also justified; and whom He justified, these He also glorified.**

Now let's do a word study according to *The Strongest NASB Exhaustive Concordance*:

Predestined=proorizo—to predetermine, foreordain.
Justified=dikaloo—show to be righteous, declared righteous.
Glorified=doxazo—to render or esteem glorious, honored.

Verse 28 describes who **verses 29-30** are talking about— "those who are the called according to His purpose". "We are predestined to be conformed to the image of His Son" (Jesus). Our free will is still intact, so we can short-circuit God's predestination plan for us to be conformed to the image of Jesus. Now, we are back to holiness.

So, here is what I personally believe in the light of those Scriptures: It is God's will, desire, plan, that everyone accept His invitation to become His adopted child, and conform to His own begotten Son, Jesus. But He loves us so much that He gives us a free will to choose whether to do so. The problem comes down to whether we love Him enough to willfully do what He requires. Man's doctrine cannot do that, but conviction of the Holy Spirit can convince you of the love that God has shown for you to the extent that you want to please Him completely.

That brings up the theological question, are we saved by works or are we saved by grace. Let's look again **at Ephesians 2:8-10—**

⁸For by grace you have been saved through faith, and that not of yourselves; *it is* **the gift of God, ⁹ not of works, lest anyone should boast. ¹⁰ For we are His workmanship, created in Christ Jesus for good works, which God prepared beforehand that we should walk in them.**

That says to me that we are saved by God's grace so that we may through His fellowship do good works. We don't do good works to get saved, we get saved to do good works. It is a result of His Holy Spirit within us, that we listen to Him and do good works.

There is another Scripture we need to look at because it has caused some confusion.

Romans 9:10-13- ¹⁰And not only *this,* but when Rebecca also had conceived by one man, *even* by our father Isaac ¹¹ (for *the children* not yet being born, nor having done any good or evil, that the purpose of God according to election might stand, not of works but of Him who calls), ¹² it was said to her, "The older shall serve the younger." ¹³ As it is written, "Jacob I have loved, but Esau I have hated."

Paul is referring here to **Malachi 1:2-3—"I have loved you," says the Lord. "Yet you say, 'In what way have You loved us?' *Was* not Esau Jacob's brother?" says the Lord. "Yet Jacob I have loved; ³ But Esau I have hated and laid waste his mountains and his heritage for the jackals of the wilderness."**

Now we will go all the way back to Genesis when the birth happened in **Genesis 25:24-28— ²⁴So when her days were fulfilled *for her* to give birth, indeed *there were* twins in her womb. ²⁵ And the first came out red. *He was* like a hairy garment all over; so they called his name Esau. ²⁶ Afterward his brother came out, and his hand took hold of Esau's heel; so his name was called Jacob. Isaac *was* sixty years old when she bore them. ²⁷ So the boys grew. And Esau was a skillful hunter, a man of the field; but Jacob was a mild man, dwelling in tents. ²⁸ And Isaac loved Esau because he ate *of his* game, but Rebekah loved Jacob.**

This becomes quite confusing, so I will attempt to get to the bottom of it. **Romans 9:10-13** tells us that God hated Esau and loved Jacob when they were first born. My Old Testament Dictionary in the back of my AMG

Hebrew-Greek Key Word Study Bible says the Hebrew word "sane," is translated as "hated" in the above Malachai and Genesis Scriptures. I will quote some of the explanation here, to help us get a better understanding of these Scriptures: "The word sane means to dislike, to be hostile to, or to loathe someone or something in some context. Malachi asserted that God hated Esau but loved Jacob to explain how God had dealt with their descendants; God cared for Esau and gave him offspring". Please understand that this is the conclusion of the Greek theologian, Dr. Spiros Zodhiates.

So, the question becomes, why did God dislike Esau before He did anything good or bad. Evidently, God predestined Jacob to become Israel, the father of the 12 tribes of Israel, but not something as important for Esau, who later forfeited his older son's birthright for a bowl of lentil soup. As we read the history of the two brothers, it is hard to see that Esau was that much a bigger sinner than Jacob. Both boys were blessed, so that did not indicate that God hated him so much. The main point is that God chose, and predestined Jacob for greatness but not as much so for Esau. That leaves us with the conclusion that the sovereign God predestines some of His children for greater roles in His plan than He does others. Then we can conclude that we are all predestined for some role in our lifetime, but we can choose the plan God has for us, or "do it my way" as Frank Sinatra sang.

CHAPTER 19

Is It Possible For A Christian To Forfeit His Salvation?

Most preachers will tell you no. I personally do believe that it is possible for a born-again Christian to forfeit his salvation. In a previous chapter I mentioned that I searched for a job in Christian camping and wound up on a Christian Youth Dude Ranch in California. Prior to taking that job I corresponded with a Christian Family Campground in Colorado, which was far more appealing to me, *and half as far away.* Our correspondence was getting along very good, until they sent me a copy of their statement of faith, which I would need to sign on to—This was around 1967. I studied it and was impressed with it, except for one item—once saved always saved. I responded that I liked everything on their statement except that one item and included Scripture to back up my stand. They responded with Scripture to support their stand, and that went on for weeks before we realized both parties were set and not giving in. I think both of us hoped we could work it out, but we couldn't. I mention that incident to point out that this has been an ongoing point of contention for centuries. That is not the only point of contention that the Bible leaves us with a problem of finding clarity on, so we must diligently search the Scriptures and decide for ourselves which side we are going to go with and stay with unless we get new revelation from Holy Spirit. In this case I would use my first wife's response in another case, "what if you are wrong?" I choose to play it safe.

Having explained all that, let's look at the Scripture that supports my stance on this subject.

Hebrews 6:1-8— ⁱTherefore, leaving the discussion of the elementary principles of Christ, let us go on to perfection, not laying again the foundation of repentance from dead works and of faith toward God, ² of the doctrine of baptisms, of laying on of hands, of resurrection of the dead, and of eternal judgment. ³³ And this [a]we will do if God permits.

⁴ For *it is* impossible for those who were once enlightened, and have tasted the heavenly gift, and have become partakers of the Holy Spirit, ⁵ and have tasted the good word of God and the powers of the age to come, ⁶ if they fall away, to renew them again to repentance, since they crucify again for themselves the Son of God, and put *Him* to an open shame. ⁷ For the earth which drinks in the rain that often comes upon it, and bears herbs useful for those by whom it is cultivated, receives blessing from God; ⁸ but if it bears thorns and briers, *it is* rejected and near to being cursed, whose end *is* to be burned.

Jesus even gave a hint of this in His last-minute instructions to His disciples in **John 15:4-8—⁴Abide in Me, and I in you. As the branch cannot bear fruit of itself, unless it abides in the vine, neither can you, unless you abide in Me. ⁵ I am the vine, you are the branches. He who abides in Me, and I in him, bears much fruit; for without Me you can do nothing. ⁶ If anyone does not abide in Me, he is cast out as a branch and is withered; and they gather them and throw them into the fire, and they are burned. ⁷ If you abide in Me, and My words abide in you, you will ask what you desire, and it shall be done for you. ⁸ By this My Father is glorified, that you bear much fruit; so you will be My disciples.**

Hebrews 12:12-17-¹²Therefore strengthen the hands which hang down, and the feeble knees, ¹³ and make straight paths for your feet, so that what is lame may not be dislocated, but rather be healed. ¹⁴ Pursue peace with all *people,* and holiness, without which no one will see the Lord: ¹⁵ looking carefully lest anyone fall short of the grace of God; lest any root of bitterness springing up cause trouble, and by this many become defiled; ¹⁶ lest there *be* any fornicator or profane person like Esau, who for one morsel of food sold his birthright. ¹⁷ For you know that afterward, when he wanted to inherit the blessing, he was rejected, for he found no place for repentance, though he sought it diligently with tears.

James 5:19-20— ¹⁹Brethren, if anyone among you wanders from the truth, and someone turns him back, ²⁰ let him know that he who turns a sinner from the error of his way will save a soul from death and cover a multitude of sins.

2 Peter 3:14-18— Therefore, beloved, looking forward to these things, be diligent to be found by Him in peace, without spot and blameless; ¹⁵ and consider that the longsuffering of our Lord *is* salvation—as also our beloved brother Paul, according to the wisdom given to him, has written to you, ¹⁶ as also in all his epistles, speaking in them of these things, in which are some things hard to understand, which untaught and unstable *people* twist to their own destruction, as they *do* also the rest of the Scriptures. ¹⁷ You therefore, beloved, since you know this beforehand, beware lest you also fall from your own steadfastness, being led away with the error of the wicked; ¹⁸ but grow in the grace and knowledge of our Lord and Savior Jesus Christ. To Him *be* the glory both now and forever. Amen.

I rest my case.

CHAPTER 20

God's Attitude Towards Marriage And Divorce

In the first chapter of the Bible, we see that God created the first man and woman to populate and subdue the earth, so we have the first two people on earth (1 man and 1 woman) were married. The first marriage was announced in **Genesis 2:24—**

Therefore a man shall leave his father and mother and be joined to his wife, and they shall become one flesh.

The term "joined to his wife, and they shall become one flesh" thus throughout the Bible refers to a man and woman being married and having children. "Become one flesh" obviously refers to sexual intercourse. In the Old Testament that is sometimes the only indication *the Bible gives* of a couple getting married.

Throughout much of the Old Testament, we see many of the patriarchs having more than one wife. Not much was said about it being a problem with them or God, but I personally cannot fathom why any man in his right mind would want to do that. Solomon, whom God blessed with the wisdom to lead Israel, topped them all with 700 wives and 300 concubines. I guess that made sense to Solomon, but it sure doesn't to me. Anyway, that practice appeared to go away eventually.

Obviously one man and one woman appears to be the rule in the New Testament, and certainly was the law in the United States and most of the world until recently. Jesus taught that the marriage bed was sacred. Look at **Matthew 5:31-32— ³¹"Furthermore it has been said, 'Whoever divorces his wife, let him give her a certificate of divorce.' ³² But I say to you that whoever divorces his wife for any reason except sexual immorality causes her to commit adultery; and whoever marries a woman who is divorced commits adultery.**

This is from the "Sermon on the Mount", where Jesus was laying out His description of The Kingdom of God on earth. So early on He made Himself clear on exactly where He stands on the sanctity of the marriage bed. Today, the younger you are, for the most part, the less value you place on this subject. **That doesn't change the Scripture or how God regards it. Customs can change, but God's word does not.** Sin then and sin today in our society is sin. The way some people look at it does not change Scripture. I am one of those weird characters, and there are many more in my generation just like me, who respected the Scripture, our own bodies, and that of our spouse too much to mess it up. If that offends you, don't get mad at me, because I didn't make the rules. Thankfully, we have a loving Lord and Savior who is willing to forgive us of our sins when we confess them to Him and repent. **1 John 1:9— If we confess our sins, He is faithful and just to forgive us *our* sins and to cleanse us from all unrighteousness.**

I confess that I divorced my first wife. She had been injured and traumatized by her parents and members of her family, and had a tough time coping with life. Thirty-two years into our marriage, I made some bad decisions and changed jobs. That job did not work out, and I had a difficult time finding another one. She, in her woundedness, hammered me so hard night and day, that I lost all self-confidence and will to live. One hour before I planned to carry out my plan to take my own life, (I was in a completely hopeless state) Holy Spirit told me it would be better to leave than take my own life. I fled to South Florida and took a menial job that would barely meet my expenses. I worked on a resort island as a boat captain and maintenance man for $500.00 per month plus room and board. My wife had a good job when I left, and during the time I was gone. I had no intention of divorcing her when I left, but she harassed me so much that it interfered greatly with my job performance. I had to divorce her and sever all ties or lose my job. After 2 1/2 years on the island, I decided I had regained enough self-confidence and sanity, to put the marriage back together, and I did. Our marriage survived until she passed away, two months before the 60th anniversary of our original marriage. We both kept the marriage bed sacred during our separation.

Even though some of the instructions of Jesus seem too hard to deal with in today's environment, that does not mean that God feels any different about it today than He did 2000 years ago. But, the good news is found in **1 John 1:9 If we confess our sins, He is faithful and just to forgive us *our* sins and to cleanse us from all unrighteousness.**

That Attitude and Mindset of God shows how much He loves us. He loves us so much that there is hardly anything we can do that is so bad that if we repent (turn away from the desire to sin and ask for forgiveness), He will reinstate us in good standing with Him.

From the Scripture from Matthew 5 that we looked at earlier, we also saw that Jesus considered adultery serious enough that it could be considered reason enough for one mate to divorce the other. The Apostle Paul explains why that is such a serious offense in **1 Corinthians 6:15-20—** **[15]Do you not know that your bodies are members of Christ? Shall I then take the members of Christ and make them members of a harlot? Certainly not! [16] Or do you not know that he who is joined to a harlot is one body with her? For "the two," He says, "shall become one flesh." [17] But he who is joined to the Lord is one spirit with Him. [18] Flee sexual immorality. Every sin that a man does is outside the body, but he who commits sexual immorality sins against his own body. [19] Or do you not know that your body is the temple of the Holy**

Spirit who *is* in you, whom you have from God, and you are not your own? [20] For you were bought at a price; therefore glorify God in your body and in your spirit, which are God's.

CHAPTER 21

God's Attitude About Homosexuality

The Scripture is crystal clear on God's Attitude and Mindset about homosexuality, both in the Old Testament and the New Testament. The account of Abraham and his nephew, Lot, in chapter 18 of the book of Genesis gives a very clear indication of His attitude: **Genesis 18:16-23, 19:1-13, & 23-25—**

16Then the men rose from there and looked toward Sodom, and Abraham went with them to send them on the way. 17 And the Lord said, "Shall I hide from Abraham what I am doing, 18 since Abraham shall surely become a great and mighty nation, and all the nations of the earth shall be blessed in him? 19 For I have known him, in order that he may command his children and his household after him, that they keep the way of the Lord, to do righteousness and justice, that the Lord may bring to Abraham what He has spoken to him." 20 And the Lord said, "Because the outcry against Sodom and Gomorrah is great, and because their sin is very grave, 21 I will go down now and see whether they have done altogether according to the outcry against it that has come to Me; and if not, I will know." 22 Then the men turned away from there and went toward Sodom, but Abraham still stood before the Lord. 23 And Abraham came near and said, "Would You also destroy the righteous with the wicked?

19: ¹Now the two angels came to Sodom in the evening, and Lot was sitting in the gate of Sodom. When Lot saw *them*, he rose to meet them, and he bowed himself with his face toward the ground. ² And he said, "Here now, my lords, please turn in to your servant's house and spend the night, and wash your feet; then you may rise early and go on your way." And they said, "No, but we will spend the night in the open square."³ But he insisted strongly; so they turned in to him and entered his house. Then he made them a feast, and baked unleavened bread, and they ate. ⁴ Now before they lay down, the men of the city, the men of Sodom, both old and young, all the people from every quarter, surrounded the house. ⁵ And they called to Lot and said to him, "Where are the men who came to you tonight? Bring them out to us that we may know them carnally."

⁶ So Lot went out to them through the doorway, shut the door behind him, ⁷ and said, "Please, my brethren, do not do so wickedly! ⁸ See now, I have two daughters who have not known a man; please, let me bring them out to you, and you may do to them as you wish; only do nothing to these men, since this is the reason they have come under the shadow of my roof." ⁹ And they said, "Stand back!" Then they said, "This one came in to stay here, and he keeps acting as a judge; now we will deal worse with you than with them." So they pressed hard against the man Lot, and came near to break down the door. ¹⁰ But the men reached out their hands and pulled Lot into the house with them, and shut the door. ¹¹ And they struck the men who were at the doorway of the house with blindness, both small and great, so that they became weary trying to find the door. ¹² Then the men said to Lot, "Have you anyone else here? Son-in-law, your sons, your daughters, and whomever you have in the city—take them out of this place! ¹³ For we will destroy this place, because the outcry against them has grown great before the face of the LORD, and the LORD has sent us to destroy it."

²³ The sun had risen upon the earth when Lot entered Zoar. ²⁴ Then the LORD rained brimstone and fire on Sodom and Gomorrah, from

the LORD out of the heavens. ²⁵ So He overthrew those cities, all the plain, all the inhabitants of the cities, and what grew on the ground.

In the New Testament we have these Scriptures, which makes God's position on the subject clear:

Romans 1:18-32- ¹⁸ For the wrath of God is revealed from heaven against all ungodliness and unrighteousness of men, who suppress the truth in unrighteousness, ¹⁹ because what may be known of God is manifest in them, for God has shown *it* to them. ²⁰ For since the creation of the world His invisible attributes are clearly seen, being understood by the things that are made, even His eternal power and Godhead, so that they are without excuse, ²¹ because, although they knew God, they did not glorify *Him* as God, nor were thankful, but became futile in their thoughts, and their foolish hearts were darkened. ²² Professing to be wise, they became fools, ²³ and changed the glory of the incorruptible God into an image made like corruptible man—and birds and four-footed animals and creeping things.

²⁴ Therefore God also gave them up to uncleanness, in the lusts of their hearts, to dishonor their bodies among themselves, ²⁵ who exchanged the truth of God for the lie, and worshiped and served the creature rather than the Creator, who is blessed forever. Amen. ²⁶ For this reason God gave them up to vile passions. For even their women exchanged the natural use for what is against nature. ²⁷ Likewise also the men, leaving the natural use of the woman, burned in their lust for one another, men with men committing what is shameful, and receiving in themselves the penalty of their error which was due.

²⁸ And even as they did not like to retain God in their knowledge, God gave them over to a debased mind, to do those things which are not fitting; ²⁹ being filled with all unrighteousness, sexual immorality, wickedness, covetousness, maliciousness; full of envy, murder, strife, deceit, evil-mindedness; they are whisperers, ³⁰ backbiters, haters of God, violent, proud, boasters, inventors of evil things, disobedient

to parents, ³¹ undiscerning, untrustworthy, unloving, unforgiving, unmerciful; ³² who, knowing the righteous judgment of God, that those who practice such things are deserving of death, not only do the same but also approve of those who practice them.

1 Corinthians 6:9-10— ⁹ **Do you not know that the unrighteous will not inherit the kingdom of God? Do not be deceived. Neither fornicators, nor idolaters, nor adulterers, nor homosexuals, nor sodomites,** ¹⁰ **nor thieves, nor covetous, nor drunkards, nor revilers, nor extortioners will inherit the kingdom of God.**

The above Scriptures give us plenty of information on what is God's Attitude and Mindset on unrepentant sin, including homosexuality. I believe it is quite clear. Because I was molested by three different men (who professed to be friends) when I was growing up, and still feel the shame and deceit of it, I choose not to say any more about it. The Scripture is very clear on the subject, and I see no need to add further comment. During my professional career in the Boy Scouts of America, we professionals had to be alert to keep homosexuals out of the movement and train the troop leadership to do the same. When troop leaders found out a homosexual was molesting boys, he was immediately expelled and placed on a watch list to not be eligible for membership in the BSA. Sadly, as I reported earlier, emphasis in the professional service was placed on membership and money to the neglect of quality programs by trained leaders, which has led to the situation we see the BSA in today. That's my opinion, and I am sticking with it. So very much has changed in our country since I exited the profession in 1965.

CHAPTER 22

God's Attitude Towards Parenting And Children

The whole Bible puts forth an attitude of our God considering children precious in His sight. The Bible, and Hebrew culture, also place the responsibility on the parents to teach their children to respect God's word. The book of Proverbs devotes many verses to the upbringing of the children and instructs the young men to be smart and follow God's instructions *and their parent's instructions*. Much to the surprise of many, there are several versus that recommend disciplining children with the "rod". Here are a few samples:

Proverbs 1:8 &10— ⁸My son, hear the instruction of your father, And do not forsake the law of your mother; ¹⁰ My son, if sinners entice you, Do not consent.

Proverbs 13:1 &24— ¹A wise son *heeds* his father's instruction, But a scoffer does not listen to rebuke. ²⁴He who spares his rod hates his son, But he who loves him disciplines him promptly.

Proverbs 19:18— Chasten your son while there is hope, And do not set your heart on his destruction.

Proverbs 22:6 & 15— ⁶**Train up a child in the way he should go, And when he is old he will not depart from it.** ¹⁵**Foolishness** *is* **bound up in the heart of a child; The rod of correction will drive it far from him.**

Proverbs 23:13-14 & 24— ¹³**Do not withhold correction from a child, For** *if* **you beat him with a rod, he will not die.** ¹⁴**You shall beat him with a rod, And deliver his soul from hell.** ²⁴**The father of the righteous will greatly rejoice, And he who begets a wise child will delight in him.**

Of course we have one of the Ten Commandments that specifically commands us, even as adults, to honor and respect our parents—"the only commandment with a promise". **Exodus 20:12— "Honor your father and your mother, that your days may be long upon the land which the L**ORD **your God is giving you.**

I do not remember reading anything in the New Testament that specifically recommending whipping a child. Hebrews 11, which we looked at earlier, made it clear that God, our heavenly Father, will discipline us if He deems it is needed for our own good. Whether we like it or not, it is illegal to whip a child in most states. I told you earlier about my early childhood. Although my dad whipped me harder and more often than was warranted, I am glad now that he did that rather than nothing. Self-discipline is one of my main character strengths to this day. Of course, at the time it happened, I did not feel glad. The most important guideline for parents disciplining children is that it be done with love for the benefit of the child. The Bible makes it clear that discipline should never be administered in anger. Perhaps the worst sin a parent can commit in disciplining a child, is to put it off until the parent becomes so mad that they strike the child in anger. Many Scriptures emphasize this.

My first wife and I disciplined our two sons by spanking them, and they turned out to be men that we were and are proud of. My sons are 70 and

66 years old, and I and my new wife have a great relationship with them and their wives.

Here are some Scriptures from the New Testament that show Jesus' attitude toward children:

Matthew 18:1-5— ¹At that time the disciples came to Jesus, saying, "Who then is greatest in the kingdom of heaven?" ² Then Jesus called a little child to Him, set him in the midst of them, ³ and said, "Assuredly, I say to you, unless you are converted and become as little children, you will by no means enter the kingdom of heaven. ⁴ Therefore whoever humbles himself as this little child is the greatest in the kingdom of heaven. ⁵ Whoever receives one little child like this in My name receives Me.

Matthew 19:13-15— ¹³Then little children were brought to Him that He might put His hands on them and pray, but the disciples rebuked them. ¹⁴ But Jesus said, "Let the little children come to Me, and do not forbid them; for of such is the kingdom of heaven." ¹⁵ And He laid His hands on them and departed from there.

Paul, in Ephesians 6:1-4 and Colossians 3:21-22 admonished children to obey their parents. This is repeated several times throughout the epistles: **Ephesians 6:1-4—** ¹Children, obey your parents in the Lord, for this is right. ² "Honor your father and mother," which is the first commandment with promise: ³ "that it may be well with you and you may live long on the earth."⁴ And you, fathers, do not provoke your children to wrath, but bring them up in the training and admonition of the Lord.

In 1 Timothy, when the Apostle, Paul was giving instructions to his young assistant, Timothy, concerning the selection of church leadership, he obviously rated a man's success in raising his children as an important qualification. **1 Timothy 3:1-5—** ¹This *is* a faithful saying: If a man desires the position of a bishop, he desires a good work. ² A bishop then must be blameless, the husband of one wife, temperate, sober-minded, of good behavior, hospitable, able to teach; [3] not given to wine, not violent, not greedy for money, but gentle, not quarrelsome, not covetous; [4] one who rules his own house well, having his children in submission with all reverence [5] (for if a man does not know how to rule his own house, how will he take care of the church of God?);

Paul repeated these instructions for the different church leaders in chapter 5 of 1 Timothy, as well as in Chapters 1 and 2 of his letter to Titus, another one of his leaders.

My oldest son recently celebrated his 70th birthday (January 20, 2022). That really made me feel like an old man. As you would imagine, it made me think back on his life, with many pleasant memories. I remembered a shocking experience I had in the fall before his 8th birthday (1959). I was a District Scout Executive in Athens Georgia. I had learned to use a very successful method of organizing new Cub Scout Packs and taught it to my district volunteers. With the school's permission, I would print up invitations to all the boys 8-10 years old to attend a meeting on a certain night with their parents, learn how to become a Cub Scout, and organize a Cub Scout Pack. At those meetings, I would show a filmstrip with a recording that explained the program and how to organize a Cub Scout Pack. After the film strip program, I would help the families organize themselves into neighborhood groups for the Cub Scout Dens, and then select the leadership for the Dens and the Pack, if we were able to move that far that night. On a good night, I would leave the meeting with a pack charter application filled out with all the leadership positions filled. Whether or not we succeeded in moving that far that night, a new Cub Scout Pack usually was born from those meetings. I might be the only leader there, and school personnel were usually absent unless they had a son within that age group. That sounds like an invitation for total chaos, and today I would believe it would be. Back then it had been working very well; up until that night. On that night, and nearly every time after that, it was bedlam. Kids running all over the place crawling over seats, kids and parents yelling across the room at each other, with the kids completely out of control.

When I returned home that night, totally frustrated and exhausted, I told my late wife to mark that date as the date that discipline in the home had broken down. From that date forward, I basically experienced the same type of breakdown of parental discipline. We moved from Athens, Georgia to Orangeburg, South Carolina a couple of years after that and found the same situation. In discussing the problem with other professional Leaders, I found that their experiences had been similar.

My wife and I have observed that many children grow up today with very few if any, boundaries. We consider establishing boundaries one of the most important responsibilities of parents. Between us, we have 5 grandchildren and 7 great-grandchildren. Frankly, we consider the current time as the toughest time we have witnessed for raising children and do not envy the job our grandchildren are having in accomplishing their tasks. We pray for them often and admire them for the way they are handling their difficult tasks. As if things were not already bad enough, now we have satanically influenced people trying to push "woke" language, CRT theory, homosexual behavior, gender confusion, and false national heritage down everyone's throat. According to what I read in the Bible, all that stuff is straight from the pits of hell. The church and parents are going to have to do a lot more than they are currently doing if they are going to succeed in stopping this vicious attack. Children's minds are simply not up to the task of mentally processing all that trash without a lot of parental coaching and close investigation. Our government appears to be using the public schools to wrest the children away from the parent's influence.

I heard a smart and influential young man recently make a very revealing statement. He observed that too many parents had quit parenting, and they simply needed to get back to parenting. Selah (go figure). The fact that over half of the households do not have a father present is a very serious problem. All too often, this is caused by people not respecting the sanctity of the marriage bed. Sex is often seen as simply another source of recreation, without accepting the consequences of the outcome.

I believe that at least part of this problem has its roots in World War II. So many fathers went to war, leaving their jobs and families. Mothers had no choice but to go to work to supplement the shortened income, keep the businesses running, and supplying the needs of the war effort. This forced mothers to leave their children home for part of the day, while at the same time there was no father in the household. Others went to work simply to support the war effort. In my opinion, this created the second biggest tragedy of World War II, with the death of hundreds of thousands of our men being killed being the worst tragedy. Two things happened in that situation. First, families adjusted to the children having more unsupervised time, and second, families got accustomed to having two household incomes. The war ending in 1945 did not change those two situations very much. Mom didn't take a job until I was in high school, and Mom's younger sister was living with us. My first wife did not take a job until our boys were in junior high and high school, and then she worked part-time so that she was home before the boys came home from school. The second tragic outcome of the war was that families become accustomed to mothers working and raising the family's standard of living. Mothers very seldom worked before the war, and a fatherless home was a rare and unusual home. Without consciously intending to do it, families started placing more importance on the family standard of living than maintaining a Christian home and raising children to grow up with Christian values. Thus, the general strength of the family and the church has been in decline ever since. The sooner Christians come to understand this and commit to changing the situation, the sooner we can get our once-Christian nation back to the stability we once had. Stable homes create a stable nation.

Sadly, we find ourselves at this time (10/22), in a situation where our national and some state governments are controlled by a group of people who are evidently under satanic influence and doing everything they possibly can to destroy the institution of family, which in turn would destroy the nation. People, we are in one horrible mess of our own making because of our complacency. If we don't quit ignoring the situation and act quickly, we are doomed by our inaction.

CHAPTER 23

God's Attitude Towards Our Handling Money

It should not be necessary to bring this up after what has already been said, but I decided to add this chapter in case some needed it. The "tithe", or tenth, is established in the Old Testament as the standard for returning to God what He has blessed you with. When we consider all God and His Son, Jesus, have done for us and everything we have is from Them, that is a very small price to pay. Oddly, in the New Testament, no specific amount is given. We will show some Scriptures that give some suggestions, but I believe this one covers the subject pretty well:

Matthew 26:36-40. [6] **"Teacher, which *is* the great commandment in the law?"**

[37] Jesus said to him, "'You shall love the LORD **your God with all your heart, with all your soul, and with all your mind.' [38] This is *the* first and great commandment. [39] And *the* second *is* like it: 'You shall love your neighbor as yourself.' [40] On these two commandments hang all the Law and the Prophets."**

It seems to me that if we really loved God with all our heart, soul, and mind and loved our neighbor as ourselves, we would naturally give at least a tithe of our income to God and those who needed help. Thankfully, before I married and left my parent's home, I realized the importance God places on giving, and started tithing. That made it easier to tithe when I Got Married. I must confess that there were times in my married life that I did not tithe, but when that happened, I was uncomfortable until I got back into the habit of it.

Although the New Testament doesn't say specifically that we should give a tithe, it does offer many suggestions. Here are a few:

Luke 22:38. Give, and it will be given to you: good measure, pressed down, shaken together, and running over will be put into your bosom. For with the same measure that you use, it will be measured back to you.".

Luke 18:18-25. [18] Now a certain ruler asked Him, saying, "Good Teacher, what shall I do to inherit eternal life?"

[19] So Jesus said to him, "Why do you call Me good? No one *is* good but One, *that is,* God. [20] You know the commandments: 'Do not commit adultery,' 'Do not murder,' 'Do not steal,' 'Do not bear false witness,' 'Honor your father and your mother.'"

[21] And he said, "All these things I have kept from my youth."

[22] So when Jesus heard these things, He said to him, "You still lack one thing. Sell all that you have and distribute to the poor, and you will have treasure in heaven; and come, follow Me."

[23] But when he heard this, he became very sorrowful, for he was very rich.

[24] And when Jesus saw that he became very sorrowful, He said, "How hard it is for those who have riches to enter the kingdom of God! [25] For it is easier for a camel to go through the eye of a needle than for a rich man to enter the kingdom of God."

Now, before you think Jesus was harsh and cruel to this man, go back and read **Matthew 26:36-40,** above. Jesus recognized that the man was selfish or greedy, did acknowledge Him as Lord, but he did not want to do what Jesus had just told him to do.

2 Corinthians 9:6-15. [6] But this *I say:* He who sows sparingly will also reap sparingly, and he who sows bountifully will also reap bountifully. [7] *So let* each one *give* as he purposes in his heart, not grudgingly or of necessity; for God loves a cheerful giver. [8] And God *is* able to make all grace abound toward you, that you, always having all sufficiency in all *things,* may have an abundance for every good work. [9] As it is written: "He has dispersed abroad, He has given to the poor;

His righteousness endures forever." [10] Now may He who supplies seed to the sower, and bread for food, supply and multiply the seed you have *sown* and increase the fruits of your righteousness, [11] while *you are* enriched in everything for all liberality, which causes thanksgiving through us to God. [12] For the administration of this service not only supplies the needs of the saints, but also is abounding through many thanksgivings to God, [13] while, through the proof of this ministry, they glorify God for the obedience of your confession to the gospel of Christ, and for *your* liberal sharing with them and all *men,* [14] and by their prayer for you, who long for you because of the exceeding grace of God in you. [15] Thanks *be* to God for His indescribable gift!

James 2:14-17.. [4] What *does it* profit, my brethren, if someone says he has faith but does not have works? Can faith save him? [15] If a brother or sister is naked and destitute of daily food, [16] and one of you says to them, "Depart in peace, be warmed and filled," but you do not give them the things which are needed for the body, what *does it* profit? [17] Thus also faith by itself, if it does not have works, is dead. [18] But someone will say, "You have faith, and I have works." Show me your faith without your works, and I will show you my faith by my works.

Philippians 4:10-19.. [10] But I rejoiced in the Lord greatly that now at last your care for me has flourished again; though you surely did care, but you lacked opportunity. [11] Not that I speak in regard to need, for I have learned in whatever state I am, to be content: [12] I know how to be abased, and I know how to abound. Everywhere and in all things I have learned both to be full and to be hungry, both to abound and to suffer need. [13] I can do all things through Christ who strengthens me.

[14] Nevertheless you have done well that you shared in my distress. [15] Now you Philippians know also that in the beginning of the gospel, when I departed from Macedonia, no church shared with me concerning giving and receiving but you only. [16] For even in Thessalonica you sent *aid* once and again for my necessities. [17] Not that I seek the gift, but I seek the fruit that abounds to your account. [18] Indeed I have all and abound. I am full, having received from Epaphroditus the things *sent* from you, a sweet-smelling aroma, an acceptable sacrifice, well pleasing to God. [19] And my God shall supply all your need according to His riches in glory by Christ Jesus.

Verse 19 above is often quoted alone. The Bible does not teach that that verse stands alone. It is very clear to me that verse 19 is a response to verses 10-18.

CHAPTER 24

And The Glory Which You Have Given Me, I Have Given Them, That They May Be One, Just As We Are One... John 17:22

Fifteen or twenty years ago, I was studying the book of John, and when I got to John 17:20-23, I got stuck. I have been stuck there ever since and I am not making any effort to get unstuck. I don't want to. Oh, I study other Scriptures, but I keep coming back to John chapters 13-17. I know I have read them over a hundred times, and probably much more. They still feed me. Look with me at 17:20-23, meditate on it, and see how important it can be to you.

John 17:20-23- [20] "I do not pray for these alone, but also for those who will believe in Me through their word; [21] that they all may be one, as You, Father, are in Me, and I in You; that they also may be one in Us, that the world may believe that You sent Me. [22] And the glory which You gave Me I have given them, that they may be one just as We are one: [23] I in them, and You in Me; that they may be made perfect in one, and that the world may know that You have sent Me, and have loved them as You have loved Me.-

Do you see how important those verses can be to you? Can you feel the impact of what your Lord and Savior asked Father God to make available to you and me? Do you remember how many times Jesus said: "I only say what My Father tells me to say"?

As you read this chapter, go back and restudy chapter 12, The Kingdom of God, and see how the two chapters work together to create a picture of provision for a life worth living while walking this earth. Review the book of Acts and the epistles to see how those early disciples (learners, students, followers, apprentices of Jesus) functioned in The Kingdom of God. Every provision that Jesus provided for them; He has provided for you. There is nothing those disciples did that you are not capable of if you only take advantage of all that Jesus provided for you. The more I study the Bible and meditate on these things, the more I am convinced that today's disciples of Jesus have the power and ability available to them to do everything we see the disciples doing in the book of Acts and the epistles. Tie these two chapters together and spend hours studying them and the Bible, to see how to walk in The Kingdom of God and have the same close relationship Jesus experienced with Father God that they had. Selah. (Go figure.)

For the fifteen or twenty years since Holy Spirit opened my spiritual eyes to this Scripture, this Scripture has been the object of my quest. In Chapter 14, of this book, Praying for a Miracle, I related an experience I had recently, in which Holy Spirit told me several prayers I had made a couple years previous were now beginning to be answered and gave me a sign. I looked down at my feet, and my right foot that had been deformed for 6-8 years, was instantly straightened. Well, I didn't tell you everything that happened that morning. Holy Spirit also told me that I had reached my quest, the gradual fulfillment of the above Scripture. He explained that I had made a breakthrough, and complete fulfillment would start materializing immediately, which it has. I can't express the joy I am experiencing as that comes to pass. I am spending a lot of time thanking God for such a fantastic gift.

To really understand fully the above Scripture, it will be very helpful to spend a lot of time in Chapters 13-17 of John. Remember that John had a very close relationship with Jesus, and he is the only gospel writer who records the important events of that night prior to Jesus' arrest in the Garden of Gethsemane. Peter and Matthew were also there, but for whatever reason they do not mention it. It is obvious Jesus stayed up all night, but the disciples evidently sneaked in a few catnaps. The setting starts in the upper room with the feast of Passover and the introducing the sacrament of The Lords Supper or Communion but follows Jesus and the disciples as they leave there, go down into the Kidron valley, across the Brook Kidron, up to the Mount of Olives, and into the Garden of Gethsemane. It was such a thrill for me to go there in 1998 and walk part of that route.

One of the most important aspects of these 5 chapters, is that this is the only place in the gospels that we have instructions on experiencing the indwelling Holy Spirit. Paul and Peter speak of some aspects of that experience in their epistles, but here in these 5 chapters we have more direct instructions. This is all the information the disciples would have prior to Pentecost, which would come 50 days later.

In John Chapter 13, Jesus introduced the sacrament of foot washing. If you have never experienced that, I suggest you consider it. We find that in **John 13:2-5 & 12-17— ² And supper being ended, the devil having already put it into the heart of Judas Iscariot, Simon's son, to betray Him, ³ Jesus, knowing that the Father had given all things into His hands, and that He had come from God and was going to God, ⁴ rose from supper and laid aside His garments, took a towel and girded Himself. ⁵ After that, He poured water into a basin and began to wash the disciples' feet, and to wipe them with the towel with which He was girded.**

¹² So when He had washed their feet, taken His garments, and sat down again, He said to them, "Do you know what I have done to you? ¹³ You call Me Teacher and Lord, and you say well, for so

I am. ¹⁴ If I then, your Lord and Teacher, have washed your feet, you also ought to wash one another's feet. ¹⁵ For I have given you an example, that you should do as I have done to you. ¹⁶ Most assuredly, I say to you, a servant is not greater than his master; nor is he who is sent greater than he who sent him. ¹⁷ If you know these things, blessed are you if you do them.

Thus, Jesus demonstrated the role He had lived, and the role He expected His disciples to live. In verses 34 & 35 He issues a new commandment as a follow-up to the foot washing:

John 13:34-35—³⁴ A new commandment I give to you, that you love one another; as I have loved you, that you also love one another. ³⁵ By this all will know that you are My disciples, if you have love for one another."

In 14:9-11, Jesus made clear to His disciples the completeness of His relationship to His Father. **John 14:9-11-** ⁹ Jesus said to him, "Have I been with you so long, and yet you have not known Me, Philip? He who has seen Me has seen the Father; so how can you say, 'Show us the Father'? ¹⁰ Do you not believe that I am in the Father, and the Father in Me? The words that I speak to you I do not speak on My own *authority;* but the Father who dwells in Me does the works. ¹¹ Believe Me that I am in the Father and the Father in Me, or else believe Me for the sake of the works themselves.-

In 14:12-14, Jesus introduced a new way to pray. **John 14:12-14-** ¹² "Most assuredly, I say to you, he who believes in Me, the works that I do he will do also; and greater *works* than these he will do, because I go to My Father. ¹³ And whatever you ask in My name, that I will do, that the Father may be glorified in the Son. ¹⁴ If you ask anything in My name, I will do *it.*-

Jesus introduces the Holy Spirit to His disciples in the remainder of chapter 14. **John 14:15-24—** ¹⁵ **"If you love Me, keep My** commandments. [16] And I will pray the Father, and He will give you another Helper, that He may abide with you forever— [17] the Spirit of truth, whom the world cannot receive, because it neither sees Him nor knows Him; but you know Him, for He dwells with you and will be in you. [18] I will not leave you orphans; I will come to you. [19] "A little while longer and the world will see Me no more, but you will see Me. Because I live, you will live also. [20] At that day you will know that I am in My Father, and you in Me, and I in you. [21] He who has My commandments and keeps them, it is he who loves Me. And he who loves Me will be loved by My Father, and I will love him and manifest Myself to him." [22] Judas (not Iscariot) said to Him, "Lord, how is it that You will manifest Yourself to us, and not to the world?" [23] Jesus answered and said to him, "If anyone loves Me, he will keep My word; and My Father will love him, and We will come to him and make Our home with him. [24] He who does not love Me does not keep My words; and the word which you hear is not Mine but the Father's who sent Me.

Chapter 15 begins by Jesus telling His disciples the importance of staying connected to Him. **John 15:1-11—** [1]"I am the true vine, and My Father is the vinedresser. [2] Every branch in Me that does not bear fruit He takes away; and every branch that bears fruit He prunes, that it may bear more fruit. [3] You are already clean because of the word which I have spoken to you. [4] Abide in Me, and I in you. As the branch cannot bear fruit of itself, unless it abides in the vine, neither can you, unless you abide in Me.

[5] "I am the vine, you *are* the branches. He who abides in Me, and I in him, bears much fruit; for without Me you can do nothing. [6] If anyone does not abide in Me, he is cast out as a branch and is withered; and they gather them and throw them into the fire, and they are burned. [7] If you abide in Me, and My words abide in you, you will ask what you desire, and it shall be done for you. [8] By this My Father is glorified, that you bear much fruit; so you will be My disciples.

⁹ "As the Father loved Me, I also have loved you; abide in My love. ¹⁰ If you keep My commandments, you will abide in My love, just as I have kept My Father's commandments and abide in His love. ¹¹ "These things I have spoken to you, that My joy may remain in you, and that your joy may be full.

In 16:7 Jesus dropped a bombshell that I imagine absolutely blew the disciples' minds. **John 16:7—** ⁷ **Nevertheless I tell you the truth. It is to your advantage that I go away; for if I do not go away, the Helper will not come to you; but if I depart, I will send Him to you.**

Your imagination can go wild, thinking about what went through the individual disciple's minds. They have been following Jesus for over three years, completely devoted and dependent on Him, and while they are trying to process the fact that He is about to leave them, He tells them they will be better off.

But forget about the disciples for a moment and think about what that means to you. How often have you thought, "Oh, I would love to have been around when Jesus walked the earth and could have spent time with Him". Well, according to this verse you can have something better. You can have Him living within you all the time. It is more than worth all the Bible study I have done to get to this point. Please don't think it is going to take you 65 years to get there. I assure you that millions have gotten there much faster. God has a reason for dealing with every one of us individually, and that just happens to be the route He chose for me. I have never been accused of being the sharpest knife in the rack, but I have been accused of being determined, so those factors figure into the equation. The bottom line in my opinion is, regardless of how hard or how long the quest turns out to be, the return is much greater.

There is so much meat that can be gathered out of these five chapters of the Bible. If you have never investigated them, I urge you to do so, because it can prove to be one of the biggest blessings to you that you can imagine.

Notice how many times in these chapters that Jesus stated in different ways, "If you love Me, you will keep My commandments". Notice that that was connected to the promise of the Holy Spirit several times. Connect this with what I wrote in chapter 11 on holiness. I believe a point Jesus was trying to get across in these chapters is, that your holiness results from your love of God, not trying to buy a ticket to go to heaven and miss hell. We seldom hear from the pulpit about holiness being a result of our depth of love of God. Perhaps that helps to account for the weak condition of the church in America today. Love of God is obviously the key to life in The Kingdom of God. I'm personally convinced that a serious study of the Bible as opposed to listening to someone else, is the best way to understand God to the point that you love Him as much as He deserves. It is most important that you love Him so much that He rewards you with a closer relationship with Him through His constant indwelling Holy Spirit.

I thank God that I discovered the importance of studying the Bible with the help of Holy Spirit 65 years ago. Nothing else has changed my life for the better more than that one event. Every other blessing that I have received since then came because of that one event. I feel sorry for the people who have not yet made that discovery, and I pray that this book will convince many of those individuals of how to receive what they have missed up to this time. Our time on this earth is limited, and in the scope of eternity, it is a very short time. Use wisely what time you have left.

I would like to pray for you now:

Most gracious Heavenly Father, I come to You in the wonderful name of your son, Jesus the Messiah, asking you to bless this reader of this book with a renewed love and understanding of You, Your Son, Jesus, Your Holy Spirit, Your Word, the Bible and Your Rhema Word, and that You speak to each one of us more than we have ever experienced. I ask you to fill us to overflowing with Your Holy Spirit, to the extent that our life is changed forever with a new relationship with you. Give each of us a richer experience in Your Kingdom of God than we ever thought possible. I thank You and praise You. Amen

CHAPTER 25

Why I Believe The Bible Is True

Short answer: God has proven to me that His word, the Bible, is true many times. I have studied the Bible for 65 years, studied Bible history and church history, and have become convinced that although the Bible was written by many different authors over a long period of time, it has become obvious to me that every one of those writers were inspired by God's Holy Spirit to write exactly what they wrote. The many wonders of the natural environment prove to me that only a loving God could put all of that together and make it work and continue to reproduce itself.

I have listed many miracles in this book that I have experienced and witnessed. About seven years ago when I was shopping for new shoes, the saleslady was having difficulty satisfying me, and asked me to walk on their recording treadmill. When she reviewed the recording, she showed me how my right foot was turned outward slightly when I walked. A few months after that, I discovered that every morning when I was getting dressed, I had less control of my feet and legs than I had had the day before. That was very scary, and I had no idea what was going on in my body. I explained to my wife, Patricia what was going on. I told her we needed to pray about the condition because I felt like I could wind up in a wheelchair in a couple of weeks because of the rapid deterioration of my ability to stand and walk. We prayed, and that halted the progress of the infirmity. My brother, who had suffered from similar problems for years, called me to say that he finally found out what had been causing similar problems in him for years. He discovered he had Charcot-Marie-Tooth Disease. CMT, as it is referred to, is a neurological disease that is rare, hereditary, and incurable. Basically, it damages the peripheral nerves or nerve sleeves. When the command nerves cease to command muscles to function, the muscles atrophy. When the sensory nerves cease to function, you lose feeling and control in the affected body part. My right foot has been affected worse than any other appendage, although the left foot and both hands have suffered some damage also. My right foot had turned out, and for years has been turned out 30-45 degrees. I could not lift the front of my right foot properly when I walked, and that caused me to stumble frequently.

I explain all this so that you can grasp at least some of the joy I felt recently that I alluded to earlier. I mentioned this story earlier, but it does bare repeating. As I was praying one morning recently, Holy Spirit told me that prayer requests I had made 3 years ago, regarding several serious physical problems plaguing my wife and me, were beginning to be answered. Then He said, "I am giving you a sign to confirm that what I say today is true." I looked down, and to my amazement, my right foot was completely straight! The "foot drop" is still bad, so I am exercising those muscles in my feet daily to build them up. Another serious physical problem that I prayed about 3 years ago was regarding my digestion and elimination. I suffered from gastric reflux, loose bowels, and diarrhea. That was the main reason we had to stop going to Haiti and Dominican Republic to teach at the pastors' conferences. Holy Spirit told me one day to stop drinking that glass of red wine every evening, which I had done for years for health reasons. So, I stopped drinking wine, that stopped the acid reflux. All the other digestive and elimination problems were all clearing up in the meantime. I apologize if these personal experiences I relate to you offend you, and they are hard for me to relate. I relate them because they were such big, life-changing miracles that I received. They show God's love for us, and His power that works in us who believe.

Ephesians 3:20-21 ²⁰Now to Him who is able to do exceedingly abundantly above all that we ask or think, according to the power that works in us, ²¹ to Him *be* glory in the church by Christ Jesus to all generations, forever and ever. Amen.

Because our lifestyle has become more sedentary recently, I have started doing some exercises that are waking up these slack muscles and making me more flexible. I feel much better and less stiff after only a few days of this. Walking has been awkward for quite some time, but I am believing that my prayer for it to again become one of my big pleasures in life. There are still several prayers for healing of our bodies that have not been answered yet, but I know they soon will be, because of the word Holy Spirit gave me and the miracle of my right foot being straightened instantly.

As many times as God has miraculously healed me, and healed others through me, how could I not believe the Bible? But a more precious blessing than all those miracles I have mentioned in this book and many more that I have not mentioned, is the almost constant fellowship I have with God through His Holy Spirit. In **John 17:20-23**, which was the subject of the preceding chapter, Jesus made that available to all His followers who sought it. I would be an ungrateful, blind idiot if I did not believe the Bible after what God has done for me! I still do not understand all the Bible, but the more I study, the more of it I understand. God has shown His love for me in so many ways and my daily Bible study reveals more of His love for each of us, that my love and respect for Him and our personal relationship is growing daily.

CHAPTER 26

In Conclusion

As I begin this final chapter of this book, it is July 4, 2022. I would like to give you my opinion of what is happening. At this time our country is in the worst predicament that I have seen it in in my 91 years. It is worse than the great depression, World War II, and the Viet Nam War. I say this because the country is so divided with threats of violence, with a national government that has proven it is determined to destroy our democratic form of government and make it a part of a global socialistic government. My guess is that it can better be compared to the shape we were in just before the Civil War. I can't say for sure, because that happened a few years before I arrived on the planet. We are saddled with a government that has come into power under questionable circumstances, that managed to sweep all evidence of fraudulent election activity under the table, passed laws and regulations that are not allowed under our constitution, and use government entities to attack the people opposing their unlawfulness. The Department of Justice refuses to stop the invasion of millions of immigrants (including terrorists, murders, drug traffickers, and human traffickers), or stop the unlawful attacks on our Supreme Court Justices, Pregnancy Centers, and churches.

In case you question anything I just said, let me give you a wake-up call. On July 1, CBN shared a quote made by the president's economic advisor, Brien Deese. He answered a CNN anchors' question about the escalating high price of gasoline by saying, "This is about the Liberal World Order, and we have to stand firm. But at the same time, what I'd say to that family and to Americans across the country is, you have a president in the Administration that is going to do everything in his power to blunt those price increases and bring those prices down." (https://www1.cbn.com/cbnnews/politics/2022/july/critics-scald-biden-admin-for-saying-high-gas-prices-are-about-the-liberal-world-order) Really? The president who created this high rate of inflation, partially by slowing domestic petroleum production and Canadian imports, making us once again dependent on our enemies for petroleum, is doing everything he can to bring prices down? Like Adolph Hitler's propaganda czar, Goebbels said, "If you tell a lie big enough and keep repeating it, people will eventually come to believe it." (https://www.inspiringquotes.us/quotes/TzEs_7CxEctuv) They obviously think we are blubbering idiots to believe those obvious lies. But they have already proven that they will continue repeating those lies with the expectation that some people will believe them.

Several conservative media outlets report daily on the methods being used to change our country. CRT, racism, the free flowing of drugs into the country, and gender confusion, are all being used to destroy the sanity of our children and young people, including our military. They have destroyed our security by cutting back on the use of fossil fuels without having supplies of alternate fuels up and running. They have weakened our military by cramming "woke" principals down their throat to destroy their manhood and womanhood, to the point that manly men and real women want no part of it. They have abandoned the law enforcement personnel and supported the criminals so that good, capable men and women no longer want the unthankful jobs. I am curious to see how long this is going to go on before we put a stop to it. We have a proven ample supply of very clean burning natural gas that could be utilized to take up the slack, and that valuable resource is being grossly under-used. Even though gasoline and diesel fuel shortage are what drove the high prices up, this administration is emptying our precious reserves to send ship loads of it to China, our most threatening adversary. Of course, if you only watch the liberal media (ABC, NBC, CBS, CNN, NPR, and

NYT), you do not hear about the things I have mentioned here. You will have to check out conservative news outlets to hear about these atrocities. It is said "ignorance is bliss," and I guess too many people are like many church members: If they are hearing what they want to hear, they listen to them only. We addressed this subject in a previous chapter. Why should we tolerate people in our midst who are advocating the destruction of our country? Why do we not move them to Cuba, Venezuela, or China if that is what they want? I was recently saddened by the video of a 100 plus year-old World War II decorated veteran breaking down when he considered the condition of our country today that he and his comrades fought, bled, and died for so long ago. FOR WHAT? Russia and China, who obviously would like to destroy America as we know it, are obviously clapping their hands and jumping up and down with glee as they watch us destroy ourselves from within without them having to fire a shot.

Christians must pray for those individuals in position of authority to move swiftly to stop this madness before it is too late. We are admonished to do this in **1 Timothy 2:1-4—**

Therefore I exhort first of all that supplications, prayers, intercessions, *and* giving of thanks be made for all men, ² for kings and all who are in authority, that we may lead a quiet and peaceable life in all godliness and reverence. ³ For this *is* good and acceptable in the sight of God our Savior, ⁴ who desires all men to be saved and to come to the knowledge of the truth.

The bright spot in the picture is that these deceived people are getting so self-confident that they are getting more and more careless about covering up their evil actions. That gives me hope that they will get careless enough to create an opportunity for someone to figure out how to charge them with treason and lock them up.

It is not hard to figure out exactly who is behind this sinister movement, although many players are obvious. If you "follow the money", it usually goes back to China. Satan is the obvious author of the plan. It is obvious that it has been in the works for many years, working through our university system and federal government undercover, and only recently busted out into the open. There are many new books out by people in positions to see the sinister workings of the movement and identify the main perpetuators. One thing is clear, and that is that they have been working through our education system, including most major universities for many years.

August 24, 2022 reality check: We have seen one effort after another by different entities to remove all responsibility and control of our children away from the parents and into the hands of the government. Now we are seeing our administration trying to push a bill through congress that adds on to the previous bill known as 'Title 9" provisions that would strip parents of any right to protect their own children from gender confusion teachings. Hopefully, we are successfully thwarting that effort. There is much more going on than what I have mentioned that is general knowledge, not to mention devious plots that are not yet general knowledge. Due to the fact the acknowledged destroyers of our country have most of the news media parroting their lies and propaganda, our beloved country is on the verge of being destroyed if righteous men and women do not rise up and stop it.

Having said all of that to express the sadness of the situation we are caught up in, I will turn to what we can do to get ourselves out of this mess. I would think that the first thing that a Christian would think about is prayer. Let's think about that for a minute. How many prayers have you made this year that you did not get answered? Have you gone back to your Bible and tried to figure out why your prayer was not answered? I have found that if I really want to get my prayer answered, I best use a sniper rifle rather than a shotgun approach. By sniper rifle approach I mean choose my weapon carefully, one with a good telescopic sight that can put a single bullet right where I need it to go, rather than a shot gun that sprays a bunch of pellets in a general direction, one of which may hopefully hit the target, and may accomplish the desired objective. I go to my Bible and find Scripture that promises a solution to the problem, whatever it is. I am already convinced that the Bible is God's Word, and God cannot lie. That is the sniper rifle approach. I get much better results with the sniper rifle approach. Before I pray, I study the Scripture to find Biblical reasons for my prayer to be answered, and then act on that. The Old Testament is loaded with instances of the Israelites finding themselves in deep trouble like we are in now and praying for and receiving deliverance. Studying those accounts may give us some direction on how to pray. The best suggestion I can give you about receiving answers to your prayers, is to pray according to the Bible and believe, really believe, what the Bible says. I certainly do not profess to be an expert on getting my prayers answered, but I do have a decent track record. We need to buckle down and get "survival mode" serious about how to pray for the critical situation our nation as we know it is in currently, pray with faith and expect positive answers. Look to the Old Testament, the history of our nation in 1775 and 1812 and years following, as well as the history of the new nation of Israel in 1948 and years following. I am convinced it is going to take that kind of miraculous intervention of God to get us through this desperate situation. We also need to be alert for opportunities to speak up and do whatever we have opportunity to do to reverse the madness of these satanic influenced individuals who are doing everything within their power to destroy the United States of America.

One action that I haven't addressed, that is important to speak up about, and that is our responsibility as followers of Jesus to be "light to the world" and "salt of the earth". Jesus had a lot to say about that as our individual responsibility. I will confess that in the current atmosphere I have tended to "lay low" on my Christian principles. I don't talk about it with strangers, for fear of starting an argument. Nowadays it is not difficult to do that. I have been recently convicted of trying to avoid a confrontation at the expense of neglecting my responsibility. I have put more emphasis on being a peacemaker than being a light to the world. I confess my sin and repent of it. I might get a negative response sometimes, but I would not be guilty of failing to fulfill my main responsibility as a disciple of Jesus Christ. So, as I endeavor to be more obedient to God's word, I will be more alert to discuss my convictions with strangers. Hey, if I start an argument, at least I gave that person something to consider. I have not been accused of being the most diplomatic disciple around (as if you have not figured that out by now), but that is no excuse for not trying harder. Jesus willingly tolerated having some of the people He bled and died for to mock Him, deride Him, insult Him, and to beat Him unmercifully. Why should I be so reluctant to be offended for speaking up for Him? I am going to make a concerted effort to do better in this responsibility and encourage you to do likewise. After all Jesus did for us, why should His followers be reluctant to take a chance on being offended by a negative response to our sharing our faith with someone who might not agree with us?

When you study the history of the founding of this once great country and the 1948 re-establishing of the country of Israel, you would naturally figure out that no reasonable person could possibly expect them to win their independence without a lot of miraculous help from all mighty God. The bottom line is enough righteous individuals prayed with enough faith that God wrought miracle after miracle to make victory happen. Friends, we are in such a time as that. Are we going to rise to the challenge, or do nothing and watch the great USA be destroyed?

We need to do a better job of controlling our emotions, which is one of the characteristics of "The Fruit of the Spirit". Pure hate is obviously driving much of the behavior of many in our country today. That should be the subject of prayer for the concerned Christian. As we state our convictions, we need Holy Spirit guidance to do so with humility yet be factual and truthful.

I believe that the weak condition of the church in America today is because church as we know it and participate in, for the most part, holds no resemblance to the New Testament Church. Far too many Christians pray with shallow hope instead of Bible educated confident faith. How many of the last several church services you attended had definite evidence of the power of the Holy Spirit? The main difference is that the power and miracles of the Holy Spirit recorded in the New Testament are non-existent in many churches today, and most churches don't even expect them to occur. Many churches don't even think it is possible for God to perform miracles through the Holy Spirit today, even though evidence abounds that He does. The fact is that most church members today have not seen a miracle that they recognized, and so assume that that they do not occur today. At least that has been my observation in the many different churches I have attended and been active in. If no one expects a manifestation of the power and exercise of the Holy Spirit, there is little reason for the Holy Spirit to show up. Evidently, that is starting to change. Many Christians have been praying for the biggest outpouring of the Holy Spirit since the great outpouring on the original disciples on Pentecost, and there is evidence it has started. There are scattered churches and ministries today witnessing miracles on a regular basis, while others are seeing them occasionally. It is a very encouraging sign, indeed. LORD, BRING IT ON! If ever there was a time for Christians everywhere to begin to seriously pray for a great outpouring of the Holy Spirit all over the world, it is now. I am asking you, what are you going to do about it? Please understand this: If your reading of this book doesn't cause you to take action to try to save our nation as we know it, I have wasted my time writing it and you have wasted your time reading it! I pray that it will move every reader to wake up and do everything within his or her power to save our once great nation.

I will finish by bringing you up to date on my personal journey, because I have shared so much of it with you up to this point. I was recently diagnosed with a seriously irregular heartbeat and scheduled to receive a pacemaker. I had prayed about this condition without seeing any results, so I reluctantly submitted to having the pacemaker installed July 18. It made about a 50% difference initially but seems to have lost some of that progress. I am not happy with the situation, so am simply depending on God to fix it. I have not previously had a heart problem, up to this point. My preference is for God to heal it. Patricia had an endoscopy to see why she chokes so much. They stretched her esophagus, which has helped but not eliminated the problem. The bottom line is that we are comfortably walking in God's presence, even though we are not really experiencing as much of His miraculous healing power as we expect. I fell off a ladder nearly five years ago and broke my floating rib on my right side. A couple of weeks later, I discovered that it had completely separated about two inches from my spine and has been floating around loose ever since. My uneducated guess is that the little bugger (a 6–10-inch flat, curved bone, pointed on one end and ragged on the other) may be involved in these heart and digestive problems. X-rays have failed to locate the rib. I am also happy to report that God has completely healed me of an allergy to corn, and walking is feeling a little more natural. Since the original diagnosis of the Charcot-Marie-Tooth disease 8 years ago, walking has been awkward and clumsy. My digestion is still improving and is 95% perfect. So, at the ripe old age of 91, I feel that God has blessed me tremendously. I have come to realize that much of our physical problems are caused by demonic activity, basically because we are desperately trying to get this book to the printer and on to distribution. As I come to grips with this factor and spend more effort rebuking demonic forces than praying for healing, I am getting more positive results. In the last month, before I received the pacemaker, it seemed that I was getting weaker every day. I must admit that I am doing better than most 91-year-old codgers, so for that, I am thankful.

My wife has decided that she is not comfortable with her 91-year-old husband dragging our home up and down the busy highways, so we are in the process of switching to our plan B. We have had this plan ever since we sold our house and "hit the road" in an RV. We have been living in an RV now for about 8 years and are beginning to feel we would like a little more living space and establish a more permanent address than we have been living with. We are also feeling the need to settle down and be used more by God in serving Him and our church community. We anticipated eventually reaching that point, and that point has arrived. We are searching for something within our limited budget in a rural setting near the Raleigh, NC area. When I say limited budget, I mean very limited budget. We have a small amount of cash on hand and depend entirely on our two Social Security accounts and a small equity account for our day-to-day expenses. That leaves us with very limited options. I had originally considered that we would simply find us a suitable lot and park our RV on it, and we would be fine. We ran into two problems with that: We were burnt out with living in the limited space of an RV; and we could not find a lot that we could get approved for an RV as the permanent residence. We decided on the area we would like to settle down in, and God miraculously provided us with a Christian realtor who is just as dedicated as we are to finding the exact place God has already selected for us.

Our "angel realtor" as Patricia refers to him as, showed us a property over a month ago that we immediately fell in love with, and I picked out the spot where I said, "this is where I will put my house". The property was further from our church than we wanted to be, but otherwise it felt ideal. We quickly realized that the price of the property was pushing the limits of our total budget for the property and the house, and there was no house on the property. There was on the property several small spring-fed ponds, two wells, and two septic systems that had been used up to about 40 years previous. But the most important feature was that it was sitting on top of a fantastic aquifer that was not very far below the ground and was serving hundreds of homes in the area. The lot is in the Sandhills, (an ancient seashore) region of North Carolina. From East to West the geographic sections of the state are known as "Coastal Plain, Sandhills, Piedmont, and Mountains. I had felt the need to get out of the very metropolitan Piedmont into the Sandhills and further South, to find easier ground to garden and a warmer climate.

After seriously considering the cost, we sadly walked away from the idea of purchasing that property and started looking for houses and lots together that we felt were within our budget. We found several that we thought we could live with, but as we checked them out one by one, we turned them down. Then the whole situation changed! Our realtor was a friend of the owner of the property we had originally fallen in love with. Our realtor felt as we did that that parcel of land that he had originally shown us was what God wanted us to have. He was a good friend of the landowner, who lives in Washington state, and persuaded him to drop the price considerably! New ball game! That price still did not leave us enough in our budget for our house, but we felt God was working in it, so we filed the paperwork and put forth the "due diligence" money to get the process started.

I remember seeing a quotation somewhere that said, "The caterpillar thought his life was over, but he became a beautiful butterfly", or something close to that. When we considered we would slow down and retreat to a quiet place in the country for our twilight years, we found God leading us to start a small Christian community, a place of refuge, rest, and ministry. The project of finding us a place to live has evolved into a place for ministry. We envision starting with our home, which would also be the ministry headquarters, then add cottages around the ponds to house those that were being ministered to, or folks who were dealing with "burnout" to come and spend a few days or weeks in a very relaxing, Christian environment. As we mention this to our Christian friends, we are stirring up a lot of interest and getting much encouragement. God gave a wonderful friend of ours vision and passion for ministry to individuals and families who were in difficult times, and needed community and encouragement. She is working right alongside us and it will be interesting to see what God does with the vision He has given her and how it relates to this property. What started out as a mundane chore of finding a home, God has turned into an exciting adventure to establish a new ministry. And we thought we were winding down.

My fellow minister who helped me with the publishing of my first book, *Attitudes and Mind Sets of Christians who Walk in Peace, Joy, and Victory*, called me recently from the shop of another fellow minister who had printed my first book, desperately pleading for my help. Because I had worked on office equipment for over forty years, they hoped I would be able to fix the bookbinding machine, which had broken down. So, now am I not only considering starting another ministry, but I am also back to working on office machines. The fact that I know nothing about a bookbinder, doesn't seem to matter.

The plan is for this book to be ready for the printer in a few weeks., so you will need to wait for my autobiography, *90+ Years of Walking in God's Love*, to find out "the rest of the story".

As I close, I want to leave you with an important thought. The prophets of the church have been very much in agreement lately in prophesying that we are on the brink of the greatest outpouring of the Holy Spirit since Pentecost, as recorded in chapter 2 of the book of Acts. They are also in agreement that America will be saved. Despite the dismal situation that I see our once great country in currently, I have enough faith in God and His prophets to believe that the prophets are right on. We see signs around us of the great world-wide revival starting. That behooves us to build up our faith in God and His Word and help pray in this great revival and restoration of our great republic. Join us, please!

APPENDIX

Quoted Scripture

PREFACE
  2 Chronicles 7:14

CHAPTER 1
  Matthew 6:19-34

CHAPTER 2
  Matthew 10:28
  Matthew 22:36-40

CHAPTER 3
  2 Corinthians 2:1-7
  Matthew 10:34-39
  Luke 2:14
  John 17:20-23
  Revelation 3:14-16
  1 Corinthians 13
  Matthew 15:14

CHAPTER 4
  1 Corinthians 14:26-33
  1 Corinthians 1:26-31

  I Corinthians 11:17-22
  I Corinthians 12:4-14
  I Corinthians 12: 27-31

CHAPTER 5
  1 John 4:7-8
  Revelation 3:20-22

CHAPTER 6
  Galatians 5:22-25
  Acts 2:46,47
  Acts 5:41,42
  Acts 20:20
  Romans 16:3-5
  I Corinthians 16:19
  Colossians 4:14
  Philemon 1:2

CHAPTER 7
  2 Timothy 3:1-5
  2 Timothy 4:3-4
  John 17:20-23

CHAPTER 8
Acts 2:1-6
Acts 2:14-18
Acts 2:40-42
Acts 3:1-16
Acts 4:1-4
1 Corinthians 2:1-5
Matthew 13:54-58
Mark 8:22-26
2 Chronicles 7:14
Ephesians 1:13-14
1 Corinthians 12:12-31
John 17:20-23

CHAPTER 9
Genesis 1:1-31
Matthew 16:26-27

CHAPTER 10
Luke 4:16-21
Mark 16:15-20
Romans 1:18-2:11
Malachi 3:6
Hebrews 13:8
Matthew 22:34-40
Matthew 23:1-36
John 8:31,32
John 3:1-21
John 7:40-52
John 19:38-42
Hebrews 12:1-11
Revelation 3:19-21
Matthew 10:28
Matthew 10:24-27
Matthew 13:10-17

2 Peter 1:2-4
2 Peter 3:9
Matthew 7:13-14

CHAPTER 11
Acts 26:20b
Matthew 22:14
Genesis 6:5-8
Deuteronomy 6:5-7
Matthew 5:17
Matthew 22:36-40
Matthew 6:48
1 John 1:9-2:3
James 5:12
Matthew 12:34-37
Matthew 15:10,11
Romans 8:5-8
Romans 8:12-16
John 14:15-16
Matthew 7:21-23

CHAPTER 12
Matthew 6:10
Matthew 3:1-2
Luke 17:20-21
Galatians 5:22-25
Ephesians 1:13-14
Mark 1:14
Luke 9:2
Luke 10:9
Luke 24:9
Acts 1:8
Matthew 16:13-20
1 Corinthians 2:1-5

1 Corinthians 2:9
1 Corinthians 2:12-13
1 Corinthians 4:20
Ephesians 1:13,14
Luke 18:16-17
John 3:5
Mark 1:14-15
Matthew 13:44-45
Mark 4:30-32
Luke 17:20-21
Mark 9:1
Luke 24:49
Acts 1:8
Romans 11:29
Luke 9:1-6
Romans 11:29
Matthew 14:25-31
Matthew 16:5-12
Matthew17:14-20
John 20:21-22
Acts 2:1-4
Acts 4:29-31
Luke 17:20-21
Acts 8:4-8
Acts 8:14-17
Acts 10:44-48
Romans 12:1-2
Galatians 5:22-26
Mark 16:14-20
Matthew 11:12
Matthew 11:20-24
John 21:24-25
John 17:20-23

CHAPTER 13
Isaiah 53:1-5
Matthew 8:16-17
1 Peter 2:24
Isaiah 52:13-14
Isaiah 50:4-7
Matthew 26:26-28
Luke 22:19-20
Luke 3:18-19
Mark 11:22-25
Matthew 13:54-58
Mark 8:22-25

CHAPTER 14
1 Corinthians 6:19-20
Isaiah 55:11
Romans 11:29
Romans 8:28
Matthew 7:7-11
Luke 11:13
Luke 8:43-48
Matthew 28:18
John 16:23-24
Mark 16:15-20
Mark 11:23-25
1 John 5:14-15
Matthew 18:19-20
John 10:10
Romans 8:28
Acts 3:1-9
Acts 4:8-10
James 5:14-16
Mark 2:4-5
Mark 2: 9-12
Matthew 26:39

CHAPTER 15
- Luke 13:1-5
- Psalm 115:16
- Romans 8:28
- 2 Corinthians 1:3-4

Chapter 16
- Matthew 11:12
- Mark 16:17-18
- James 4:7-8
- 2 Corinthians 10:3-6
- I John 2:16
- 1 Peter 5:6-9

CHAPTER 17
- Matthew 6:33
- 2 Corinthians 1:8-11

CHAPTER 18
- Ephesians 1:1-14
- 2 Peter 3:9
- John 6:47-65
- Matthew 7:13-14
- Ephesians 1:4
- Ephesians 2:8-10
- Romans 8:28-30
- Romans 9:10-13
- Malachi 1:2-3
- Genesis 25:24-28

CHAPTER 19
- Hebrews 6:1-8
- John 15:4-8
- Hebrews 12:12-17
- James 5:19-20
- 2 Peter 3:14-18

CHAPTER 20
- Genesis 2:24
- Matthew 5:31-32
- 1 John 1:9
- 1 Corinthians 6:15-20

CHAPTER 21
- Genesis 18:16-23, 19:1-13, & 19:23-25
- Romans 1:18-32
- 1 Corinthians 6:9-10

CHAPTER 22
- Proverbs 1:8 & 10
- Proverbs 13:1 & 24
- Proverbs 19:18
- Proverbs 22:6 & 15
- Proverbs 23:13-14 & 24
- Exodus 20:12
- Matthew 18:1-5
- Matthew 19:13-15
- Ephesians 6:1-4
- 1 Timothy 3:1-5

CHAPTER 23
- Matthew 26:36-40
- Luke 22:38
- Luke 18:18-25
- 2 Corinthians 9:6-15
- James 2:14-18
- Philippians 4:10-19

CHAPTER 24
    John 17:20-23
    John 13:2-5 & 12-17
    John 13:34-35
    John 14:9-11
    John 14:12-14
    John 14: 15-24
    John 15:1-11
    John 16:7

CHAPTER 25
    Ephesians 3, 20,21

CHAPTER 26
    1 Timothy 2:1-4